I0540325

The Mystical
Gospel of Thomas

The Mystical Gospel of Thomas: Revelation of the Inner Christ

© 2025 Jamie C. Dunston

All rights reserved, printed in the United States of America. No part of this publication may be reproduced, stored, or transmitted in any form or by any means, electronic, mechanical, photocopying, recording, scanning, or otherwise without written permission from the publisher. It is illegal to copy this book, post it to a website, or distribute it by any other means without permission.

ISBN 979-8-218-66310-0

Library of Congress Control Number: 2025907632

Publisher's Cataloging-in-Publication Data

Names: Dunston, Jamie C., author.

Title: The mystical gospel of Thomas : revelation of the inner Christ / Jamie C. Dunston

Description: Includes bibliographical references. | Colorado Springs, CO: Sacred Luminary Press, 2025.

Identifiers: LCCN: 2025907632 | ISBN: 979-8-218-66310-0

Subjects: LCSH Gospel of Thomas (Coptic Gospel)--Criticism, interpretation, etc. | Bible. Gospels--Criticism, interpretation, etc. | Mysticism. | Bible. New Testament--Theology. | BISAC RELIGION / Gnosticism | RELIGION / Mysticism | RELIGION / Biblical Studies / New Testament / General

Classification: LCC BS2860.T52 .D86 2025 | DDC 229/.8--dc23

Scripture quotations marked (NIV) are taken from the Holy Bible, New International Version®, NIV®. Copyright © 1973, 1978, 1984, 2011 by Biblica, Inc.™ Used by permission of Zondervan. All rights reserved worldwide. www.zondervan.comThe "NIV" and "New International Version" are trademarks registered in the United States Patent and Trademark Office by Biblica, Inc.™

Scripture quotations are from the King James Version (KJV) of the Bible. Public domain.

A Note on Permissions

All images used in this publication are either in the public domain or used with permission from the respective copyright holders. Every effort has been made to identify and credit original sources where possible. Some icons and artworks remain unattributed due to their historical or anonymous origin; however, they are believed to be in the public domain and are used respectfully in accordance with fair use and scholarly reference.

Any excerpts from sacred texts are quoted with reverence, under fair use for educational and spiritual commentary. This work is offered in the spirit of devotion, study, and sacred reflection.

This is a work of spiritual reflection based on true mystical experience…

Please visit: jamiecdunston.com

The Mystical Gospel of Thomas

Revelation of the Inner Christ

JAMIE C. DUNSTON

Sacred Luminary Press

For the Beloved,
who revealed Himself in Light, Cloud, and Word—
and made my heart a temple.

The Mystical Gospel of Thomas: The Revelation of Christ Within
A sacred journey into the hidden sayings of Jesus—unveiling the divine
light within the soul, where the eternal Christ speaks in silence,
mystery, and truth.

Table of Contents

Preface

To Those Who Hear the Whisper Within

This book is not a scholarly commentary, nor is it a doctrinal defense. It is, above all, a witness. A witness to the ineffable. A testimony to the living Christ who speaks not only through words, but through silence, through creation, and through the soul's awakening.

The Gospel of Thomas is a collection of sayings—logia—that invites a different kind of hearing. It doesn't explain; it reveals. It is not concerned with belief, but with *being*. It does not lead us outward, but inward—to the place where the Divine Light flickers quietly behind the veil of ordinary life.

The writings that follow emerge from a direct encounter, a theophany that unfolded in the quiet fields of Avondale, Colorado. What began as an ordinary day in spring became the threshold to something eternal. Beneath the sky, amidst garlic rows and ditchwater, I encountered the Christ—not as an idea or a memory, but as the radiant center of all things. The sayings of Jesus in the Gospel of Thomas came alive—not as riddles, but as living flames of truth. They mirrored the inner unfolding I experienced, where the Kingdom of God revealed itself within and all around me.

This work is part vision, part meditation, part remembrance. It is an offering, not to define the mysteries, but to open the heart to them. It is written for the mystic and the seeker, for those who have tasted the sweetness of divine nearness and for those who have wandered long, thirsting for the waters of truth.

May the words within these pages draw you closer to the Light that is hidden in all things. May they lead you, not to answers, but to intimacy with the living Christ who speaks in silence, abides in mystery, and dwells within the soul.

— In the Light of the Unseen Image

 *Acknowledgments*

I would like to express my heartfelt gratitude to all those who have supported and inspired me throughout the creation of this work. First and foremost, I thank the Divine for the revelation and guidance that led me to the profound wisdom of the Gospel of Thomas, and for the grace that has illuminated my path.

I am deeply grateful to my family and friends, whose unwavering love and encouragement have been a source of strength. To those who have walked alongside me in the mystical journey, your shared insights and prayers have been invaluable.

A special thank you to the scholars, mystics, and theologians whose works on early Christian texts, mysticism, and the Gospel of Thomas have shaped my understanding. Your profound contributions to the field have been a light in the darkness, guiding me in my own contemplations.

Lastly, I acknowledge the ancient voices of the Gospel of Thomas itself, whose words echo across time, speaking of mysteries that transcend the material world and inviting us into a deeper, more intimate relationship with the Divine.

May this work be a small offering in the eternal pursuit of wisdom, truth, and love.

Introduction

I didn't seek God in Avondale. But Avondale sought me out. In the quiet of that small town, I had lived for years, where the landscape stretched wide and the sky felt like a thin veil, separating earth from heaven.

Avondale means "valley of the river," and in many ways, it wasn't just the land that reflected this meaning, but the inner terrain within me. It was here that the waters of divine light flowed, in ways both subtle and profound. The veil between the visible and invisible realms was torn, revealing something far beyond anything I could have imagined.

It was in Avondale that I encountered Christ, not as a figure confined to time or history, but as an eternal presence within.

As the Gospel of Thomas teaches, "I am the light that is over all things. I am the All. The All came forth from me, and the All reaches unto me. Cleave a piece of wood; I am there. Lift up the stone, and you will find me there" (Thomas 77).

I didn't cleave wood or lift stones that day, but I felt His presence in the quiet corners of my heart, in the air that circled the valley, and in the space between each breath. His light revealed the truth: that the Christ is not a figure apart from us, but the inner flame of divinity burning at the center of all things. The Kingdom of God, as Jesus says in Thomas, "is within you and it is outside you" (Thomas 3). And there, in Avondale, I came to understand that the river of divine presence was flowing both inside me and through all things around me.

Seeing With The Soul What The Eyes Cannot Behold

When I reflect on the moment the Divine revealed itself to me, I recall the truth expressed in Saying 83: *"The images are visible to humanity, but the light within them is hidden in the image of the Father's light. He will be revealed, but his image is hidden by his light."* I saw what my eyes could not fully comprehend—yet the inner knowing, the deep seeing with the soul, revealed something far beyond my perception. The visible world, with its trees, the earth, and the sky, contained a light not of this world, a light that shone through every visible form, pointing back to the eternal source.

In Avondale, I encountered this hidden light. As the water flowed through the valley, so too did the living light flow through all things. I saw the Father—not as a distant image but as the water that sustains all life, an eternal river whose source was the deep mystery of divine love. I saw Christ as the light over all things, radiant like the sun, yet also shimmering in the form of a man—the Son of Man, sitting at the right hand of the Father. The rainbow-like presence of the Blessed Holy Spirit encircled them, with colors of carnelian, amber, and emerald green radiating around the throne of divinity.

The Burden of the Unseen Image

In the Gospel of Thomas, Jesus also speaks of a burden in Saying 84: *"When you see your likeness, you rejoice. But when you see your images that came into being before you did – which don't die, and aren't revealed – how much you'll have to bear!"* This saying echoes the deep mystery I encountered. The likeness of the Divine was revealed to me not as an image to behold with my eyes, but as the inner truth of all things, hidden yet present in every moment. When I saw the Trinity, the Holy Presence enveloping me, I saw beyond my own limited image into a vast ocean of divine light and wisdom. It was as if I was seeing the "unseen image" that existed before time, the eternal essence of God, of which all creation is an outpouring.

The burden Jesus speaks of wasn't a weight of despair, but the weight of realizing that the images we see—the ones we rejoice in—are but a shadow of the greater reality. It is the burden of seeing through the surface of things and encountering the Divine in all that is unseen. This was the revelation of the Trinity to me: the eternal Christ, the living light, the Holy Spirit, and the Father, whose presence was a flowing river of life that moved through the very core of all existence. Each image, each reflection, each element of creation held the hidden light, waiting to be revealed through the soul's inner sight.

This land—this vast stretch of land—is not merely part of the earth, but a sacred space with layers of history, each as ancient as the wind itself. Before the arrival of settlers, long before the expansion of agriculture and towns, the plains were home to various Native American tribes. The Southern Cheyenne, Ute, and Arapaho people traveled across these lands, tracing paths that had been followed by their ancestors for generations. The land was not just a place to live—it was a space woven into their myths, stories, and spiritual traditions.

But with the arrival of settlers, the landscape began to change. It was the late 19th century when a new kind of transformation began to take root in Avondale. The Bessemer Ditch, a pivotal piece of irrigation infrastructure, was completed in 1887. This canal, named after the Bessemer Coal and Iron Company, was a marvel of engineering at the time. It brought water from the Arkansas River, fed by the melting snow of the nearby Rockies, and channeled it into the farmlands of the region. This was no small feat, for the plains are parched and unforgiving without water. The snowmelt from the mountains—cold, clear, and pure—became the lifeblood of Avondale, transforming the barren land into a patchwork of fertile fields.

The ditch became the artery of life for the farmers who settled in the area, allowing them to grow crops that could not otherwise survive in the arid climate. Corn, wheat, alfalfa, and the infamous Pueblo Chile flourished where only dust and dry grasses had stood before. The Bessemer Ditch, with its steady flow of water, allowed Avondale to thrive as an agricultural community. Farmers carefully tended to the water that coursed through the ditches, irrigating their fields, watching as the fertile soil came alive with crops that fed not only their families but the surrounding communities.

As the town grew, Avondale became a small but significant agricultural village, nestled just outside of Pueblo, Colorado. It was here that the pulse of the earth, now nourished by the water of the mountains, seemed to synchronize with the rhythms of human life. But even as the town expanded and flourished, it was impossible to ignore the ancient energy of the land. The whispers of the past still lingered in the winds that swept through the fields, in the shade of the cottonwoods, and in the space between the great plains and the towering Rockies.

And so, it was here, in this intersection of ancient wisdom and modern growth, that I found myself standing, beneath a **Sacred Name of God**, beneath the cloud that seemed to contain the divine essence of the universe itself. The cloud was not just a mere formation; it was the breath of God, hovering above the earth, filling the space between the heavens and the earth. As I stood beneath it, I felt it drawing me in, enfolding me in its warmth, its light.

The world around me seemed to disappear, as if the mountain and the plains had shifted, opening up a doorway to something eternal, something greater than this moment. The wind whispered secrets, and the grass seemed to bend in reverence to the cloud. Even the sky—vast, endless, and impossibly blue—felt like a living presence. It was as if everything had conspired to bring me to this very spot, at this precise moment, to witness the divine.

I was not just in Avondale; I was *within* it. The place itself had become sacred, alive with the divine presence. And within that sacredness, I encountered the truth that had always been hidden beneath the surface: that this land, these plains, these mountains, and this sky were not merely part of the earth—they were part of the *Heavenly Kingdom*, manifest in time and space.

This was the place of the Apparitions of Avondale, where the veil between the visible and the invisible grew thin, and the divine revealed itself in a way that was both overwhelming and intimate. And in that moment, I knew that the Kingdom of God was not distant, but was here, in the heart of the plains, beneath the Rockies, in the silence of the wind, and in the divine cloud above. The Kingdom was in my heart, within me as much as it was in the world around me, a living presence that connected the earth and heaven, and I felt it pulsing through my very being, filling the space between the sacred and the mundane.

I was an organic vegetable farmer and seedman at the time. It happened in the evening, as the sun began its slow descent behind the distant mountains. The last day of March arrived with a familiar, tender warmth, where the earth's pulse quickened, coaxing the dormant life to stir. The worms, hidden deep beneath the soil, awoke from their winter slumber, burrowing and wriggling, as if knowing that the earth was ready to receive new life. It was a moment of rebirth, of anticipation. The world, it seemed, held its breath as spring approached, a time of renewal and transformation.

The air was thick with the scent of moisture, fresh from the irrigation that had begun to flow through the Bessemer Ditch, nourishing the crops that had been planted the previous year. The garlic, already established, lay in neat rows, its single cloves from the prior season having grown into clusters of plump bulbs. What was once one clove was now a harvest waiting to be gathered in the coming months, its transformation a quiet miracle of nature. The land was rising, stretching toward the sun, awakening from its long winter's rest.

As the evening shadows lengthened and the warmth of the sun faded into the cool embrace of twilight, Easter's stirrings could be felt in the air. The bunnies, too, were giving birth. New life was everywhere—on the farm, in the soil, in the hearts of those who tended the land. It was a time of rising, of new beginnings. The old was passing away, making way for the new. The cycle of life and death, of planting and harvesting, was beginning once again.

My box turtles, Nube and Mundo, came out of their dens for the first time to warm themselves by the sun and feast on fresh strawberries and grasshoppers. It was as if the earth herself was gently coaxing them out into the light, just as she was coaxing the seeds and bulbs to sprout. Their emergence seemed synchronistic in the truest sense. For in their names, too, there was a deeper truth—the world cloud, the divine presence, was preparing to reveal itself. Nube, meaning "cloud," and Mundo, meaning "world," held a prophetic resonance. It felt as if the turtles' appearance marked a moment when the heavens themselves were about to touch the earth, when the veil would grow thin, and the divine would break through into the visible world.

The Gospel of Thomas: Origins and Significance

The Gospel of Thomas is one of the most famous and controversial texts found among the collection of early Christian writings known as the *Nag Hammadi library*. Discovered in 1945 in Egypt, this collection contains ancient Gnostic scriptures, many of which were previously unknown to modern scholars. The Gospel of Thomas, specifically, is a non-canonical text that is believed to have been written in the early centuries of the Common Era, possibly as early as the second century.

The Gospel of Thomas is unique because it consists of 114 sayings, many of which are attributed directly to Jesus. Unlike the canonical Gospels, which recount the life, death, and resurrection of Jesus, the Gospel of Thomas focuses almost entirely on his teachings, presenting them as sayings, often cryptic and enigmatic. It does not contain a narrative structure, nor does it mention the crucifixion or resurrection. Rather, it emphasizes the transformative power of spiritual knowledge—*gnosis*—and the way in which the seeker can discover the divine presence within.

Some scholars believe that the Gospel of Thomas may have been a part of early Christian oral traditions, and it shares many similarities with the synoptic Gospels (Matthew, Mark, and Luke), though it diverges sharply in its emphasis on esoteric teachings and inner spiritual transformation. The Gospel of Thomas is considered by many to be a Gnostic text because it highlights the importance of direct, experiential knowledge of the divine over orthodox beliefs or practices. This aligns with Gnostic thought, which tends to prioritize inner enlightenment and self-discovery over ritualistic faith.

The text was not included in the biblical canon and was suppressed by early Church authorities due to its perceived heretical teachings. However, its rediscovery has offered modern readers a glimpse into an early, mystical, and alternative vision of Christian spirituality.

The Gospel of Thomas: Knowledge as the Gateway to Immortality

This opening statement from the Gospel of Thomas encapsulates a fundamental Gnostic theme: spiritual knowledge as the gateway to immortality. Unlike the canonical Gospels, which emphasize faith in Christ's death and resurrection as the means to eternal life, the Gospel of Thomas suggests that understanding—*gnosis*—grants transcendence over death.

This idea aligns with Johannine theology, where eternal life is linked to knowledge of God and Christ. As it is written in **John 17:3**: *"This is eternal life, that they may know You, the only true God, and Jesus Christ whom You have sent."*

However, while the Gospel of John emphasizes relational knowledge through faith, the Gospel of Thomas presents enlightenment itself as the transformative key to immortality. In this text, spiritual insight is the mechanism through which one awakens to a higher reality, beyond the constraints of physical death. It is through *gnosis*—deep, personal knowledge— that one transcends the limitations of the mortal body and enters into a state of eternal, spiritual awakening.

Chapter 1

The Hidden Kingdom: A Journey of Discovery (Sayings 1-3)

These are the secret sayings which the living Jesus spoke and which Didymos Judas Thomas wrote down.

The name Thomas comes from the Aramaic "T'oma", and the Greek name Didymos means "twin." Thus, Thomas is known as "the Twin," but not merely in a physical sense. His name points to a deeper spiritual bond with Jesus, the Living Word. Thomas is not just the twin of a man; he is the twin of the Divine, linked to Christ in a profound, mystical way.

In the Gospel of Thomas, Thomas is not merely a follower but the one entrusted with recording the secret sayings of the Living Jesus. These teachings were not meant for all, but preserved for those with the spirit to hear beyond words and see the unseen, entering into the deeper truths of the Divine.

Saying 1: The Living Word

Jesus said, "Whoever uncovers the meaning of these words will never taste death." (1)

Why It's Profound

As the first saying of the Gospel of Thomas, this establishes the foundational message of the text. It is not simply about intellectual understanding—this "interpretation" invites a deeper, transformative realization. The true meaning is not something to be grasped through the mind alone, but through spiritual awakening. To "find the interpretation" is to undergo an inner transformation, one where the seeker experiences a profound shift in consciousness.

In this saying, Jesus promises that the key to eternal life lies within the interpretation of his words. This eternal life is not merely an afterlife event; it is an awakening to a higher, timeless existence that transcends physical death. It suggests that death, in its conventional sense, holds no power over the one who understands the deeper truth. This interpretation of eternal life implies that, by awakening to the divine within, the seeker moves beyond the limitations of birth and death, entering a state of union with the divine.

Mystical Insights

This notion of transcending death through spiritual awakening is echoed in mystical traditions across cultures. In Taoism, the sage who aligns with the Tao transcends the ego and worldly limitations, living harmoniously with the eternal flow of life. Similarly, in the Gospel of Thomas, true understanding opens the way to discover the eternal within the self.

The Bhagavad Gita (10.20) speaks of this divine immanence: "I am the Self, O Gudakesha, seated in the hearts of all creatures. I am the beginning, the middle, and the end of all beings." Here, the recognition of the divine Self within grants eternal life, not as a resurrection after death, but as an awakening to the realization of oneness with the divine essence. This aligns with Saying 1, which suggests that eternal life comes not through waiting for an afterlife but by understanding one's true nature and discovering the divine presence within.

Scriptural Resonance

Luke 17:21: "The kingdom of God is within you." This saying echoes the heart of the Gospel of Thomas: that eternal life is not something to come, but something that is realized in the present moment, within our own hearts. The realization of the kingdom within leads to spiritual transformation and a deeper connection to the divine.

Living Resurrection

In Saying 1, Jesus points to a transformative experience: an awakening that opens the seeker to the divine presence within. This is not about waiting for resurrection as a future event but recognizing that resurrection is an ongoing, inner transformation. It is through awakening to our true nature as divine beings, to the eternal life already within us, that we transcend the boundaries of life and death. We come to realize that we are not waiting for resurrection—we are living it now, in every breath, in every moment. The resurrection, the divine union, is happening in the very fabric of our being.

Thus, the seeker of truth is not merely on a quest for knowledge; they are invited into a deeper, spiritual experience that leads them to recognize that they are already one with the divine. This is the path to eternal life—not a future promise, but a present realization. Through this understanding, death loses its power over us, as we awaken to the eternal truth of who we are: divine, eternal, and one with the Source.

Saying 2: The Seeker's Journey to Transformation

Jesus said, "Whoever seeks must not give up until they discover. When they do, they will be shaken. In that shaking, they will be amazed—and in that amazement, they will come into mastery over all." (2)

True seekers must move beyond conventional wisdom to uncover the deeper mysteries of the divine. This theme is echoed in Jeremiah 29:13: *"You will seek me and find me when you seek me with all your heart."*

> *Proverbs 3:13-18 (NIV):*
> *"Blessed are those who find wisdom, those who gain understanding, for she is more profitable than silver and yields better returns than gold. She is more precious than rubies; nothing you desire can compare with her. Long life is in her right hand; in her left hand are riches and honor. Her ways are pleasant ways, and all her paths are peace."*

> *Mark 13:26 (KJV):*
> *"And then shall they see the Son of man coming in the clouds with great power and glory."*

> *Matthew 24:30 (KJV):*
> *"And then shall appear the sign of the Son of man in heaven: and then shall all the tribes of the earth mourn, and they shall see the Son of man coming in the clouds of heaven with power and great glory."*

> *John 14:3 (KJV):*
> *"And if I go and prepare a place for you, I will come again, and receive you unto myself; that where I am, there ye may be also."*

> *Daniel 7:13 (KJV):*
> *"I saw in the night visions, and, behold, one like the Son of man came with the clouds of heaven, and came to the Ancient of days, and they brought him near before him."*

The figure shown here is the iconic image of **Christ Pantocrator**, one of the oldest and most revered representations of Jesus in Christian art. In this sacred depiction, Christ is portrayed with a penetrating gaze—his right hand raised in blessing, and his left holding the Book of Life. This image, rich in symbolism, conveys both his divine authority and intimate presence. One eye often appears slightly different from the other, subtly illustrating the mystery of Jesus as both fully God and fully man—*the One who embodies both transcendent power and compassionate humanity.*

Alongside this traditional icon is a deeply personal image: the actual photograph I took on the day I experienced the *theophany of the LORD*. This zoomed-in view offers a closer look at the details of his face—his nose arching gently up to the brow, the prominence of his cheekbones, and the delicate outline of a mustache. Surrounding his head is a luminous halo in the shape of a mandorla, or vesica piscis—a sacred form of divine geometry that appears again in other images from that day. If you look with a discerning eye, you will notice a faint echo of his right hand raised in blessing, mirroring the gesture from the Christ Pantocrator icon.

In this vision, Jesus revealed himself as both Son of God and Son of Man (Sun of Man), standing in radiant union between the Heavenly Father and the Blessed Holy Spirit—a living manifestation of the Triune God. What had once been a painted icon became a living reality, captured not only on camera, but forever etched in spirit.

"Ancient Gaze" and "The Beloved Face" — A Contemplation of the Revealed Christ

"**Ancient Gaze**" *Christ the Pantocrator-6th Century Byzantine Icon-Saint Catherine's Monastery, Mount Sinai-Artist Unknown*

"**The Beloved Face**" *Details of Jesus' Face — "Whoever Has Seen Me Has Seen the Father" J.C. Dunston, 2015"*

Mystical Insight:

Saying 2 reveals the stages of the seeker's spiritual journey and the profound transformations that come with the discovery of truth. The first part speaks to the relentless pursuit of truth. The seeker is called to continue the search without stopping, emphasizing perseverance and commitment. The quest for truth is not passive but requires continuous effort and inner focus. This aligns with the idea that the path to wisdom is not a simple or easy one but demands dedication and persistence.

The disturbance that follows upon finding the truth symbolizes the disruption of the status quo. When one encounters a higher reality or divine knowledge, it often shakes the foundation of previous understanding. This inner disturbance is an essential part of the awakening process—without it, transformation would be incomplete. Just as the grain of wheat must be broken for the seed to grow, the soul must be unsettled for new wisdom to take root.

When the seeker moves through this disturbance, the next step is marveling—the deep sense of awe that arises when one perceives the truth of existence. This marvel is not merely intellectual but deeply spiritual, as it reflects a direct encounter with the divine. It speaks to the experience of beholding the mysteries of life with wonder and reverence.

Finally, the promise that the seeker will reign over the All points to spiritual mastery, but not in a worldly sense. It speaks to the inner sovereignty of the soul. The seeker, having gone through disturbance, awakening, and marveling, now possesses dominion over their own consciousness and experience. The "All" refers to the totality of existence, and ruling over it signifies mastery over the self and the realization of one's divine nature.

This saying closely mirrors the journey outlined in several spiritual texts. In the Gospel of Thomas, the progression from seeking, to disturbance, to marveling, and then ruling over the All, mirrors the transformative journey of the soul in the mystical and Gnostic traditions. It emphasizes that knowledge, when sought and found, brings with it both enlightenment and discomfort, which ultimately lead to spiritual sovereignty.

A parallel in the Johannine tradition can be found in John 8:32: *"Then you will know the truth, and the truth will set you free."* Here, the truth reveals the liberation of the soul, but it also requires the breaking down of previous falsehoods and illusions, which can be a painful but necessary process for spiritual growth.

Application to the Seeker:

For the modern seeker, this saying invites us to examine our own pursuit of truth and self-realization. The path is not easy, and discomfort is part of the process of awakening. Seekers are called not to stop, to remain steadfast in their quest for knowledge. The moment of disturbance should not be feared but embraced as a sign of the soul's transformation. This discomfort indicates that the ego and false perceptions are being shattered to make way for a deeper, truer understanding.

As we progress through this journey, we move from disruption to marvel, ultimately experiencing the wonder of spiritual enlightenment. In the final stage, we are called to reign—not over others—but over our own minds, hearts, and actions. This is the true mastery: ruling our thoughts and emotions, aligning them with divine wisdom, and seeing ourselves as co-creators in the unfolding of the universe.

Proverbs 25:2: "It is the glory of God to conceal a matter; to search out a matter is the glory of kings."

As I began to come into the fullness of knowing myself, it was as though I were a flower, slowly blossoming, unfurling her petals for the very first time. This journey of self-discovery was not one of simple thought but of profound revelation. It began with an inner voyage, one that led me deep into the seat of my soul.

Months before the Apparitions of Avondale, I had already been touched by the divine. One morning, just as the sun kissed the dawn, I had a visitation from the Blessed Holy Mother. I stood in my living room, warmed by the fire, watching the cows peacefully graze in the pasture below. And then, before me, appeared a radiant being of light, shrouded in living light, adorned in a blue mantle, and holding in her hands a glowing orb of pure white light.

Without a word spoken aloud, she communicated with me through a gentle telepathic message: *I am your Mother, the Mother of all humanity. And you, too, are a child of the light.* My gaze was drawn to the luminous orb in her hands, and in that light, I saw something beyond comprehension—an overwhelming love that radiated from within. She offered me this love, inviting me to witness it, to truly know it.

It was the light of Christ—magnificent, boundless, and transformative. She extended it to me, not just as a gift, but as a calling. In that moment, I understood that this love was not distant or abstract, but something I was invited to embody and carry within myself. This was the beginning of my journey into faith—a sacred initiation into the divine light that would illuminate the path ahead.

After that sacred encounter, my faith began to take root, growing quietly but steadily, like a seed longing to reach the light. I felt drawn to outward symbols of this inner stirring. I purchased a candle bearing the image of Jesus, and not long after, I printed a picture of Christ the Pantocrator—a 6th-century Byzantine icon whose name means "Almighty." The image unsettled me at first. I had never considered myself religious. I was spiritual, always, but this felt like something deeper—an inner summons I could not ignore.

I was raised in the currents of the New Age movement, a time of restoration, renewal, and exploration of the inner life. My mother identified as a cultural Catholic, having inherited the faith of my dear grandmother, who had embraced Catholicism in her late teens in the quiet landscapes of Minnesota. My father, on the other hand, was a man of science, an agnostic who encouraged critical thinking. Together, they gave me the gift of freedom—to seek my own path, to question, to wonder.

My encounters with church were occasional, mostly visits with my grandmother during Easter or Christmas. I was baptized at the age of three, later than tradition prescribed, much to my grandmother's chagrin. When my cousins were preparing for their first communion, I did not walk that path. Organized religion never felt like home to me. My heart was drawn elsewhere—to the pages of mystics and philosophers, to the words of Khalil Gibran and other voices that spoke to the soul's deep longing. The hallowed pews of the Roman Catholic Church held no allure then; I was seeking a living truth, not one bound in ritual, but one that breathed from within.

This unfolding of faith was not about adopting dogma but about awakening to something ancient within me. The image of Christ Pantocrator stirred something deep and mysterious—a recognition of divine presence beyond icons, beyond words. It was as though the outer forms pointed inward, guiding me to discover the indwelling light.

This encounter stirred within me a deep reflection on the nature of the icon itself. Though the term *icon* simply refers to an image, the venerated icon holds a distinct and sacred place within the Christian tradition. It is not merely a religious artifact or artistic representation, but a threshold—a window into the heavenly realm. A true icon serves as a sacred conduit between the earthly and the divine, inviting the viewer into a participatory relationship with the presence of God.

Venerated icons are understood not as depictions of the divine essence, but as luminous signs of divine participation—portals through which grace may be encountered. As Ouspensky and Lossky beautifully expressed, "The icon is not a representation of the Deity, but an indication of the participation of a given person in Divine life." The icon reveals the presence of holiness through light and form, drawing us into contemplation, into prayer, and ultimately, into communion.

In this sense, the icon becomes not only a visual medium but a spiritual one—a form of revelation alongside Holy Scripture and the Cross. It mediates divine reality through silence and presence, offering the beholder a path toward the eternal. "The icon is both the way and the means," they write, "it is prayer itself."

The reverence shown to an icon is not directed to the wood or pigment, but to the divine prototype it reflects. As the Catechism of the Catholic Church explains, "The honor rendered to an image passes to its prototype, and whoever venerates an image venerates the person portrayed in it." This distinction between veneration (*dulia*) and worship (*latria*) was essential in resolving the theological tensions of the Iconoclastic Controversy in the 8th and 9th centuries. Far from idolatry, the veneration of icons honors the incarnation—the mystery of God made visible in Christ.

Thus, to gaze upon an icon such as *Christ Pantocrator* is not simply to look at an image, but to open oneself to divine encounter. It is to stand before a mirror of eternity, through which the soul glimpses the light of the immortal Word.

Likewise, the Heavenly Father also used a venerated image that my mind's eye could relate to, similar to the famous fresco painting by Michelangelo known as "The Creation of Adam."

In the Creation of Adam, God appears as an old, white-bearded man conveying wisdom and authority, floating in a swirling cloak shaped like a brain with his angelic host. He swims through the sky with his whimsical beard and shows a side profile of his face, and he floats to his creation, giving consciousness to Adam, the first man.

෨෫෯෬

Saying 3: The Kingdom Within

Jesus said, "If your leaders tell you, 'The Kingdom is in the sky,' then the birds will get there before you. If they say, 'It is in the sea,' then the fish will arrive before you. Rather, the Kingdom is within you, and it is all around you. When you come to truly know yourself, you will be known, and you will see that you are a child of the Living Father. But if you do not know yourself, you dwell in emptiness, and that emptiness is your poverty." (3)

The Kingdom is not in some far-off realm, nor hidden in the unreachable depths. It is not beyond the stars or buried beneath the waves. It is closer than breath, present, luminous, and waiting to be seen. Yet so often, the misguided direct their longing outward, casting their eyes to the heavens or plumbing the oceans, mistaking distance for divinity. But if the Kingdom truly resided in the sky, would not the birds inherit it first? If it lay beneath the sea, would not the fish discover it before us?

This is the illusion of elsewhere.

The sacred truth is this: the Kingdom is within. It dwells in the innermost chamber of the heart, the hidden sanctuary where the divine presence has always resided. Jesus affirms this when he says, *"When you pray, go into your inner room, close the door, and pray to your Father, who is unseen. Then your Father, who sees what is done in secret, will reward you."* (Matthew 6:6) It is within this secret room—beyond sight, beyond noise, beyond the outer world—that the soul comes awake, and divine light pours forth.

Mystics across traditions have echoed this truth. Rumi asks, *""Why do you wander, seeking the pearl in the depths, when the ocean is within you?"* Meister Eckhart writes, *"God is nearer to me than I am to myself."* The Taoists speak of the Way not as a journey to undertake, but as the ever-unfolding harmony of reality—already present, already here.

To search beyond is to be led astray.
To turn inward is to behold the Kingdom.
To still the seeking is to arrive.

3: The Knowledge of the Self and the Living Father

> *"When you come to know yourselves, then you will be known, and you will under-stand that you are the children of the living Father. But if you do not know yourselves, then you live in poverty, and you are poverty." (3)*

The path to divine knowledge begins with the unveiling of the self. To know oneself is to awaken to the great mystery—that within the soul burns the light of the living Father. This knowledge is not the mere grasping of personal identity but the recognition of one's true nature, a child of the divine, fashioned in eternity before the foundations of the world. Jesus' words echo the ancient wisdom inscribed in the heart of all traditions. The Upanishads whisper, *Tat Tvam Asi*—"Thou art That"—a call to recognize the spark of the infinite within. The Psalmist sings, *"I have said, you are gods, and all of you are children of the Most High"* (Psalm 82:6), revealing the divine lineage embedded in every soul. Yet, to remain ignorant of this truth is to dwell in spiritual poverty, for the one who does not seek inwardly remains exiled from their inheritance. The sacred vessel of the heart, the inner chamber where the Spirit speaks, remains unopened. But to enter this hidden sanctuary, to lift the veil, is to know as we are known—to gaze into the divine mirror and see not a stranger but the radiant image of the living God.

"He who knows the Atman becomes the Atman." (Brihadaranyaka Upanishad 1.4.10)

There was a moment, quiet and unassuming, when I first caught a glimpse of this truth—not in theory, but in lived experience. I had begun to sense something sacred stirring within me, like a long-lost melody remembered. In prayer, in silence, and in the simple acts of presence, a whisper would rise: *"You are not separate."*

As I sat with the Pantocrator icon, I realized it was no longer just an image of Christ—it was a mirror reflecting the divine origin within me. A sacred recognition passed between us. I began to feel *known*—not in the surface sense of identity, but in the deep awareness that I was seen by Love itself, and that I belonged to it.

This unveiling did not come all at once, but like dawn light seeping through the cracks of a long-shut door. And with each ray came the understanding: I had never been outside the garden. I had only forgotten the way back in.

Jesus' words— "When you come to know yourselves, then you will be known"—now echo like a heartbeat. To know oneself is not to inflate the ego, but to encounter the soul's birthright. I began to understand the poverty he spoke of—not of possessions, but of perception. The poverty of forgetting the divine spark within. To know this, even for a moment, is to taste eternity.

Chapter 2

The Search for Truth and the Self (Sayings 4-10)

Saying 4: The Hidden Wisdom of the Child

Jesus said, "An old man will not hesitate to ask a child just seven days old about the source of life, and he will live; for many who are first will become last, and they shall become one." (4)

This saying reveals a profound paradox at the heart of spiritual truth: the aged, who are often seen as wise in the world, must humble themselves and seek the wisdom that resides in the child, not merely a literal infant, but the pure, uncorrupted spirit within. In Gnostic thought, and throughout the Gospel of Thomas, there is an emphasis on *returning* to a state of original, untainted being — a recovery of the primal unity with the divine. The "little child of seven days" evokes the idea of a newborn still close to the mystery of creation, still aware, intuitively, of the "place of life" — the divine source. In many spiritual traditions, the child symbolizes the pure heart, the untouched soul that knows without yet being clouded by the conditioning of the world.

When Jesus says that the elder must seek wisdom from the child, he points to the necessity of radical humility and unlearning. True life is not found through accumulation of worldly knowledge or status (being 'first'), but through simplicity, wonder, and remembrance of our innate unity with God.

There is only One of us. We do not so much *become* one as realize we have *always* been one. The seeming separation is a veil cast by forgetfulness. Spiritual awakening is thus a re-cognition, a remembrance of the truth already within us — that we are emanations of the One, and the journey is not a becoming, but a returning.

The final line, "the first shall be last, and they will become a single one," underscores the reversal of worldly values: those who cling to being first, to egoic achievement, will be humbled; those who embrace humility and spiritual poverty will be restored to unity. In the end, all separations dissolve into the divine singularity — the One Being from whom all have come and to whom all return.

Thus, the journey is not a progression toward something external, but a return inward to what has always been true. Beneath the accumulation of years and the constructs of memory, the original awareness remains — untouched, undivided. Consciousness, as we experience it, flows through the vessel of subjectivity, giving rise to the illusion of separateness. Each perspective appears distinct, shaped by time, circumstance, and memory. Yet this diversity of experience does not divide the underlying reality. The child, fresh from the mystery of being, and the man aged in days, seasoned by the world, both participate in the same unified essence. They are distinct faces of one reality, different expressions of a single originating source. To seek, to question, to wonder, is to move beyond the illusions of selfhood and to remember that behind every perspective lies the same fundamental truth: we belong to a greater wholeness that is not lost but merely hidden from view.

This recognition — that behind the apparent diversity of perspectives there remains an indivisible wholeness — prepares the way for a deeper mystery spoken of later in the Gospel of Thomas. In Saying 22, Jesus extends the vision further: the work of spiritual realization is not merely to recognize unity intellectually, but to *embody* it, to actively reconcile all opposites within oneself, until duality itself dissolves.

Saying 22 reads:

"When you bring the two together as one and when what is within you becomes like what is outside you, and what is above becomes as what is below, and when the masculine and feminine no longer divide you, so that the two become a single whole…then you will enter the Kingdom."

Here, the movement is not only about seeing through the illusion of separateness but participating in the restoration of unity at every level of being: inner and outer, spirit and body, heaven and earth, masculine and feminine. It is a call to transfigure the divided self into a living symbol of the undivided Whole. Where Saying 4 awakens the memory of unity, Saying 22 calls for the complete integration of that memory into lived experience.

Thus, the Gospel of Thomas weaves a path: from the rediscovery of what has always been true, to the active participation in the oneness of existence — a journey not merely of understanding, but of transformation.

⁂❈❀❈⁂

Saying 5: Recognition and Revelation

Jesus said, "Know what stands before your eyes, and what has been concealed from you will be made known." (5)

Revelation is not distant—it unfolds in the nearness of now. What we long to see is not concealed by absence but hidden in plain sight, veiled by inattentiveness. The sacred surrounds us, pulses through every moment, shimmers through every face, yet so often the eyes are veiled and the ears dulled by the noise of the world.

Jesus invites a return to simplicity, to presence, to the sacred gaze that truly sees. For to recognize what is before us is to pierce the veil, to awaken the eye of the heart. As he says elsewhere, *"Blessed are your eyes, for they see, and your ears, for they hear"* (Matthew 13:16).

The mystic does not escape the world but learns to look into it with clarity. The eternal is not apart from the temporal—it infuses it. When the eye becomes single, the whole body is filled with light (Luke 11:34), and in that light, what once seemed hidden stands fully revealed.

The Kingdom is not found in distant heavens but in the unfolding now. Each moment, each breath, each leaf trembling in the wind offers a portal to the Infinite.

"So we fix our eyes not on what is seen, but on what is unseen. For what is seen is temporary, but what is unseen is eternal." (2 Corinthians 4:18)

Little did I know that on the evening of March 31st, 2015, the glory of God would be unveiled before me. I was sitting in my office, finishing the day's work—cleaning seed to be planted into the rich Avondale soil, a deep, well-drained earth formed by ancient alluvium and mingled stone, a soil that yields abundance when carefully tended.

As the sun began to lower over the Rockies, I caught sight of a lenticular cloud outside my west-facing window—its shape ethereal, its presence arresting. Something stirred within me, a whisper as soft as breath, guiding me to step outside. I took my camera, the goats, and the dogs, unsure of what I would find. I wondered, half in awe and half in jest, whether it might be the Blessed Holy Mother… or perhaps something beyond this world—a craft of heavenly origin.

Just thirteen days earlier, I had prayed a strange but earnest prayer: "Lord, may I have a picture of You?" Since that request, I had felt God's nearness saturate my days, as though we were sharing the same room, the same air. His presence enveloped everything: the breeze brushing through the trees, the birds singing at dusk, the soil soft beneath my feet. It was a quiet ecstasy, a joy that made every breath feel full of divine love.

I stepped outside and lifted my camera toward the heavens. At first, I didn't see glory in the images, but I felt it. Deep within, something luminous stirred, something ancient and alive. It wasn't until later, while reflecting on the photographs, that I noticed a synchronistic sign—etched into the sky, as if by the hand of nature itself: the number 3. A sign of the Trinity. A promise.

Thirteen days after that silent prayer, the heavens answered. I was called—not with thunder or fire, but with stillness and wonder—to become a witness to the living God.

As I walked alongside the cloud, veiled in a shroud of lapis lazuli, my heart trembled, freed from all earthly bounds. A profound knowing seized me: this cloud was not a mere vapor drifting through the sky. It was aware. It was *alive*. As I gazed upon it, I sensed it gazing back. A conscious cloud—an intelligence cloaked in beauty.

Then, like a lightning strike through the soul, the realization flooded me: *This is God.* And within, a childlike cry rose—*Oh my God... that is God.*

Overcome with reverence, I called upon Archangel Gabriel, the Angel of Revelation. At once, orbs of light began to appear, suspended in the atmosphere around me, pulsing with radiant intelligence. They did not simply appear; they *responded*, as if heaven itself answered the call.

In the unfolding of my faith journey, the Spirit had drawn me to sacred texts beyond my tradition—whispers that led me to the Upanishads, the Bhagavad Gita, and the Gospel of John. Later came the Gospel of Thomas and the Gospel of Mary, like petals unfurling in the garden of awakening.

In that holy moment, something in me surrendered completely. Without thought, without effort, I began to sing. From the depths of my being rose the ancient sound—*OM*—the song of the Lord, the vibration of the eternal.

And then... the Trinity began to take form. Not in abstract concept, but in a vision my heart could behold: the Father, the Son, and the Holy Spirit unveiling themselves in a language older than words, clothed in light my spirit could finally understand.

The Heavenly Father was the first to reveal Himself—formless yet full of majesty, a presence vast and intimate, clothed in water and light. Then, from the breath of His being, the Beloved—Yeshua, the Son—was made manifest, radiant like the sun breaking through the veil of the sky. Beside Him appeared the Holy Spirit, shimmering in hues of living color: magenta, carnelian, ruby, jasper, and emerald green. The Trinity stood before me—*distinct, united, alive.*

As it is written:
"This is my beloved Son, in whom I am well pleased" (Matthew 3:17),
"The Word became flesh and dwelt among us" (John 1:14),
and **"The Spirit descended like a dove and alighted upon Him"** (Matthew 3:16).
All three bore witness in the heavens—and now, in front of my eyes.

I walked with this living cloud for approximately seven minutes—a sacred number echoing the fullness of creation and divine perfection. As I returned home, heart still trembling with wonder, I told my family with trembling joy: *I just walked with God.*

Later, as I uploaded the photographs to my computer, I was overcome with awe. The images seemed to pulse with a mystery beyond comprehension. Days passed, and yet the sense of glory did not fade—it deepened. Then, one morning, I looked at the Pantocrator icon on my desk, and my breath caught. The face in the clouds… it mirrored the image of Christ on the icon.

They used that image… I whispered. In quiet contemplation, and in awe and wonder, I lifted my question to the heavens: *Why?* And I heard the answer—not in thunder, but in the still, small voice within: **"It's the Christ in you."**

"Christ in you, the hope of glory" (Colossians 1:27).

"Do you not realize that Jesus Christ is in you?" (2 Corinthians 13:5).

It was not only a vision—it was an unveiling. A revelation not just of who God is, but of who we are in Him.

In the early days of my awakening, as faith began to stir like dawnlight in my soul, I found myself returning again and again to the image of Christ the Pantocrator. Though familiar and at times unsettling, something within me was being called forth—called inward.

In moments of stillness, I would sit before the icon and listen. Not with ears, but with the heart. As if the image itself became a mirror, reflecting something I hadn't yet known about myself: the divine spark already dwelling within me.

"Dunston, J.C. (2014) "Ink Of Faith: Dove Doodles And The Pantocrator"

One quiet afternoon, moved by a longing I could not name, I turned the icon over and began to write messages on its back—small offerings of prayer, reminders for the soul:

Nature Has Designed Us To Connect
Grace
Love One Another As I Have Loved You
*A dove with the **sacred name** of God: **I AM** etched inside.*

Each word was a seed planted in the garden of my heart. And somehow, through that simple act, the Kingdom began to speak—not from the heavens or the deep, but from within.

It was then that I began to understand: the true icon is not on the wall but etched in the soul. And when we turn inward with love and trust, we find the face of the Divine already there, waiting.

Months passed as I continued to unravel the mystical insights and divine revelations I had been blessed to witness. One day, as I turned over the Pantocrator image—an image that had become so dear to my heart—I was struck by a deep realization. I had forgotten that, in a moment of inspiration, I had written on the back of the image, etched with my hand the dove, and inscribed within it God's sacred name: *"I AM."*

As I gazed upon it, my breath caught in my chest. In the divine orchestration of these sacred moments, I realized that the dove I had drawn had appeared in the sky, painted in the very clouds I had witnessed that day. The same symbol, the same Spirit, was present both in my image and in the heavens.

It was not mere coincidence; it was a sacred sign, showing us that we, too, are co-creators with the divine. As it is written:

"Let us make man in our image, after our likeness" (Genesis 1:26).

In that divine communion, we are not mere spectators of the Creator's will, but active. This is the mirrored image God painted in the sky, reflecting the dove that I drew on the back of the Pantocrator icon. You can see that in this photograph, the Almighty "I AM" **love** and **light** is the chariot of God's temple, walking on the wings of the wind. You can see the curve of the dove's mantle, which flows out from Christ's heart chakra. This image symbolizes that we are co-creators with the Divine, participating in the sacred work of creation. We are participants, each of us bearing a spark of the eternal I AM.

"Dunston, J.C. (2015) "Chariot of Light: The Dove of Divine Love"

Isaiah 66:11-12
"For you will nurse and be satisfied at her comforting breasts; you will drink deeply and delight in her overflowing abundance."

Matthew 3:16
"As soon as Jesus was baptized, he went up out of the water. At that moment heaven was opened, and he saw the Spirit of God descending like a dove and alighting on him."

This revelation, this moment of clarity, was more than just an intellectual understanding. It was a deep, felt knowing—an awareness that as we walk in the Spirit, we are invited to shape, to create, to mirror the divine in all that we do. As Jesus Himself prayed, *"Your kingdom come, Your will be done, on earth as it is in heaven"* (Matthew 6:10).

The dove, the symbol of the Holy Spirit, was a reminder not only of the divine presence but also of the truth that we are called to embody— *I AM*—and in doing so, we join with the Creator in the ongoing act of creation.

In my encounter with the divine on that sacred evening, as the cloud veiled in lapis lazuli stretched across the sky, I felt my soul laid bare. There was no pretense, no veil between me and God. The heavens, always unflinching in their gaze, held nothing back, and I, in return, could not hide. As I walked alongside that cloud, the truth of my being was made clear— not just in what I saw, but in what was felt. The reality of God's presence stripped away the illusions I had carried, and in that moment, I realized that what had been hidden, the deep questions and doubts within me, could no longer stay hidden. The divine radiance, ever-present, revealed it all, not to condemn, but to illuminate and heal.

In the Sayings Gospel of Thomas: 'Nothing hidden will not become manifest, and nothing covered will remain without being uncovered.' I was called to see not only the cloud, not only the divine light before me, but the truth within myself. My encounter with God revealed to me that all was plain in the sight of heaven, and there was no place for dishonesty or self-deception. In this sacred unveiling, I found not just divine love, but the truth of my own soul, one not separate from the Divine, but intimately united in the Kingdom that already resides within.

❧❧❧

Saying 6: Seeking and Finding

The disciples asked him, "Should we fast? How ought we to pray? Should we give to the poor? What kind of food should we eat?"

Jesus replied, "Speak truthfully, and do not act against your true self. Everything lies open before Heaven. Nothing remains hidden that will not be revealed, and nothing concealed that will not come to light." (6)

Truth is not simply a matter of words but of life itself. When we walk in dishonesty, we shroud ourselves from the divine light, but the heavens are never deceived. In the presence of the Eternal, all is laid bare. Every hidden thought, every concealed intention, stands fully illuminated before the gaze of the Creator. The call is clear: to live with integrity, in harmony with the sacred order that runs through all creation. What is hidden will inevitably be revealed, just as a seed must break open to give rise to new life. The veils of illusion cannot last forever—the radiance of truth is inescapable. As the prophet declares, "There is nothing concealed that will not be disclosed, or hidden that will not be made known" (Luke 12:2).

To embrace what is true, one must shed all pretense. Self-deception is a poverty of the spirit, a barrier that keeps the soul from its fullness. The heart is the sacred vessel, the temple of the Kingdom, and only in sincerity does one enter its secret chamber. When the soul stands open and bare before the divine light, the false coverings we've clung to fall away, and what was once hidden becomes radiant, known in the purest form of truth.

In the sacred moment when I walked with the cloud, veiled in lapis lazuli, I felt both the weight and freedom of surrender. The passions and fears that once dominated my soul—like wild beasts, clawing for attention—were suddenly laid bare before the Almighty. The lion within me, the beast of my lower nature, had been confronted by divine love. In that instant, I understood the truth of Saying 7: blessed is the lion that becomes human. In God's presence, the lion of my instinctual desires was transformed, not devoured, and I was led into a fuller understanding of my true self.

The divine light revealed to me that these base instincts, these passions that once ruled me, were not to be denied, but transmuted. Like gold refined in fire, the lower nature could be sanctified through love. The lion, once a symbol of my primal self, now rested at peace, subdued by the radiant light of God's presence. It was in this encounter that I was called to put off the old self—the fearful, impulsive nature—and to embrace the new self, made in the image of the Creator, bathed in truth and divine light.

I recalled the teachings of Paul: 'For if you live according to the flesh, you will die; but if by the Spirit you put to death the deeds of the body, you will live.' As I stood in the divine presence, I was not consumed by my lower nature, but instead was **refined**, my soul lifted into a new and higher state of being. This divine encounter was not simply a moment of revelation; it was an invitation to master the lion within, to transform the base into the sacred, and to live fully as the person God had created me to be.

༺✿✿༻

Saying 7: Mastering the Lower Nature

Jesus said, "Blessed is the lion consumed by a human, for it becomes human. But unfortunate is the human consumed by a lion, for the lion becomes human." (7)

Blessed is the one who transforms their lower nature with love, so that they become fully human in the image of God. But unfortunate is the one who is ruled by their lower nature, for they will lose sight of their true self. The lion symbolizes the base instincts—the passions and desires that, if left unchecked, consume the soul. But when these instincts are disciplined and sanctified, they become integrated into the fullness of divine being.

This transformation echoes Paul's call to *put off the old self* and *put on the new self, created to be like God in true righteousness and holiness* (Ephesians 4:22-24). In the mystical path, the lower nature is not to be denied but transmuted, as the alchemists sought to refine base metals into gold. The one who conquers their baser impulses becomes radiant, while the one devoured by them falls into spiritual darkness. Thus, the soul's journey is one of overcoming, of becoming fully alive in the divine image, ascending from the earthly to the heavenly.

This theme echoes Paul's teaching in Romans 8:13: *"For if you live according to the flesh, you will die; but if by the Spirit you put to death the deeds of the body, you will live."*

In the *Gospel of Mary*, this is echoed in the call to clothe ourselves with the perfect human, embracing it so that we may attain perfection, just as our Heavenly Father is perfect.

Thus, saying 7 is a call to spiritual refinement—to transform the self with love and divine awareness rather than be led astray by instinctual drives.

As I stood under the radiance of the divine light, I felt a surge of understanding rise within me. It was as if the world around me faded into the background, and I was given the ability to see with new eyes. The small fish—the fleeting thoughts and distractions of life—were no longer captivating. They drifted away like mere ripples on the surface of the ocean. Instead, my heart turned toward the large fish—the divine wisdom that had been hidden beneath the surface. It was a moment of clarity, a divine invitation to embrace the eternal truth that was now shining before me.

The divine encounter was not just a passive vision—it was an invitation to engage. I felt called to dive deeper, to hear and understand in a way that transcended ordinary perception. It was no longer enough to simply see the light; I was being asked to **align myself with it**, to **live in accordance with the divine truth** that had been revealed. I had heard the calling, but now I had to fully **engage** with it, just as the fisherman chooses the large fish with unwavering certainty.

⁊❈❈❃

Saying 8: Spiritual Discernment

Jesus said, "A wise person is like a fisherman who cast a net into the sea and hauled in many small fish. Among them, he discovered one large fish, fine and valuable. Without delay, he kept the large fish and returned the small fish to the sea. Whoever has ears, let them listen." (8)

This saying metaphorically depicts the soul's journey to spiritual enlightenment. The "sea" represents the vast expanse of experience and knowledge, full of distractions, temptations, and transient concerns. The "small fish" are the fleeting, superficial aspects of life, which may captivate the mind but ultimately do not contribute to the deeper purpose of existence. The "large fish," on the other hand, symbolizes the true wisdom, the divine essence, that the seeker must recognize and embrace without hesitation.

This parable calls for spiritual discernment—the ability to sift through the many distractions and desires that life offers and choose only that which brings one closer to the divine. It echoes the wisdom of the apostle Paul, who speaks of focusing on the eternal rather than the temporary: *"So we fix our eyes not on what is seen, but on what is unseen, for what is seen is temporary, but what is unseen is eternal"* (2 Corinthians 4:18). Just as the fisherman chooses the large fish, the spiritual seeker must prioritize the eternal truth found in God's wisdom over the fleeting pleasures or distractions of the world.

In Eastern spirituality, this idea mirrors the concept of *detachment*—the ability to let go of what no longer serves one's higher purpose. The Bhagavad Gita speaks of *renunciation*, where one lets go of attachments to the material world in order to focus on the divine path (Bhagavad Gita 2:47). By making the right choice, the seeker achieves spiritual clarity and alignment with the divine will.

The phrase "Whoever has ears to hear, let them hear" invites the listener into an active participation in the revelation, urging not just hearing but a deeper understanding that transcends ordinary perception. This is not a passive instruction, but an invitation to fully engage with the truth and allow it to transform one's life. It recalls the invitation of Jesus in the Gospels, where he constantly calls his followers to *"hear and understand"* (Matthew 13:9). Thus, Saying 8 underscores the importance of discernment on the spiritual path, the act of choosing what is eternal and profound over what is temporary and illusory.

In the mystical tradition, the "large fish" can also represent the divine presence—often hidden in the world but shining clearly when the seeker has the eyes to see. Meister Eckhart speaks of the divine *"spark"* within every soul, which, when recognized, transforms all aspects of life. Similarly, Rumi suggests that the divine is like the ocean that contains everything, yet it is only when the seeker dives deep into the heart of the ocean that they discover the treasure that lies beneath the surface.

Just as on the farm, where I bury a seed in faith and wait, so too had the Holy One planted this moment in me long before it blossomed. The hundredfold harvest is not merely the vision I saw, but the way it now bears fruit: in my words, my works, my love, my surrender. When the vision came—Father in water and star cloud, Son in sunlight, Spirit in rainbow flame—it wasn't simply seen with my eyes. It took root in my whole being. The vision grew within me like a seed awakened by light. I didn't strive to make it grow. I only needed to be still and receive.

And now, it bears fruit beyond my understanding—fruit not for me alone, but for every heart who hungers for the eternal Word. *In the beginning was the Word, and the Word was with God, and the Word was God.* That divine Logos—the eternal seed—was sown into the soil of creation and the soil of my heart.

In the **Apparitions of Avondale**, a seed was planted in me that has never stopped growing. I encountered the living Logos not just as truth, but as seed, as light, as presence. What was sown that day continues to grow and flourish, bearing witness to the eternal Word that became flesh and now lives within us.

Saying 9: Spiritual Receptivity

Jesus said. "The sower went out to cast seed. Some fell on the road, and the birds came and ate it. Some fell on rocky ground, where it couldn't take root or bear fruit. Some fell among thorns, and the thorns choked it, leaving it to be consumed by worms. But some seed fell on good soil, and it grew, producing good fruit; it yielded sixty per measure and even a hundred times as much." (9)

"The One Who Sows the Living Logos"

This saying echoes the well-known parable of the sower found in Matthew 13:3-9, where Jesus speaks of seeds being scattered on different types of soil, each representing the varied responses of human hearts to the divine word. In this metaphor, the sower is the divine teacher, spreading seeds of truth throughout the world. The seeds, representing the word of God, are capable of producing abundant spiritual fruit, but only if they fall on receptive soil—the heart that is open, prepared, and willing to nurture divine wisdom.

The "good soil" symbolizes a heart that is prepared through humility, love, and devotion to receive the teachings of the divine. Just as fertile soil nourishes a seed to grow into a healthy, fruitful plant, a receptive heart cultivates the word of God, allowing it to grow and bear fruit in one's life. This fruit represents the manifestation of divine wisdom, love, and grace in the actions, thoughts, and behavior of the believer. The crop that yields "a hundredfold" reflects the immense potential for spiritual growth when one truly embraces the divine teachings.

This saying emphasizes the importance of cultivating one's inner life to be receptive to spiritual truths. It mirrors the teachings in the New Testament about being "doers of the word" rather than mere hearers (James 1:22). The "good soil" is not passive; it actively nurtures the divine seed, allowing it to grow, transform, and bear fruit. As the apostle Paul writes, *"The fruit of the Spirit is love, joy, peace, forbearance, kindness, goodness, faithfulness, gentleness and self-control"* (Galatians 5:22-23). These are the qualities that emerge from a heart that has received and cultivated the word of God.

In the mystical tradition, the fertile soil of the heart is also described as the inner sanctum where divine union can take place. Meister Eckhart speaks of the soul as a garden where God can dwell, and only when the soul is prepared to receive the divine seed can it produce the fruits of mystical union. Similarly, in Eastern spirituality, the concept of *sattva*—the quality of purity, wisdom, and spiritual clarity—aligns with the notion of good soil, where divine teachings are allowed to flourish.

Saying 9, therefore, calls the seeker to examine the condition of their heart: Is it ready to receive the seed of divine wisdom? Are the distractions and cares of the world like the thorns or rocky paths that hinder spiritual growth, or is the soil of the soul rich with intention and openness? This is a call to spiritual preparation—through prayer, contemplation, and a life of inner discipline—to allow the divine seed to take root, grow, and bear fruit in abundance.

After the vision, I did not simply return to my old life unchanged. The encounter ignited something in me—a fire I could not put out. It was as if the Logos, the living Word, had not only planted a seed, but had also cast fire upon my soul. And this fire, like the fire Jesus spoke of, did not destroy me. It refined me. It illuminated every corner of my being, exposing what was false, what was selfish, what could not remain.

Saying 10 speaks: "I have cast fire upon the world, and see, I am guarding it until it blazes." I came to see that the vision was not the end, but the kindling. The Holy One did not leave me with a memory, but entrusted me with a flame. It burned quietly at first— like the ember of a whisper—but soon it consumed my inner world. I could feel it purging the illusions I once held dear, the attachments I thought were sacred, the ego that so often stood in the way.

This was not a fire of wrath, but of mercy. It was love's fire. The same fire that descended at Pentecost. The same light that burned in the bush yet did not consume it. It burned in me to awaken me—to refine the gold from the dross. I began to understand what Jesus meant when He said He was guarding this fire until it blazes. For it blazed in me. And I was not afraid.

Like a field after controlled burning, where the old stubble is cleared and the soil made fertile, I felt a readiness I never had before. The Word that had been planted in me now found space to grow unencumbered. Love began to burn brighter. My desires shifted. What once satisfied no longer did. I was being made new.

This inner fire—the divine presence—kept calling me back to surrender. Again and again, I laid down my will. And each time, the flame grew stronger, clearer, more radiant. It was no longer just my vision to carry, but a fire to tend, just as He tends the fire of the world.

In this way, the *Apparitions of Avondale* were not only a revelation but an initiation. What I saw was only the beginning. What followed was the fire.

"Sacred Flame of the Inner Christ"

Saying 10: Destruction And Renewal

Jesus said, "I have cast fire upon the world, and behold, I am guarding it until it blazes with intensity." (10)

Fire is a central symbol in many spiritual traditions, representing purification, transformation, and the divine presence. In this saying, Jesus speaks of a fire that He has cast upon the world—a fire that will burn away the falsehoods, illusions, and impurities of the human heart, leaving only the truth of divine wisdom. The fire signifies both a challenge and a grace, for it consumes what is unnecessary while refining what is essential.

This concept resonates with Jesus' words in Luke 12:49, where He declares, *"I have come to bring fire on the earth, and how I wish it were already kindled!"* Here, fire represents the fiery passion and intense purification required for spiritual awakening. The coming of this fire is not to destroy the world in the conventional sense but to purify and refine it, allowing the soul to be purified through the flame of divine love and wisdom. Just as gold is refined in fire, so too must the soul undergo a process of purification through the divine light, which burns away the dross of ignorance and sin.

The phrase *"I am guarding it until it blazes"* emphasizes the active role of Jesus in safeguarding this transformative fire. It is not merely a passive force that will eventually ignite the world, but a fire that is being carefully nurtured, protected, and tended by the divine, ensuring it grows stronger and more widespread. Jesus' guardianship of the fire suggests a patient, ongoing process of spiritual awakening, where the fire will not flare up all at once but will steadily burn until it reaches its full intensity.

"The Spirit Came Upon Them"

This fire also reflects the Holy Spirit, who is often associated with fire in scripture, especially in Pentecost when the disciples are filled with the Spirit and tongues of fire rest upon them (Acts 2:3). The Holy Spirit ignites the soul, purging it of selfishness and sin, and empowers the seeker to live a life of truth and love. The fire is both the presence of God and the means of transformation, a refining force that prepares the soul for union with the divine.

The mystics often speak of this fire as the *inner light*, the transformative force that burns away the ego, desires, and attachments. Meister Eckhart, for instance, described the soul's union with God as an experience of fire, where the soul, in its purest form, is consumed by divine love. The Sufi poet Rumi similarly speaks of the *love fire*, which burns through the soul, purging it of all impurities, leaving only the beloved's essence.

Saying 10 invites the seeker to embrace the fire of divine wisdom, understanding that it is both a challenge and a blessing. It is a fire that transforms, purifies, and refines, making way for spiritual enlightenment and union with the divine. This fire is not destructive in the sense of annihilation but is a powerful force of renewal, burning away everything that stands between the seeker and the ultimate truth. The process of spiritual purification may be intense and uncomfortable, but it is ultimately a journey toward greater freedom and divine intimacy.

And yet, even as the fire refined me, another revelation unfolded—one even deeper. The world around me, once so solid and fixed, began to shimmer with impermanence. I felt the heavens tremble, not in fear, but in release. That which I once clung to, even the most sacred forms, began to pass away.

The next figure is an image of the Blessed Holy Spirit. The rich carnelian hue that you see is the Holy Spirit. The Father and the Son have faded out of this image, and the Holy Spirit takes center stage with its magnificent, radiant glory of love shining upon us.

"Dunston, J.C. (2015) "The Mighty One, God the LORD, speaks and summons the earth from the rising to the setting of the sun. From Zion, perfect in beauty, God shines forth" (Psalm 50:1-2).

Psalm 19:1-4
"The heavens declare the glory of God; the skies proclaim the work of his hands. Day after day they pour forth speech; night after night they reveal knowledge. They have no speech, they use no words; no sound is heard from them. Yet their voice goes out into all the earth, their words to the ends of the world."

Job 12:7-10
"But ask the animals, and they will teach you, or the birds in the sky, and they will tell you; or speak to the earth, and it will teach you, or let the fish in the sea inform you. Which of all these does not know that the hand of the Lord has done this? In his hand is the life of every creature and the breath of all mankind."

The following image is one of the last few photographs I took on the day of the Epiphany of the LORD. The Holy Spirit's visage is fading out, yet surrounding the whole. The Angelic Host appears as small celestial spheres of light, mostly seen under the luminous love that is God.

"Dunston, J.C. (2015) "Spheres of Radiant Celestials:
Archangels Revealed in Glowing Glory"

Saying 11 echoes through my spirit: "This heaven will pass away, and the one above it will pass away. The dead are not alive, and the living will not die." I saw that the vision had not come to anchor me in another illusion, but to unearth the eternal from beneath the temporal. What I had once called "life" was a living among the dead—nourished by what could never satisfy. I had consumed the world, and in consuming it, tried to keep it alive. But now, I was being consumed—by light, by love, by the flame of eternal presence.

In the light of the vision, I was asked a quiet question: "When you are bathed in light, how will you act?" It wasn't enough to see. I had to become. The divine fire did not simply reveal—it *invited*. It pulled me from the sleep of form into the awakening of essence. I began to live as one who will never die—not because the body would endure, but because something deeper had been touched by eternity.

On that day, when I saw the Father in water and star cloud, the Son in sunlight, and the Spirit in rainbow flame—I remembered what I had forgotten: that once, I was One. And in being born, I became divided. "But now that you are two, what will you do?" I understood then: the return was always the goal. Not to destroy the self, but to illuminate it. Not to flee the world, but to see it as passing shadow—a vessel through which the eternal could shine.

Like the sages who said, *"Everything perishes except the imperishable Self,"* I found in the flames of Avondale the truth of the Self that does not perish. The Logos that became flesh had taken root in the soil of my being, and what now bloomed was neither mine nor other. It was the eternal returning to itself.

Chapter 3

The Parables of the Kingdom (Sayings 11-20)

Saying 11: The Transcendent Nature Of True Life And The Impermanence Of The Material World:

Jesus said, "This heaven will pass away, and the one above it will also pass. The dead do not live, and the living will never die. When you fed on what was lifeless, you brought it to life. When you are bathed in light, how will you act? When you were one, you became two. But now that you are two, what will you do?" (11)

This saying highlights the transient nature of all things, including the heavens themselves, suggesting that everything in the material world is temporary and will eventually pass away. The idea of the heavens passing away alludes to the concept of cosmic cycles—everything, even the highest heavens, is subject to change and decay. However, true life, according to Jesus, is not found in what is temporary and fading but in the eternal truth and divine life that transcends these forms.

Jesus speaks of those who are spiritually asleep, describing them as the *dead* who are not truly alive. These are the individuals who live in ignorance of their divine essence, consumed by the fleeting world of the senses. In contrast, those who are *alive* in the spirit, awakened to the truth of their existence, are not bound by death. They live with an awareness of the eternal nature of the soul, which can never truly die. This distinction between physical death and spiritual life echoes the teachings of many mystical traditions, which assert that true life is found in spiritual awareness, not in the temporary, material existence.

The phrase, *"When you fed on what was lifeless, you brought it to life,"* speaks to the process of transformation that the seeker undergoes. Just as the body consumes food to sustain its life, so too must the soul transform what is dead within it—its ignorance, its attachments to the material world, and its false beliefs—into something that is alive with divine wisdom and understanding. When one is spiritually awakened, the dead parts of the soul are made alive, transfigured by the light of divine insight.

The question, *"When you are bathed in the light, how will you act?"* challenges the seeker to reflect on their response to spiritual enlightenment. The light represents divine truth and awareness, and once one has stepped into it, there is a responsibility to live in accordance with that truth. This question implies that true enlightenment is not merely about perceiving the light but living according to its guidance. The seeker is asked to consider how they will live now that they have seen the truth.

Finally, the saying delves into the paradox of unity and duality. Jesus says, *"When you were one, you became two, But now that you are two, what will you do?"* This points to the inherent division between the individual self and the divine essence from which it originates. In our spiritual journey, we start in unity with the divine but become separated into duality as we identify with the ego and the material world. However, the question remains: What will we do once we recognize this duality? The implication is that the journey is one of returning to oneness with the divine, transcending the illusion of separation.

Saying 11 invites deep contemplation on the nature of life, death, and spiritual awakening. It challenges the seeker to recognize the impermanence of the material world and to focus on cultivating eternal life through spiritual awakening and alignment with divine truth. It calls for a transformation of the soul, turning what is dead within us into life, and asking how we will choose to live once we step into the light of divine consciousness.

Brihadaranyaka Upanishad (1.4.10) states: "Everything perishes except the imperishable Self (Atman)."

Isha Upanishad (verse 7) states: "When one sees all beings in the Self and the Self in all beings, there is no more delusion, no more sorrow."

 මෙවැනි

Saying 12: Leadership of James the Just

The disciples said to Jesus, "We know that you will depart from us. Who will be our leader?" Jesus said to them, "Wherever you are, go to James the Just, for his sake heaven and earth came into being." (12)

This saying reflects the early Christian recognition of James as a key figure in the church's leadership. It underscores the unique position of James as a chosen leader who would guide the disciples after Jesus' departure. The title *"James the Just"* emphasizes his righteousness and moral integrity, qualities that made him a central figure for the community. His leadership was not just a matter of organizational structure but of embodying the spiritual and ethical principles that Jesus imparted.

Saint James the Just, the Brother of the Lord, 16th century.
Novgorod- Wood, gesso, tempera. 31.1x25.4 cm.

The phrase *"for his sake heaven and earth came into being"* carries profound theological implications. It suggests that James' role was part of the divine plan from the very beginning of creation. This statement may allude to the idea that James, in his righteousness and closeness to Jesus, is a key figure in the unfolding of God's salvific plan. It echoes the notion that the leaders of the church are not merely historical figures but are divinely appointed and connected to the very foundation of creation.

In early Christian writings, James is often depicted as a pillar of the church, and his role as the leader of the Jerusalem church was vital in the period following Jesus' resurrection. The *Gospel of Thomas* here emphasizes his importance in a spiritual sense, presenting him as a bridge between Jesus and the early Christian community, guiding them in truth and righteousness.

This saying also speaks to the continuity of the divine plan. Even though Jesus would depart from the disciples physically, his teachings and authority would remain present through James, who would act as a leader grounded in the values that Jesus imparted. The disciples are instructed to seek out James, emphasizing the ongoing presence of divine guidance within the community.

Saying 12 highlights the transition of leadership from Jesus to James, affirming that the community is to continue its journey of faith, anchored in the teachings of the living Word through those chosen to lead. It suggests that spiritual leadership is not just about authority but about being a vessel for divine truth and carrying forward the work of creation and redemption.

This is one of the few passages in early Christian literature that explicitly elevates James over Peter or any other disciple, which suggests that the Gospel of Thomas may have connections to early Jewish-Christian communities, such as the Ebionites, who regarded James as the true leader of Jesus' movement.

Interestingly, in the icon of James the Just, he is encased in half of the sacred vesica piscis. Just as the sunlight formed a vesica around the head of the Son in **the Theophany of Avondale**, now this half-shape near James the Just evokes the same divine geometry. It is as if the light that crowned the Son now echoes quietly in the humble righteousness of the one appointed to lead. James stands not only as a historical figure, but as a living axis between heaven and earth—a vessel for divine continuity. The vesica's arc beside him whispers of union, of a portal between the realms. The leadership of James is not political; it is cosmically rooted, for as Jesus said, "for his sake heaven and earth came into being."

In the vision, the fullness of the Trinity was revealed in light, cloud, and color—yet it is here, in the grounding presence of James, that the heavenly order finds its earthly echo. The vesica beside him reminds us: divine leadership is born not of conquest, but of interior purity, a heart that reflects the eternal.

I was named after James, though I was born a girl, so I became Jamie. My brother, Timothy. Names passed down through scripture, carried like seeds in our lives. Now, as I reflect on Saying 12 and the role of **James the Just**, I feel a quiet thread pulling through time—from ancient Jerusalem to the light that broke open in the Theophany of Avondale.

Perhaps the arc of the vesica beside James in the image is also an arc in me—a geometry of becoming. A sign of spiritual inheritance. Not just of name, but of calling. To witness. To remain close to the light. To remember that divine leadership is not loud but luminous, not power but purity. James stood as the bridge, and somehow, by name and grace, I, too, carry a glimmer of that bridge.

My name, *Jamie,* holds within it the sacred syllables of the Divine Name. It's as though even my name is wrapped in invocation. *Jamie* contains **"I am"**, the sacred declaration God spoke from the burning bush:

"I AM that I AM" (Exodus 3:14).

I was named after **James**, though born a girl, I became **Jamie**. A name that quietly holds the name of God within it, "I AM," hidden in plain sight, like a pearl within the veil. My brother is **Timothy**, his name meaning "honoring God." Together, our names formed a household where the Divine Name echoed softly in our lives, even when we didn't yet understand.

Now, as I contemplate the image of James the Just, adorned with half the vesica piscis, I see my own name nestled in that same sacred geometry. The vesica—symbol of birth, union, the space between two worlds—opens like a window to what Saying 12 reveals: divine authority passed on, not to power-hungry hands, but to the righteous one. James, the bridge. Jamie, the echo.

In the light of the *Theophany of Avondale*, I now see that this name—my name—is more than a given label. It is a quiet covenant. A whisper of identity beyond form. A door where the holy can speak.

James was chosen.
Jamie was called.

Saying 13: Recognition of Christ's Divine Nature

Jesus said to his disciples, "Compare me to someone and tell me whom I am like. "Simon Peter said to him, "You are like a righteous angel."

Matthew said to him, "You are like a wise philosopher."

Thomas said to him, "Master, my mouth is utterly incapable of saying whom you are like." Jesus said, "I am not your master. Because you have drunk, you have become intoxicated from the bubbling spring that I have measured out." And he took Thomas aside and told him three things. When Thomas returned to his companions, they asked him, "What did Jesus say to you?" Thomas said to them, "If I tell you even one of the things he told me, you will pick up stones and throw them at me; and fire will come out of the stones and consume you." (13)

This passage serves to highlight the limitations of human language in describing the divine. Simon Peter sees Jesus as akin to a righteous angel, a figure of spiritual purity and authority. Matthew compares Jesus to a wise philosopher, perhaps recognizing the deep wisdom that Jesus imparts to his followers. However, Thomas, with his profound recognition of the ineffability of Christ's nature, acknowledges that words cannot fully encapsulate who Jesus truly is.

In Gnostic thought, this moment reflects the tension between the attempt to describe the divine and the ultimate unknowability of God. Christ's true essence, being beyond earthly categories, cannot be captured by any single comparison. Each of these attempts — comparing Jesus to an angel, a philosopher, or acknowledging His ineffable nature — points to the divine wisdom that transcends human understanding. It is a reminder that the fullness of divine revelation cannot be fully expressed in finite terms.

Thus, saying 13 not only emphasizes the challenge of describing the divine with human language but also points to the deeper, transcendent nature of Christ, whose true essence is beyond any earthly comparison. It invites the seeker to look beyond surface descriptions and enter into the mystery of the living Word, the divine Logos, who cannot be fully known except through direct experience.

Thomas pauses, listens deeper, and answers, "Master, my mouth is wholly incapable of saying whom you are like." This moment holds immense weight. It's not just a confession of awe — it's a recognition that the essence of Christ cannot be contained by language, by image, or by the intellect.

And in response, Jesus does something extraordinary. He rejects the title "master," saying, "Because you have drunk, you have become intoxicated from the bubbling spring which I have measured out." This isn't just a moment of honor — it's a transmission. It's as if Jesus is saying, *You have tasted the same source I have. You no longer need to name me, because you've encountered what I AM within yourself.*

Then he takes Thomas aside and tells him "three things." When Thomas returns, he doesn't reveal them. Instead, he says, "If I tell you even one of the things he told me, you will pick up stones and throw them at me; and fire will come from the stones and burn you up." That's how sacred, how radically transformative, these revelations are. They're not meant to be spoken in ordinary terms — they're living fire, and they awaken or consume depending on one's readiness to receive.

This saying isn't just about Jesus' identity — it's about the encounter with the Divine that shatters categories, burns through illusion, and draws us into wordless union. It's a koan. A threshold. A glimpse into the revelation that Christ is not to be followed, but found within.

The Logos — the living Word — isn't just a spoken truth. It's the silent pulse at the heart of being. As John says, "In the beginning was the Word," but this isn't mere speech. It's a resonance, a presence, a light within. It's what Eastern traditions call the soundless sound — heard only in the silence beyond the mind. Not something to be explained. Something to be *beheld*. Words may fall short. But presence never does.

As for the possible words that Jesus might have used to describe Himself, several phrases from Christian mysticism and Gnostic thought come to mind:

1. **"I AM HE" (Ἐγώ εἰμι αὐτός)**: This phrase recalls John 8:58: *"Before Abraham was, I AM."* In this context, Jesus is revealing His eternal nature beyond human time and categories. *"I AM"* was the name by which God revealed Himself to Moses in Exodus 3:14, signifying an eternal, self-existent divinity. In a Gnostic sense, Jesus' use of this phrase would point to His pre-existent, divine essence, beyond the limitations of earthly form.

2. **"I AM YOU"**: This phrase reflects a nondual, mystical understanding of divinity, where the distinction between the divine and the individual is dissolved. It suggests an intimate union with the divine, an idea that finds resonance in Saying 108 of the *Gospel of Thomas*, where Jesus tells Thomas, *"Whoever drinks from my mouth will become as I am, and I myself will become them."* This deep identification with Christ mirrors the nature of divinity as it is understood in the Gnostic tradition, where the divine essence is present in all.

3. **"WORD, BREATH, LIGHT"**: These three words connect to key Gnostic and Christian theological concepts — Logos (the Word), Pneuma (the Spirit or Breath), and divine illumination (Light). In Gnostic thought, the Logos is the divine principle of order and knowledge that reveals truth to the soul. Pneuma represents the breath of life, the Holy Spirit, who guides and enlivens the seeker. Light is often a symbol of divine illumination, representing the truth and wisdom that dispels the darkness of ignorance. Together, these words encompass the full spectrum of Christ's divine nature as the revealer of truth, the giver of life, and the light that illuminates the path of salvation.

Embracing the "I AM": A Light of Consciousness Connected to the Divine

In the words of Thomas, "My mouth is utterly unable to say whom you are like." But perhaps the deeper truth is that no words are needed—because "I AM" is not just a phrase spoken by Christ, but a living, breathing presence that exists within each of us. It is the light of consciousness that connects us to the Divine, the eternal Source of all things.

"I AM" is not a distant, unreachable concept, but a reality that lives within the heart of every being. It is the light that illuminates our minds, the breath that gives life to our souls, and the Word that speaks through our actions. When we say, "I AM," we are affirming that we are not separate from the divine but are intimately connected to it—co-creators in the divine plan, living reflections of God's eternal essence.

This recognition is transformative. As we embrace the "I AM" within us, we acknowledge that we are a vessel for divine consciousness. We are not mere individuals, defined by our separate selves, but expressions of the greater whole—reflecting the light of Christ, the Logos, within us. In this way, we come to see that the ineffable nature of Christ, the mystery beyond human understanding, is not just a distant truth, but a living reality that we can experience directly through our consciousness, our very being.

Just as Jesus revealed Himself as the "I AM," we too are called to embody that same divine light. The question is not "Who is like Christ?" but rather, "How do we live in alignment with the 'I AM' within us?" As we step into the light of this divine awareness, we realize that the words of Thomas are our own: the divine essence cannot be fully captured in human language. But it can be lived, experienced, and shared in the world around us, as we embrace the eternal light within.

Another possible word choice found in the *Pistis Sophia*, is the phrase "Yao, Yao, Yao" (also rendered IAO), a sacred name or invocation spoken by Jesus during a powerful utterance or hymn of ascent. This text is part of a Gnostic Christian scripture, likely composed between the 2nd and 4th centuries CE, and reflects esoteric teachings given by Jesus to his disciples after the resurrection.

"Yao" or IAO is a form of the divine name of God used in Gnostic, Hermetic, and magical traditions. It may derive from the YHWH (יהוה) and was considered a mystical vocalization or sound-name of the divine. In ancient Greek magical texts, "IAO" was often used to refer to the highest deity, beyond all names—the unknowable Source. The sacred triple utterance echoes the mystery of movement and repose, as seen in Saying 50 of Thomas. "Yao, Yao, Yao" or IOA is an invocation of divine identity, the origin of light, a sacred echo of divine authority. It reminds us of the sacred utterance of OM. Both are cosmic utterances, sacred sounds that bridge the finite and the infinite, movement and repose, and manifestation with the unmanifest.

On March 31st, 2015, as I stood in awe and wonder, a divine epiphany unfolded before me. From the depths of my being rose a spontaneous song—the sacred OM, the primordial resonance, the song of the Lord as revealed in the *Bhagavad Gita*. In divine compassion, the *Almighty* revealed the Triune essence in a form my soul could comprehend, unveiling the splendor of magnificent love. First, the Heavenly Father appeared in a way my mind's eye could receive. Then, beloved Jesus manifested at the Father's right hand, radiant with divine sonship. Finally, the Holy Spirit—subtle, luminous, and nearly invisible—made its gentle presence known.

Bhagavad Gita 8:13
"Uttering the single-syllable OM, the eternal sound of Brahman, and remembering Me, he who departs leaving the body attains the supreme goal."

Bhagavad Gita 9:17
"I am the Father of the universe, the Mother, the Supporter, the Grandsire... I am the sacred syllable OM..."

Many historians, atheists, and believers alike have questioned whether the canonical gospels accurately reflect the historical Jesus and if these texts can be considered reliable sources. The Catholic Church maintains that there are no hidden teachings of Jesus and rejects texts like the Gospel of Thomas as heretical. This is largely because such writings emphasize the divine light within each person, suggesting that divinity is not exclusive to Jesus but shared among humanity. In contrast, the Church teaches that only Jesus is divine and that to be considered a Christian, one must profess belief in his death and resurrection through the traditional creed.

In other Gnostic writings, such as the Gospel of Mary, Jesus presents a radically different understanding of sin. He says, "There is no sin, but it is you who make sin when you do the things that are like the nature of adultery, which is called sin." In this context, sin is not viewed as a moral failing judged by external law, but as a misstep of the soul—a failure to perceive and live from the divine truth already present within.

This emphasis on inner transformation and direct knowledge of the divine is echoed powerfully in the Gospel of Thomas, especially in Saying 14. Here, Jesus challenges conventional religious practices—not to reject them outright, but to expose the hypocrisy that can lie beneath them when they are severed from true spiritual insight.

Saying 14: Spiritual Transformation

Jesus said, "If you fast, you may invite sin upon yourselves; if you pray, you risk judgment; if you give charity, you might damage your own spirit. But when you travel through any land and are welcomed, accept what is given and heal the sick among them. It is not what enters your mouth that makes you unclean, but what flows out from it." (14)

In this passage, Jesus challenges us to move beyond the externalities of religious ritual and delve into the essence of our inner spiritual life. He says, *"If you fast, you may invite sin upon yourselves; if you pray, you risk judgement; if you give charity, you might damage your own spirit."* At first glance, these words might seem paradoxical, as fasting, prayer, and charity are often seen as virtuous practices. However, Jesus is pointing us toward a deeper, more profound understanding of spiritual transformation — one that is not rooted in outward displays or rigid rituals but in the state of the heart.

In Gnostic thought, the path to salvation and enlightenment comes not through external practices, but through direct knowledge of the self and an inner awakening. Rituals, while they can have their place, should not become a substitute for true transformation. They become empty when they are divorced from a heart that seeks divine truth and purity. Jesus makes it clear that what matters is the inner alignment with divine will, not the mere act of performing religious duties. *"It is not what enters your mouth that makes you unclean, but what flows out from it."* This is a call to examine the motivations behind our actions and words. It is not what we eat, nor what we wear, that shapes our spiritual state — it is the condition of our hearts, the truth we speak, and the love we embody.

Jesus emphasizes that it is our *intentions* — the root cause of our actions — that truly define us. The outer world may reflect our inner state, but it is the inner purification that is the true path to holiness. This teaching challenges us to reflect on the sincerity of our religious practices. Are we performing these actions to fulfill an external expectation, or are they born of a genuine desire for transformation and divine connection?

This theme finds resonance in the words of the prophets in the Hebrew Scriptures. In **Isaiah 58**, the prophet rebukes the people for fasting while perpetuating injustice, saying, *"Is this the kind of fast I have chosen?… Is it not to share your food with the hungry and to provide the poor wanderer with shelter?"* The fast that God desires is one that is rooted in mercy, justice, and compassion — a fast that transcends ritual and touches the lives of others in meaningful ways. Similarly, in **Hosea 6:6**, God declares, *"For I desire mercy, not sacrifice, and acknowledgment of God rather than burnt offerings."* These statements echo Jesus' teaching that it is not through external rituals or sacrifices that we draw closer to the divine, but through the integrity of our hearts and actions.

The transformative journey, therefore, is not one that begins with outward acts, but with an internal shift. True spiritual growth happens when we cleanse our hearts, align our will with divine truth, and allow the love of God to flow through us. It is this alignment of inner and outer life — the harmony between what we believe and how we act — that defines true holiness. **Spiritual transformation** begins within, as we become more attuned to our authentic selves, shedding false beliefs, ego-driven motivations, and worldly distractions.

In our day-to-day lives, this means that we are called to live with a higher awareness of our inner state. Are our actions motivated by love, compassion, and justice? Do we speak with sincerity, kindness, and respect? Are we guided by the truth that lives within us — the divine spark — rather than by societal expectations or the approval of others? The transformation that Jesus speaks of is not about conforming to external standards but about embodying divine love in the world around us. This alignment of action with intention purifies the soul, bringing us closer to God, and allowing us to heal not just ourselves but others as well.

Jesus' teaching in this passage offers a radical invitation: to *look within*, to recognize the truth of our inner nature, and to align our words, actions, and intentions with that divine essence. It calls us to transcend religious formalism and live a life that is authentically connected to the divine light within us. **True devotion** is not measured by what we give or do for appearances' sake, but by the transformative love we express through our words and deeds.

In conclusion, Saying 14 urges us to turn our attention away from the external trappings of religion and toward the purification of the heart. It challenges us to ask ourselves: *What are the intentions behind our actions? What truth do our words reflect? Are we living in alignment with the divine love that exists within us?* The journey toward spiritual transformation is one of awakening — to the truth of our being, to the love that unites us, and to the divine essence that is the source of all.

Saying 14 dismantles the external performance of religion when it lacks inner authenticity, emphasizing that what truly defiles a person is not what enters the mouth but what flows from it—words, intentions, and actions born from the heart. This mirrors Jesus' teaching in Matthew: "Do not swear an oath at all... let your 'Yes' be 'Yes,' and your 'No,' 'No'" (Matthew 5:34–37). Integrity and truthfulness are not optional virtues—they are foundational to spiritual clarity. Likewise, in John 15:4, Jesus urges, "Remain in me, as I also remain in you," pointing to the source of all true transformation: union with the divine. It is not religious ritual, but this abiding presence that bears fruit. To be "salt of the earth" and "light of the world" (Matthew 5:13–14) is not about self-righteous display but about preserving truth and illuminating love wherever we go. As Jesus prays in John 17:21, "That they may all be one, Father, just as you are in me and I am in you," unity in divine essence is both the goal and the ground of our being. Together, these teachings echo through Saying 14, reminding us that healing, hospitality, and authenticity are what make one truly spiritual—not outward rituals, but the light within made manifest.

Proverbs 2:6
"For the Lord gives wisdom; from his mouth come knowledge and understanding."

Bridging Reflection: From the Unborn to Inner Transformation

To behold the One not born of woman is to awaken to the reality of divine presence that transcends form — to recognize that we, too, carry the imprint of the Eternal within us. As children of the Unborn, we are called not only to reverence but to transformation. For to truly see the Father is to be changed by the vision. This recognition invites us to embody the divine in our lives — not through empty ritual, but through the inward journey of purification, love, and integrity. Thus, the next saying becomes a natural extension: if we have seen the Source, how then shall we live?

Saying 15: The Recognition of the Divine Through the Unborn One

Jesus said, "When you encounter the one not born of woman, bow down and honor him. That one is your true Father." (15)

In this enigmatic saying, Jesus calls upon his listeners to recognize the presence of the Divine in a form beyond human birth—one **"not born of woman."** This is a revelation of the Eternal, the Uncreated One, the ineffable source from which all things arise. The call to **fall in worship** is an acknowledgment that this Being is beyond all earthly limitations, beyond flesh and time, dwelling in the realm of pure Spirit.

The prophets glimpsed this mystery, for **Isaiah declared**: *"Before Me no god was formed, nor shall there be after Me. I, even I, am the LORD, and apart from Me there is no savior."* (Isaiah 43:10-11). This is the Unborn One, the Eternal "I AM" who appeared to Moses in the burning bush (Exodus 3:14), a fire that burned yet was not consumed—**a symbol of existence beyond all material constraints**.

The Gospel of John echoes this same truth: *"In the beginning was the Word, and the Word was with God, and the Word was God."* (John 1:1). Christ, the Logos, comes from beyond time and space, manifesting as light into the world, yet His essence is uncreated. To see **the One not born of woman** is to perceive the source of all being, the Father, whom no eye has seen yet who is revealed in the Son (John 1:18).

The mystics, too, have spoken of this great mystery. In the Gospel of Mary, Jesus tells his disciples that the soul must rise beyond the powers that bind it to the material world, ascending through the realms until it reaches repose in the Eternal. The journey of the soul is not toward something newly created, but toward the recognition of its true origin, the Divine One who was never born and will never die.

Thus, this saying is not only a statement about the nature of God—it is an invitation. It calls us to see with **spiritual eyes**, to recognize that beyond all appearances, beyond flesh and form, there is the Radiant One who has always been. And in this recognition, we do not stand—we fall in reverence, for we have encountered the Source of all life.

The "unborn one" represents the divine Father in His most transcendent form — not born, not created, but eternally existent. This aligns with mystical ideas of God as the "ground of being" (as in the writings of philosophers like Plotinus) or the unmanifest aspect of the divine, from which all creation flows.

Saying 16: The Division of the Light: A Prophetic Vision

"Jesus said, 'Perhaps people think that I have come to cast peace upon the world. They do not know that I have come to cast divisions upon the earth: fire, sword, and war. For there will be five in a house: three will be against two and two against three, father against son and son against father, and they will stand alone.'" (16)

Jesus' words, spoken in the ancient mystic tradition, resound with the paradox of the divine revelation. To the uninitiated, the light He brings may seem like a balm, a harbinger of peace and unity. But He, the Living Logos, knows that His presence will sow not merely peace, but the deep, cutting fire of transformation.

Fire, Sword, and War:

In the mystical realm, **fire** is not only destruction but purification — a divine conflagration that burns away the veil of illusion. **Sword** is the sword of discernment, the word of truth that divides the light from the darkness, the real from the false. In the language of the soul, **war** signifies the inner battle — the war between the ego and the spirit, between attachment and liberation. This sacred conflict, though born in suffering, is the very crucible of spiritual enlightenment.

In the Gnostic Gospel tradition, fire is often the symbol of divine illumination. The soul, caught in the fetters of material existence, must endure this fire to be reborn in the divine light. In Eastern thought, particularly in Buddhism, the path to enlightenment is one fraught with internal conflict — the battle of the self dissolving into the great void of non-attachment, where even familial ties become distractions to the higher self.

The Prophetic Division of the Family:

"Father against son, son against father." These words echo the prophetic writings of the Old Testament, where the coming of the Messiah divides hearts. In the book of Micah 7:6, it is written: *"For a son dishonors his father, a daughter rises up against her mother, a daughter-in-law against her mother-in-law; a man's enemies are the members of his own household."* Here, the prophet speaks of the rupture that divine truth can cause, even within the most sacred of bonds.

In Eastern teachings, particularly in the Bhagavad Gita, the divine revelation arrives with profound tension. Arjuna, the warrior, is torn between his duty to his family and the call of the soul. Krishna's counsel is not one of worldly peace but a call to internal victory, to transcendence beyond attachment. Jesus, too, speaks of this transcendence — when one chooses the kingdom of God, the world must lose its hold.

This "division" in the family is not the violence of human hate, but the necessary separation from the bonds that tether the soul to the fleeting, earthly plane. It is a spiritual division, a detachment that is not of the body but of the mind — the soul choosing God over the world. In Matthew 10:34-36, Jesus says: *"Do not think that I came to bring peace on earth. I did not come to bring peace but a sword. For I have come to 'set a man against his father, a daughter against her mother, and a daughter-in-law against her mother-in-law; and a man's enemies will be those of his own household.'"*

Standing Alone: The Path of the Seeker

"And they will stand alone." The path of the divine seeker is solitary, for it requires one to stand apart from the world, away from the comfort of familiar ties. In Eastern traditions such as Sufism, the mystic speaks of standing alone before God, lost in the divine presence. The soul, like the Buddha under the Bodhi tree, must face its deepest shadows and illusions in solitude.

This aloneness is not loneliness, but the profound realization of oneness with the eternal. In Christian mysticism, this standing alone is mirrored in the experience of the Desert Fathers, who withdrew from society to encounter God in silence. The soul, though standing alone, is not abandoned, but is led into union with the Divine.

The Cost of Divine Revelation:

To embrace the light, one must accept the division it brings. The Tao Te Ching teaches that the Tao (the Way) can only be understood when one is willing to follow it beyond the ordinary, beyond the comfortable, beyond the familial and the material. Lao Tzu says, *"The Tao is like a great river. It flows without hesitation, yet many try to hold it back. The one who is wise goes with the flow of the river and is not bound by the banks of the river."*

The same holds true for the followers of Christ. The fire of Christ's truth will burn through the illusions of the world. The sword of His wisdom will sever the attachments of the flesh. The war He speaks of is the ultimate war for the soul — a war not against flesh and blood but against the forces of ignorance and ego.

Mystical Reconciliation: Fire and Sword as Purification

In the cosmic drama, the fire of divine truth is both a destructive and creative force. It is the same fire that consumes the dross of the soul and refines it in the crucible of love. **John 1:5** tells us, *"The light shines in the darkness, and the darkness has not overcome it."* Christ's light will pierce the darkness of the world, bringing the conflict that leads to ultimate peace — peace in union with God.

In the end, the path of spiritual awakening is one of radical transformation, where the self must die to be reborn. And in that rebirth, one will stand alone, yet paradoxically, one will also be one with all. This is the essence of non-duality — the recognition that in the deepest solitude, we are not alone but united with the Divine.

Conclusion: The Awakening Fire

Thus, Jesus' words echo through time as a call to those who are willing to stand alone in the fire of divine truth. The divisions He foretells are the necessary upheavals of the soul — the dismantling of false identities, the breaking of illusions, and the spiritual war that purifies the seeker. The peace that follows is not a peace of the world, but a peace that surpasses all understanding, a peace found only in the full embrace of the Divine.

As the Bhagavad Gita teaches: *"The one who is steadfast in mind, who has renounced worldly desires, and who seeks refuge in the Supreme Divine, transcends the conflicts of the world and finds peace in union with God."* May we walk this path, casting aside all that binds us, to stand in the light — alone, yet united in the Divine.

Prelude to the Inconceivable Gift: A Threshold of Divine Encounter

Before the soul can receive the gift that no eye has seen or mind imagined, it must be emptied of all that it clings to — perception, control, and the illusion of knowing. This saying stands as a threshold between the finite and the Infinite. Here, Jesus is not merely offering insight, but initiation into the mystery of the divine. The language he uses points to a realm of experience that cannot be entered through thought, tradition, or flesh, but only through surrender — the surrender of self, of form, of expectation. Like Moses removing his sandals before the burning bush, we are asked to step barefoot onto holy ground, stripped of all faculties except the open heart. Only then can we receive the divine gift that transcends seeing, hearing, touching, and thinking — for it is not a gift among many, but *the Gift*, the Presence of Godself poured into the soul.

Saying 17: Divine Gift: The Unseen, Unheard, Unfelt, Unimagined

"Jesus said, 'I will give you what no eye has seen, what no ear has heard, and what no hand has touched, and what has never occurred to the human mind.'" (17)

In this profound saying, Jesus promises a divine gift that transcends the limits of human perception and understanding. The words echo the ineffability of divine wisdom and the unimaginable nature of the gifts of the Spirit. What He offers is not of this world, nor can it be comprehended by the ordinary senses or intellect. This divine gift is beyond the grasp of sight, hearing, touch, and thought, signifying that it belongs to a higher realm, a transcendent reality that is only accessible through direct spiritual experience.

Unseen by the Eye:

The "eye" here symbolizes **earthly perception** — our ability to perceive the physical world. Yet, the divine gift Jesus speaks of is not a tangible object or a worldly experience. It is a spiritual vision that surpasses the limits of our physical senses. This aligns with the mystical traditions across cultures, where the eye of the soul is said to perceive a higher reality beyond the material plane. In the Gnostic tradition, this "unseen" vision corresponds to the ability to perceive the Logos, the divine mind that underlies all creation, beyond the superficial appearances of the world.

In the Hebrew Bible, Elijah's vision of the still small voice of God in 1 Kings 19:11-12 represents this transcendent sight — the ability to behold God not in the whirlwind or the fire, but in the subtle and hidden movements of divine presence. This inner sight requires spiritual awakening, and as Matthew 5:8 says, *"Blessed are the pure in heart, for they will see God."*

Unheard by the Ear:

The "ear" represents our ability to hear the sounds and voices of the world, but the divine gift transcends this capacity. True wisdom, as revealed by Jesus, is not the sound of words, but the Word itself — the Logos, which is unspoken, beyond any human language or understanding. In John 1:1, we read: *"In the beginning was the Word, and the Word was with God, and the Word was God."* This Word is not just speech; it is divine communication that resounds in the depths of the soul, not in auditory form but in the transcendent experience of oneness with the Divine.

In Eastern thought, this is mirrored by the silence of the mind, which is the key to receiving true wisdom. In Buddhism, the soundless sound or the *"unheard"* teachings are those that can only be perceived when one attains stillness and silence in the mind. It is not the external voices that bring the message of truth, but the silence that speaks louder than any words.

Untouched by the Hand:

The "hand" here refers to physical touch, the ability to interact with the world through the senses. But what Jesus offers is a gift that cannot be grasped by the hand, for it is spiritual and immaterial. It cannot be held or contained by the body. True divinity, as expressed in the mystical traditions, is not something we can hold onto, but something that holds us, enveloping the soul in divine light and love.

In Sufism, this is expressed as the divine embrace — the soul yearning to be united with the Beloved, but realizing that this union is not of physical nature. It is a union of hearts, of divine essence, not physical proximity. Isaiah 55:8-9 reflects this as God says, *"For my thoughts are not your thoughts, neither are your ways my ways... as the heavens are higher than the earth, so are my ways higher than your ways and my thoughts than your thoughts."* The divine gift cannot be contained by earthly hands but is embraced by the heart.

Unimagined by the Mind:

The final part of the saying speaks to the human intellect — the mind that is constantly striving to grasp and categorize everything within its reach. The divine gift Jesus speaks of is beyond the rational mind and cannot be conceived by human thought. It is not something that can be deduced or imagined through intellectual effort.

In Eastern traditions, this corresponds to the non-conceptual knowledge that transcends dualistic thinking. It is the direct experience of reality as it truly is, free from the limitations of thought and language. The Upanishads speak of Brahman, the ultimate reality, as beyond all concepts and intellectual formulations. It is the ineffable — the experience of the divine that defies all mental categorization.

1 Corinthians 2:9 echoes this idea: *"No eye has seen, no ear has heard, no mind has conceived what God has prepared for those who love him."* Here, Paul speaks of a mystical wisdom that is beyond the grasp of human intellect but is revealed to those who are spiritually awakened.

The Divine Gift as the Path to Unity:

Jesus' divine gift is not just an abstract concept, but a transformative force that brings the soul into union with God. This union is not an intellectual or sensory experience, but a deep, mystical participation in the divine nature. The mystical experience of Christ, where the soul encounters the living God in direct communion, is the ultimate gift — it cannot be grasped, it cannot be described, but it can only be experienced in the depths of the soul.

John 17:21 — *"That all of them may be one, Father, just as you are in me and I am in you. May they also be in us, so that the world may believe that you have sent me."* This unity is the divine gift Jesus promises — a unity that transcends the divisions of the material world and brings the soul into oneness with the Divine.

Conclusion: A Mystical Invitation

The divine gift Jesus offers is an invitation to enter into mystical union with the Divine — a gift that transcends all worldly understanding, surpasses the limits of the senses, and cannot be captured by the mind. This is the ultimate revelation — not of something external, but of the eternal truth that resides within. To receive this gift is to enter the Kingdom of God within, where the soul experiences the infinite depths of divine love, wisdom, and light.

Thus, Jesus beckons us to go beyond the limits of the material world, to rise above the illusions of the senses and intellect, and to step into the eternal mystery of the divine presence. In doing so, we experience the **unseen**, **unheard**, **untouched**, and **unimagined** —

the very essence of God, which no human mind can fully comprehend but only encounter in the transformative experience of divine union.

Saying 18: The Cyclical Nature of Existence: The End and the Beginning

"The disciples said to Jesus, 'Tell us how our end will be.' Jesus said, 'Have you discovered, then, the beginning, that you seek after the end? For where the beginning is, there the end will be. Blessed is he who shall stand at the beginning, and he shall know the end, and shall not taste of death.'" (18)

The next figure shows the Triune nature of God made of Mind, Body, and Spirit. Jesus is encased in a self-illuminating halo with the Holy Spirit and the Heavenly Father between him.

"Dunston, J. C. (2015) "THE EMBODIED DIVINE: UNVEILING THE HEART OF GOD'S MANIFESTATION IN THE WORLD"

In this profound saying, Jesus responds to His disciples' question about the end of their lives with a paradox that invites a deeper reflection on the cyclical nature of existence. Instead of offering a linear answer, He points to the beginning — a timeless and eternal truth — suggesting that the key to understanding the end is rooted in the first step, the origin, the source of all things. This saying calls attention to the interconnectedness of beginning and end, echoing the eternal circle of life, where the end is not a finality but a return to the source.

The Beginning and the End: A Cyclical Journey

The nature of existence is often perceived in terms of linear time — from birth to death, from creation to dissolution. However, in mystical teachings, the true nature of reality is revealed to be cyclical. The beginning is not distinct from the end, but rather inseparable. The circle of life, which turns continuously in both creation and destruction, suggests that all things return to their origins, as the Tao and Eastern philosophies assert. The Yin and Yang in Taoism symbolize this cyclical motion, the interplay between opposites that are, in truth, reflections of the same eternal flow.

In Christian mysticism, this cycle is reflected in the Alpha and Omega — the first and last letters of the Greek alphabet, which symbolize Christ as the beginning and end of all creation. In **Revelation 22:13**, Jesus declares: *"I am the Alpha and the Omega, the First and the Last, the Beginning and the End."* This vision points to the ultimate truth that all of creation is contained in the divine purpose, beginning in Christ and culminating in His return, which is not the end, but a restoration and renewal of the original creation.

Standing at the Beginning: The Timeless Moment

Jesus teaches that blessed is he who stands at the beginning, for to be in touch with the origin is to be in touch with the eternal nature of existence. The "beginning" represents spiritual awakening, the point where the soul reconnects with the divine source — the Christ within that is both the origin and fulfillment of all creation.

In the Gnostic tradition, the beginning is often represented as the Pleroma, the fullness of divine consciousness, from which the soul emanates. To stand at the beginning is to experience union with this divine fullness, which transcends time and space. This aligns with the mystical understanding that the soul, in its deepest essence, is not bound by the temporal flow of past, present, and future but exists in an eternal present, where the beginning and the end converge in a continuous circle of divine union.

In Eastern spirituality, particularly in Buddhism, there is the understanding of samsara — the cycle of birth, death, and rebirth. However, ultimate nirvana is the liberation from this cycle, a return to the beginning, the original oneness from which all things emerge.

In this state, the individual transcends the temporal distinctions between life and death, beginning and end.

Knowing the End: The Eternal Now

To know the end is to realize that it is already present in the beginning. This is not a mere intellectual understanding but a spiritual realization that the cycles of life and death, creation and destruction, are not separate from our essential being. In mystical Christianity, this is captured by the concept of the resurrection — the ability to transcend death by entering into a state of divine union with the Source, where the soul is no longer bound by the limitations of the physical world.

Jesus' message here is that the end is not to be feared. The one who stands at the beginning — the awakened soul — knows that death is not an ultimate separation but a transformation into the eternal. **John 8:51** echoes this: *"Very truly I tell you, whoever obeys my word will never see death."* In this sense, the end is not an event but a realization of eternal life, where the soul recognizes its unbroken connection to the divine.

Not Tasting Death: The Immortality of the Soul

The promise that the blessed one "will not taste death" is an invitation to transcend the fear of mortality. In mystical traditions, death is seen not as the end of life but as a transition to a higher state of being. This can be understood as spiritual immortality — the idea that the soul, once awakened to its divine origin, is beyond the grasp of physical death.

In Eastern thought, this is reflected in the atman (the individual soul) and its union with Brahman (the ultimate reality). Once the soul realizes its oneness with the divine, it is no longer subject to the cycle of birth and death. Bhagavad Gita 2:20 echoes this idea: *"The soul is neither born, and nor does it die."* Similarly, Christian mysticism emphasizes that those who are united with Christ are already partakers of eternal life, transcending physical death through their participation in the divine nature.

The Prophetic Voice: A Call to Transformation

Jesus speaks here with the voice of a prophet, inviting His disciples to look beyond the surface appearance of life and death and to recognize the eternal nature of their souls. His words challenge us to reconsider our understanding of time, existence, and the afterlife. The key to this understanding is not merely intellectual knowledge but spiritual awakening, a return to the divine origin that transcends time and space.

In the mystical tradition, the awareness of this eternal present is the key to true liberation. When the soul recognizes its oneness with the divine, it no longer perceives death as a separate event, but as a transformation into a higher state of being. This is not an abstract doctrine but an experiential truth — to stand at the beginning is to live in the eternal now, where the end and the beginning are one.

Conclusion: The End is the Beginning

The paradox that Jesus presents in Saying 18 calls us to transcend time and to see the circle of existence as a reflection of the divine. The beginning and the end are not separate events but interconnected moments in the eternal dance of creation. To stand at the beginning is to know the end, for both are contained in the eternal present, where life and death, creation and destruction, are part of the same divine reality.

This teaching invites us to awaken to the divine within, to recognize that in our deepest essence, we are beyond the cycles of time. When we realize our eternal nature, we will no longer fear death but will embrace the eternal life that is already within us — the gift of spiritual immortality. In the end, we return to the beginning, and in the beginning, we find the end.

Ecclesiastes 3:1-2 says, "There is a time for everything, and a season for every activity under the heavens: a time to be born and a time to die..."

The Seed That Remembers

The vision passed,
but it did not fade.

I walked back across the same soil—
the same dust, the same wind, the same branches swaying
but I was not the same.

Something had been planted in me,
or rather, something had awakened—
a seed that had been waiting since before your birth,
before the shaping of the stars,
before even time dreamed of itself.

It was not just a memory.
It was a knowing.

And now,
each moment was pierced with revelation.

I could see it in the eyes of a child,
in the shadow play of leaves,
in the quiet weight of dusk settling over the field.

I could see it even in sorrow—
how even grief bends toward light.

I remembered that all things are nesting dolls,
and every form hides the formless.
Every question bears the echo of an answer
already whispered at the root of Being.

The kingdom had come.
It had always been here.

It was never in the sky or beneath the sea,
but within—
not locked, but waiting
for me to turn inward
with eyes that see
and ears that hear.

The pearl was never lost.
The mirror was never broken.
The Voice was never silent.

It is all still here.
He is still here.
And we are still in Him.

Forever enfolded,
forever one.

ଽଌଌଌ

Saying 19: The Eternal Origin and the Five Trees of Paradise

"Jesus said, 'Blessed is he who was before he came into being. If you become disciples of mine and hear my words, these stones will minister to you. For you have five trees in Paradise, which remain unmoved summer and winter, and whose leaves do not fall. Whoever becomes acquainted with them will not taste death.'" (19)

This enigmatic saying invites us into the realm of **pre-existence** and **eternal life**, concepts that transcend the human understanding of time and existence. Jesus speaks of a state of being that precedes even the physical birth, pointing to a **divine origin** that exists outside the constraints of temporal creation. His words suggest that there is a deeper spiritual reality, one that exists before the soul's earthly manifestation. The phrase, *"Blessed is he who came into being before he came into being,"* is a paradox that invites us to explore the **mystery of eternal life** and the **timeless nature** of the soul.

"Came into Being Before He Came Into Being": The Mystical Birth

This phrase echoes the profound mystery of the Logos, the divine Word that existed before time itself, as spoken of in John 1:1: *"In the beginning was the Word, and the Word was with God, and the Word was God."* The idea that one can "come into being before coming into being" suggests that the true essence of a person exists in an eternal state, before being manifest in the physical world. This pre-existence aligns with the Gnostic understanding that the soul's true nature is part of the divine realm before descending into the material world.

In Eastern spirituality, particularly within Hinduism and Buddhism, this idea finds resonance in the concept of Atman (the true self) and the eternal Brahman (the ultimate reality). Before the soul enters the cycle of samsara (birth and rebirth), it is already part of the divine source, untouched by time and change.

"Stones Will Serve You": The Power of Divine Words

Jesus speaks of stones serving His disciples, a mystical concept that implies the transformation of the material world when one is aligned with divine wisdom. The stones here symbolize the material world, which, when understood through the lens of divine truth, is no longer an inert and lifeless substance but becomes a reflection of the spiritual realm. The disciples, through their connection with Jesus and His teachings, can command the material world, recognizing its deep, spiritual significance.

In biblical tradition, stones often represent spiritual truths or milestones of faith. In 1 Peter 2:5, believers are referred to as "living stones," being built into a spiritual house. The stones serving the disciples reflect the transformation of the material world through spiritual insight, where everything aligns with divine purpose.

The Five Trees in Paradise: The Mystical Significance of the Trees

Jesus mentions five trees in Paradise that remain undisturbed by the changing seasons, whose leaves do not fall. The number five holds significant mystical meaning in many spiritual traditions. In biblical tradition, five often symbolizes grace and the fullness of divine favor. It may also represent balance between the material and spiritual worlds, as the five senses are gateways through which we experience the physical world.

The five trees can be understood as symbols of spiritual nourishment, offering sustenance that is not affected by the passing seasons, representing the eternal and unchanging truths of the divine. The idea that their leaves do not fall suggests a constant renewal of spiritual life and wisdom, unaffected by the corrupting influences of time. This eternal fruitfulness is a sign of the immortality of the soul, nourished by the divine Word and wisdom.

Immortality and the Knowledge of the Trees

The statement, *"Whoever becomes acquainted with them will not taste death,"* ties the knowledge of the five trees to the gift of eternal life. This is not simply an intellectual understanding but a spiritual awakening that connects the soul to the divine source, to the Paradise of God, which is both within and beyond the material world. The five trees can be seen as symbols of spiritual truths that offer nourishment to the soul, life that transcends death.

This next photograph captures the majestic beauty of the Rocky Mountains, a reflection of the divine image and likeness in which we are all made. Within the veiled shroud of the clouds, the Holy Spirit appears to the left of Yeshua—subtle and luminous in fiery hues—while the Heavenly Father rests on the right, with **hair as white as wool**, radiant and ancient, full of eternal presence. They are both enveloped in mystery and light, and **the radiant Dove is their chariot**, carrying the divine presence through the heavens like living fire and breath.

Surrounding Jesus, you can see the halo—the **cosmic egg of creation**—a self-illuminating radiance that shines with the light of a **menorah**, each ray like a branch extending divine wisdom and presence into the world.

This sacred scene once overlooked a farm where Catalpa trees once grew—broad-canopied trees with showy white blossoms, massive heart-shaped leaves, and long, bean-like seed pods hanging from their gently twisting trunks.

"Dunston, J.C. (2015). "There He Was Transfigured Before Them.
His Face Shone Like The Sun, And His Clothes Became As White As The Light"

In Christian mysticism, this reflects the Tree of Life in the Garden of Eden, which grants eternal life to those who partake of it. The leaves of the trees symbolize healing and eternal renewal, as seen in Revelation 22:2: *"On either side of the river was the tree of life, bearing twelve crops of fruit, yielding its fruit every month. And the leaves of the tree are for the healing of the nations."*

In Eastern traditions, the concept of eternal life is tied to spiritual awakening, where the individual is freed from the cycle of birth and death (samsara) and attains moksha (liberation). The knowledge of the five trees aligns with this idea of discovering eternal truth, which liberates the soul from the limitations of temporal existence.

The Prophetic Voice: A Call to Transformation

Jesus' words carry a prophetic message to His disciples, calling them to recognize their divine origin and the eternal truth that sustains all things. He emphasizes that spiritual knowledge is the key to immortality, not just in a future sense, but as a present reality. The five trees in Paradise symbolize the living truths of the divine that can sustain and renew the soul in the eternal now.

In this prophetic voice, we are invited to reconnect with our divine source, to recognize that the material world, when seen through the lens of divine wisdom, becomes a reflection of the eternal truth. We are called to experience immortality through knowledge, through transformation, and through the eternal presence of the divine.

Conclusion: The Blessing of Pre-Existence and Eternal Life

Saying 19 invites us into a mystical vision of pre-existence, spiritual nourishment, and eternal life. Jesus calls His disciples to recognize their origin in the divine, to seek the knowledge of the five trees in Paradise, and through this knowledge, to transcend death. These trees, symbolizing spiritual truths, offer a way to reconnect with the divine source and to find eternal life not only in the afterlife but in the present moment.

As we heed Jesus' words and seek to understand the eternal truths represented by the five trees, we are transformed, nourished, and made immortal — no longer bound by the limitations of time and space. The divine, in all its fullness, is available to those who seek, and through this divine knowledge, we partake in the eternal life that transcends death.

Bhagavad Gita 9.22 – "To those who are constantly devoted and always remember Me, I give the understanding by which they can come to Me."

"The Seed and the Sanctuary"

Saying 20: The Kingdom of Heaven: The Mustard Seed

"The disciples said to Jesus: 'Tell us what the kingdom of heaven is like.' He said to them, 'It is like a mustard seed, the smallest of all seeds, but when it falls on tilled ground, it grows and becomes a great tree, and the birds of the heaven come and make nests in its branches.'" (20)

In this saying, Jesus uses the mustard seed as a symbol for the kingdom of heaven, emphasizing its humble beginnings and vast potential for growth. The mustard seed, despite being the smallest of all seeds, contains within it the power to transform and expand into something great and expansive. This imagery invites the listener to understand the kingdom not as an immediate or worldly power, but as a spiritual force that begins within and gradually grows to encompass all things.

The Mustard Seed: A Symbol of Divine Potential

In Christianity, the mustard seed has traditionally been interpreted as a symbol of faith—small, yet capable of growing into something of great importance. In Matthew 17:20, *Jesus says, "If you have faith as small as a mustard seed, you can say to this mountain, 'Move from here to there,' and it will move. Nothing will be impossible for you."* This connects the mustard seed to the transformative power of faith, suggesting that even the smallest measure of faith can unleash immense spiritual power when planted in the right conditions.

In this saying, however, the mustard seed is used to illustrate the kingdom of heaven, a divine spiritual realm that begins small, almost imperceptibly, but grows beyond all expectation when nurtured in fertile ground. The tilled ground represents the heart and soul that is prepared and ready to receive the divine truth. The growth of the mustard seed into a great branch that provides shelter for the birds of heaven indicates the kingdom's vastness, which provides refuge, peace, and spiritual shelter for all who seek it.

The Kingdom of Heaven: An Expanding Spiritual Reality

The kingdom of heaven is not a physical or earthly realm in the conventional sense. Rather, it is the inner kingdom, the realization of the divine within the heart of the individual and the world at large. The great branch signifies the growth of divine wisdom, and the shelter provided to the birds of heaven symbolizes the protection and comfort of the divine for those who seek it.

In Eastern thought, there is a similar recognition that spiritual awakening is a process that begins with a small, subtle shift in consciousness. Whether viewed through the lens of Hinduism (where the spiritual journey begins with a small spark of divine consciousness) or Buddhism (where the mind and heart are cultivated toward enlightenment), the idea of a humble beginning leading to vast spiritual growth is universal.

The Birds of Heaven: Divine Shelter and Protection

The birds of heaven mentioned in the saying are a symbol of those who seek the kingdom—spiritual seekers, souls in search of truth, and those who align themselves with divine wisdom. The birds taking refuge in the tree's branches represent individuals who find spiritual shelter within the kingdom of heaven. This shelter can be understood as divine protection, peace, and the spiritual nourishment found when one aligns oneself with the divine will.

This image echoes the Psalmic vision of divine refuge, as seen in Psalm 91:4, *"He will cover you with his feathers, and under his wings you will find refuge."* Similarly, in Eastern mystical traditions, the imagery of sheltering wings often represents the protection of divine wisdom and the care offered by the spiritual guide or teacher.

The Tilled Ground: Preparation for Spiritual Growth

The tilled ground is crucial to this image. It represents the spiritual preparation of the heart, mind, and soul to receive divine truth. In biblical terms, this idea is similar to the parable of the sower (Matthew 13:3-9), where the condition of the soil (heart) determines whether the seed (truth) will take root and grow. Tilling the ground speaks to the spiritual discipline of purifying the heart, making it ready to receive the divine message and allow it to grow.

In Eastern traditions, this concept aligns with the practice of meditation or contemplation, which prepares the individual to receive enlightenment. Mindfulness, discipline, and self-awareness are key to cultivating the ground of the soul, making it fertile for the planting of wisdom.

The Growth of the Seed: Spiritual Transformation

The growth of the mustard seed into a great tree represents spiritual transformation. The mustard seed's power to grow from a tiny seed into a large tree reflects the divine potential within every person. Just as the seed contains the blueprint for the future tree, each individual carries within them the potential for spiritual growth and enlightenment.

The great branch that emerges symbolizes the spiritual fruits of this growth, including peace, wisdom, compassion, and love. As the tree provides shelter for the birds, the individual who has nurtured the seed of divine wisdom becomes a vessel of peace and a source of refuge for others.

The Kingdom is Within: A Universal Spiritual Truth

In this saying, the kingdom of heaven is not an external reality that must be sought outside, but an inner reality that can be accessed through spiritual practice, faith, and self-awareness. Jesus' message is clear: the kingdom begins as something small, seemingly insignificant, but when tended with care, it grows into a vast and encompassing presence, offering shelter and peace to all who seek it.

This concept is consistent with Eastern spirituality, where the ultimate realization of the divine is within the individual. The kingdom, like the mustard seed, is often hidden until it is cultivated, but once it begins to grow, it transforms the person and the world around them.

Prophetic Voice: The Call to Inner Transformation

Jesus' words in this saying are a prophetic invitation to spiritual awakening and growth. The mustard seed represents the initial step—an act of faith, a spark of divine truth, a moment of clarity—that, when nurtured, can grow into something far beyond the individual's initial understanding. This message speaks to the potential for spiritual transformation in every individual, no matter how small or humble their beginning might be.

In a world that often seeks grandiose, external signs of power and greatness, Jesus reminds us that the kingdom of heaven grows silently and humbly, through spiritual discipline and inner cultivation. The tree that grows from the mustard seed offers a vision of hope: that even the smallest step toward spiritual truth can have a profound impact, both on the individual and on the world.

Personal Reflection: Planting Seeds Among the Rocks

On my own journey, I often planted seeds into the rocks, where a foundation for awakening did not grow. There were times I offered my faith, my love, and my efforts into places or people not ready to receive them—hearts un-tilled, souls hardened by pain, or even moments when I myself was not fully prepared to receive what the Spirit was sowing in me. In these barren places, the mustard seed could not yet take root. But this, too, was part of the journey. For in witnessing the absence of growth, I came to more deeply understand the necessity of the tilled ground—the inner readiness to receive the kingdom.

Conclusion: A Journey of Spiritual Growth

In Saying 20, Jesus teaches us that the kingdom of heaven is not something distant or external but is instead something that grows within. Like the mustard seed, it begins small and humbly, but when nurtured with faith, awareness, and spiritual practice, it expands, offering spiritual shelter to those who seek it. The message is clear: even the smallest beginning can lead to great transformation, and through this process, we are all invited to partake in the divine kingdom that resides within us all.

Chapter 4

Light, Knowledge, and Divine Revelation
(Sayings 21-30)

Saying 21: Spiritual Vigilance and Readiness

"Mary said to Jesus, 'What are your disciples like?'He said, 'They are like little children who have settled in a field that is not theirs. When the owners of the field come, they will say, "Give us back our field." They take off their clothes in front of them in order to give it back to them and return their field to them. Therefore I say, if the owner of a house knows that a thief is coming, he will keep watch before he comes and will not let him break into his house of his domain to carry away his goods. You, then, be watchful over against the world. Gird your loins with great strength lest the robbers find a way to reach you, for the advantage for which you look, they will find. May there be among you a person of understanding. When the grain ripened, he came quickly, sickle in hand, and reaped it. Whoever has ears to hear, let him hear.'" (21)

This saying, like many teachings of Jesus, speaks to the necessity of spiritual vigilance and readiness. In the first part of the parable, Jesus compares his disciples to children who live in a field that does not belong to them, a subtle but potent metaphor for the transient nature of worldly existence. The field, like all material things, is not permanent and will be reclaimed by its rightful owner when the time comes. The disciples, or those seeking to follow Christ, must be ready to relinquish what they do not truly possess when the true Master returns.

The mention of a thief coming in the night amplifies the urgency for preparedness: as in the biblical parables of the faithful servant (Matthew 24:43-44), Jesus warns that the world—like a thief—can stealthily invade the heart, leading one astray unless one is spiritually vigilant. This spiritual alertness reflects an essential quality for those who are trying to remain in harmony with the divine, resisting the pull of worldly distractions and misdirections.

The Field: The World and the Soul

The field in this context is symbolic of the world and the human soul. The disciples—children or spiritual novices—may seem innocent in their engagement with this world, yet they have settled in a place that does not truly belong to them. The worldly life is not their eternal home. This reflects the teaching found in 1 John 2:17, where it is stated that "the world and its desires pass away, but whoever does the will of God lives forever." As such, Jesus calls his followers to be aware of the impermanence of material things and the spiritual danger of clinging to what is temporary.

The action of returning the field signifies relinquishment—the letting go of material attachments when the True Owner comes to claim what is His. Spiritual maturity involves recognizing the fleeting nature of worldly possessions and the eventual return to the Divine Source, who is the true possessor of all things.

The Thief: Spiritual Deception and Temptation

The thief serves as a symbol of spiritual deception and the subtle temptations of the world that can infiltrate and take away what is most precious: the soul's focus on the divine. The warning to be watchful echoes the parable of the wise and foolish virgins in Matthew 25:1-13, where vigilance is required for the arrival of the bridegroom. The thief in the night is the metaphor for the unexpectedness of spiritual threats that can rob the unprepared. The robbers in this passage represent the distractions of materialism, ego, and sin that seek to take away the soul's true treasure—the connection with God.

This warning also invokes the Eternal Watchfulness that Eastern traditions such as Buddhism and Hinduism speak of: a state of mindfulness and awareness in the present moment that resists the distractions of the material world. In these traditions, the illusion of the material world (Maya) must be transcended through awareness and vigilance in order to reach spiritual liberation.

Gird Your Loins: Spiritual Preparation and Strength

To gird your loins is an ancient metaphor for preparation and readiness. In ancient times, this phrase referred to the act of gathering one's garments and preparing for action, particularly in battle. Spiritually, it signifies the need to prepare oneself for the challenges and distractions that will inevitably arise on the path. It is the call to strengthen oneself spiritually through prayer, meditation, discipline, and detachment from worldly concerns, to ensure that one is not caught unawares.

In Ephesians 6:14, Paul writes, *"Stand firm, then, with the belt of truth buckled around your waist, with the breastplate of righteousness in place."* This imagery complements Jesus' teaching, urging believers to be ready and equipped with spiritual strength and truth. The girding of the loins represents the spiritual discipline and alertness necessary to withstand the constant threat of worldly distractions and to remain focused on one's eternal purpose.

The Grain Ripened: The Moment of Spiritual Harvest

In Christian tradition, Christ is often depicted as the harvester at the end of the age—the one who comes when the soul is ready, to gather it into the eternal Kingdom. The image of the sickle in hand evokes both divine discernment and mercy.

The final image of the grain ripening and being reaped suggests the spiritual harvest—the moment when one's soul, having been nurtured in the field of the world, reaches its full maturity in the kingdom of heaven. The person of understanding is the one who recognizes when the time has come for spiritual transformation and is able to act decisively, with wisdom and discernment. This is the moment when spiritual maturity allows the disciple to gather the fruits of their labor and return to the Divine Source.

In Eastern thought, the ripening of the grain corresponds to the maturation of spiritual wisdom. In Buddhism, this would align with the ripening of the fruits of enlightenment, where one's spiritual journey reaches its culmination and the seeker attains nirvana, the complete liberation from suffering. Similarly, in Hinduism, this aligns with the realization of moksha, the state of liberation from the cycle of birth and rebirth, where one recognizes their oneness with the Divine.

Understanding and Readiness: The Call to Discernment

The call for a person of understanding is a call for spiritual discernment. It is not enough to simply follow a path blindly; one must be alert and conscious of the signs of spiritual maturation. Those who can discern the right time for action—whether in the moment of prayer, service, or inward transformation—are those who are best equipped for the spiritual harvest. The disciple who understands the times will respond with wisdom and prepare themselves for the coming of the Divine Kingdom.

Prophetic Voice: A Warning and a Call to Action

This saying carries a prophetic tone as it warns of the inevitable coming of the Kingdom and the spiritual reckoning that will accompany it. It urges followers to remain vigilant, to prepare themselves spiritually, and to stay awake to the subtle movements of the soul. The prophetic nature of the saying is clear: spiritual deception, material distractions, and the temptation to fall asleep spiritually will always be present, and the faithful must be ever ready to respond with strength, wisdom, and faith.

To walk this path is to live with the eyes of the soul open, ready to surrender the field, and to reap with joy when the grain of the spirit ripens.

Conclusion: The Path of Vigilance

In saying 21, Jesus calls us to spiritual vigilance, urging us to remain alert to the spiritual dangers that threaten our connection with the Divine. The world, like a thief, can steal away the soul's treasure, but through preparedness, understanding, and discernment, we can be ready for the harvest of the Kingdom. The path of spiritual readiness is one of constant awareness, where we live in the present moment while always looking ahead to the fulfillment of the divine promise.

> *Matthew 24:43-44 – "But understand this: If the owner of the house had known at what time of night the thief was coming, he would have kept watch and would not have let his house be broken into. So you also must be ready, because the Son of Man will come at an hour when you do not expect him."*

> *Dhammapada 327-328 – "Just as a farmer channels water to his fields, just as a fletcher shapes his arrows, just as a carpenter carves wood, so the wise master themselves."*

Saying 22: The Unity of Opposites, the Kingdom Within, and the Path of Co-Creation

"Jesus saw some infants being nursed. He said to his disciples, 'These infants being nursed are like those who enter the kingdom.' They said to him, 'Then shall we enter the kingdom as infants?' Jesus said to them, 'When you make the two one, and when you make the inside like the outside and the outside like the inside, and the upper like the lower, and when you make the male and the female into a single one, so that the male will not be male nor the female be female, when you make eyes in place of an eye, a hand in place of a hand, a foot in place of a foot, an image in place of an image—then you will enter [the kingdom].'" (22)

In these profound words, Jesus reveals a mystery hidden since the foundation of the world: the Kingdom of God is not reached through striving outwardly but through an inward transformation—a return to original innocence, wholeness, and unity. Just as the infants being nursed are pure, unselfconscious, and close to the source of life, so too must the soul become: stripped of illusion, reconciled within itself, and one with the Divine.

The disciples' question—"Shall we enter the kingdom as infants?"—is not met with a simple yes or no. Instead, Jesus invites them into a deeper mystery: the making of the two into one. This is not merely a call to childlike simplicity; it is a call to transcendence, to the dissolution of false separations within ourselves and in the world around us.

To make the two one is to awaken to the truth that what appears separate was never truly divided. The world of inner thought and the world of outer action, the spiritual realm and the material realm, heaven and earth—these are not distinct realities in opposition, but different expressions of the same eternal essence. When we make the inside like the outside and the outside like the inside, we live in integrity. Our thoughts and actions reflect one another. We are no longer fragmented beings at odds with ourselves, but whole, unified, and transparent to the light of God.

When Jesus speaks of making the above like the below and the below like the above, he is calling us to recognize the sacredness woven through the entire cosmos. The heavens mirror the earth, and the earth reflects the heavens. The great and the small are interwoven in the Divine tapestry, each revealing the other, each bearing witness to the hidden unity that binds all things together.

This unity also extends to the energies we experience as masculine and feminine. In the mystical tradition, male and female are not merely biological distinctions but symbols of polarities within the soul: activity and receptivity, strength and compassion, logic and intuition. To make the male and female into a single one is to transcend opposition, not by erasing difference, but by recognizing their deeper harmony. In the Divine, there is no separation between Father and Mother, for God contains all things in unity. When we heal these polarities within ourselves, we reflect more perfectly the image of the One from whom we come.

The process of co-creation, therefore, is not just about transforming the self but about realizing the divine potential within us all. As we do so, we participate in the unfolding of the Kingdom on earth, helping to shape a world that reflects the divine truth, beauty, and love.

Thus, the Kingdom of God is not a distant place beyond the stars. It is a state of being, a consciousness of unity, where the soul rests in the eternal embrace of the Divine. In this state, distinctions of race, class, gender, and status dissolve—not because diversity is erased, but because the deeper truth of oneness outshines all division.

As Paul writes in his letter to the Galatians:
"There is neither Jew nor Gentile, neither slave nor free, nor is there male and female, for you are all one in Christ Jesus." (Galatians 3:28)

And as Jesus himself teaches elsewhere:
"At the beginning, the Creator 'made them male and female,' and said, 'For this reason a man will leave his father and mother and be united to his wife, and the two will become one flesh.' So they are no longer two, but one flesh." (Matthew 19:4–6)

John 17:21 – *"That all of them may be one, Father, just as you are in me and I am in you."*

Tao Te Ching, Chapter 42 – *"The Tao gave birth to One. The One gave birth to Two. The Two gave birth to Three. The Three gave birth to all things. All things carry Yin and embrace Yang. They achieve harmony by balancing these forces.*

The call to unity is a call to return—not to a past innocence, but to the eternal present where all things are already reconciled in God. It is not an erasure of individuality but a realization that all individualities find their root and fulfillment in the One.

Mystics across traditions have glimpsed this truth. Paul Brunton wrote: *"The first step in spiritual realization is to see that we are one with the world, that we are part of the whole. The second step is to realize that this oneness is not merely a concept but a living truth."*

And Swami Prabhavananda echoed:
"True knowledge is the realization of the unity of all things. When we experience this oneness, we know the deepest truth of existence: there is no distinction between the self and the universe."

To enter the Kingdom is not to go elsewhere, but to awaken here and now to the divine unity that always is, always was, and always will be. It is to see that every breath we take is a breath of the Divine. Every life we encounter is a face of the Divine. Every moment is woven into the vast, radiant fabric of God's being.

When we make the two one, when we live with the eyes of the heart open, when we act from the wholeness we already are, then—and only then—do we find ourselves standing in the Kingdom, even now, even here.

When we harmonize dualities, we are not simply dissolving them; we are integrating them in such a way that the fullness of the divine can be realized and expressed in the world. This spiritual union opens us to the role of co-creators, where we are no longer passive recipients but active participants in the divine flow of life. As the masculine and feminine energies unite within, so too do we, as humanity, co-create with God in the ongoing work of shaping the world in divine light.

This idea of co-creation is central to the Gnostic worldview, which views human beings not as mere creations but as divine sparks capable of participating in the cosmic unfolding. Just as the Logos (the divine Word) brings creation into being, so too are we invited to speak and act in alignment with the divine will, becoming agents of creation in the world. This is not a passive acceptance of fate but an active, conscious participation in the creative process.

Finally, when Jesus speaks of an image in place of an image, he points to the true divine nature that humanity is called to embody. The false self, shaped by ego and earthly desires, must be replaced by the true self—the divine image in which we were originally created. This transformation is part of the co-creative process, where humanity is invited to become who they truly are—not mere reflections of the world around them, but expressions of the divine essence that brings the world into being.

As part of the Apparitions of Avondale, I beheld a vision where Jesus revealed his image in place of an image from the ancient Pantocrator icon to a living divine manifestation working through nature itself to bear his love and light to the world. In this divine encounter, he renewed his commandment: that we love one another as God has loved us.

Saying 23: The Hidden and the Revealed

"Jesus said, 'I shall choose you, one from a thousand and two from ten thousand, and they will stand as a single one.'" (23)

This saying reveals the mystery of divine election and spiritual unity, where the chosen ones are those who awaken to their divine origin. They are called to co-create with the Divine, weaving heaven and earth into oneness. As Paul wrote, *There is neither Jew nor Greek, slave nor free, male nor female, for you are all one in Christ Jesus* (Galatians 3:28).

This mystery of divine selection echoes the esoteric traditions where the few are called to awaken, not in isolation, but in unity with the whole. The chosen ones are those who transcend separation, dissolving the illusion of duality to become *a single one*. This is the great restoration—the reunification of what was scattered, the healing of the primordial rift.

Jesus speaks of the *one from a thousand and two from ten thousand*—a remnant, a hidden seed of divine consciousness that grows into a mighty tree, much like the mustard seed of Saying 20. It is a call to spiritual vigilance, to deep remembrance, to the recognition that the soul is not merely an exile in the world but a bearer of divine light.

This echoes the words of Isaiah: *A remnant will return, a remnant of Jacob, to the mighty God* (Isaiah 10:21). It is not a selection of privilege but of preparedness, of those who have attuned themselves to the voice of the Spirit. As Jesus said, *Many are called, but few are chosen* (Matthew 22:14), not because God withholds, but because few open themselves to receive.

The chosen ones are not set apart by external distinction but by the *inner eye that sees, the inner ear that hears.* They recognize the secret voice calling them home, much like Elijah, who found God not in the earthquake or fire but in *the still, small voice* (1 Kings 19:12). These are the ones who perceive the hidden light, who stand as the *single one—* whole, undivided, restored in divine unity.

In the Gospel of Thomas, this theme of oneness recurs. Saying 22 speaks of making the *two into one*—the reconciliation of opposites, the healing of fragmentation. It is the path of theosis, of divine union, where humanity ceases to see itself as separate from God. As Christ himself prayed: *That they may be one, as We are one* (John 17:22).

To be chosen is to be awakened. To be awakened is to *stand as a single one.* This is the mystery of the Kingdom, the hidden call to return to the Source.

> *Lankavatara Sutra – "Few are those who awaken to the supreme wisdom and stand firm in the truth."*

ଛଟ୍ଟତ

Saying 24: The Light Within

"His disciples said, 'Show us the place where you are, since it is necessary for us to seek it.' He said to them, 'Whoever has ears, let them hear! There is light within a person of light, and it shines on the whole world. If it does not shine, it is darkness.'" (24)

This saying unveils the paradox of seeking and finding, of presence and absence. The disciples desire to know *where* Jesus is—as though the Kingdom were a distant realm, a hidden sanctuary set apart from the world. Yet Jesus redirects their gaze inward, calling them to recognize that the Light they seek is already within. The Kingdom is not found in external geography but in the awakened soul.

The light within is the divine spark, the indwelling radiance of God that illuminates all things. This recalls the Prologue of John: *The true light, which gives light to everyone, was coming into the world* (John 1:9). It is the Logos, the eternal Word, present from the beginning and now revealed in Christ. This light is not a foreign addition to the soul but its very essence—the Imago Dei, the image of God within.

Yet Jesus gives a warning: *If it does not shine, it is darkness.* This echoes his words in Matthew: *If then the light within you is darkness, how great is that darkness!* (Matthew 6:23). A hidden light is a lost light. The one who fails to awaken to the divine presence within is trapped in spiritual blindness, unable to perceive the radiant mystery that pervades all things.

The disciples' question—*"Show us the place where you are"*—is the perennial cry of the seeker. Where is the divine? Where does Christ dwell? The answer is both transcendent and immanent: *The Kingdom of God is within you* (Luke 17:21). To see the Light, one must become light. To know Christ's dwelling, one must awaken to His presence within.

The mystics of all traditions have testified to this interior illumination. St. Symeon the New Theologian, in his *Hymns of Divine Love*, describes encountering the divine as a luminous fire arising from within:

"He suddenly appeared inside my poor heart,
As the sun rising in the morning sky."

Similarly, Rumi writes: *"Why do you seek the light outside? Light yourself, and the whole world will shine."* The Buddha, too, speaks of the awakened one as a *lamp unto themselves*, a being who radiates wisdom from within.

Saying 24 is a call to *awaken to the divine light already present*, to let it shine forth and illuminate the world. It is not found in a distant realm but in the very ground of one's being. The path is not outward but inward—*the place where He is* is the place where the soul meets God.

As the Psalmist declares: In Your light, we see light (Psalm 36:9).

Brihadaranyaka Upanishad 4.3.6 states:
"Now, when he sees himself as the Self, as the Lord of all that is, then he is free from sorrow."

Saying 25: The Love That Guards

"Jesus said: 'Love your brother like your own soul; guard him like the pupil of your eye.'" (25)

This saying distills the essence of divine love into a simple yet profound command. To love another as one's own soul is to recognize the deep unity that binds all beings. It echoes the greatest commandment: *Love your neighbor as yourself* (Mark 12:31). Yet, here, Jesus intensifies the call—not merely to love as one loves oneself, but to love as one loves the very essence of their being, their soul, the divine breath within.

The second part of the saying—*"guard him like the pupil of your eye"*—reveals the protective nature of true love. The eye is among the body's most sensitive and vital parts, instinctively shielded from harm. Just as the body reflexively guards the pupil from dust and danger, so must one safeguard the well-being of their brother, ensuring that no harm befalls them, whether physically, emotionally, or spiritually. This recalls the Psalmist's prayer:

"Keep me as the apple of your eye; hide me in the shadow of your wings." (Psalm 17:8)

"The Shepherd's Love"

To love and guard another in this way is to participate in the very nature of God, who is described as a Shepherd, a Guardian, a Protector of souls. In the Gospel of John, Jesus declares: *I am the good shepherd. The good shepherd lays down his life for the sheep* (John 10:11). To love in this manner is to lay down one's life, to be wholly devoted to the well-being of another, as Christ is devoted to humanity.

This saying also reflects the mystical truth that love is not separateness but oneness. To love another as one's own soul is to recognize that in the Divine Reality, there is no distinction—what we do for another, we do for ourselves; what we do for ourselves, we do for another. This echoes Paul's words: *If one member suffers, all suffer together; if one member is honored, all rejoice together* (1 Corinthians 12:26).

Thus, saying 25 is a call to a love that is not merely affection or kindness, but a sacred duty—an unwavering commitment to the well-being of others, a guardianship of their soul as one would guard the light of their own being.

> *Mark 12:31: "Love your neighbor as yourself."*

> *Deuteronomy 32:10: "He guarded him as the apple of His eye."*

> *Bhagavad Gita 6.9: "He who sees the same Supreme Lord dwelling equally in all beings, in the superior and the inferior alike, is regarded as a perfect yogi."*

Saying 26: The Vision to See Clearly

"Jesus said: 'You see the speck that is in your brother's eye, but you do not see the beam that is in your own eye. When you remove the beam from your own eye, then you will see clearly to remove the speck from your brother's eye.'" (26)

This saying is a call to inner purification and spiritual discernment. It reveals the paradox of human nature—how quick we are to recognize the faults in others while remaining blind to the greater obstacles within ourselves. Jesus speaks here in the language of prophetic wisdom, echoing the psalmist's cry:

> *"Who can discern his errors? Cleanse me from hidden faults." (Psalm 19:12)*

The beam represents the illusions, attachments, and unacknowledged faults that obscure one's vision. It is the veil over the heart, the cataract that dims the soul's perception. Only when this obstruction is removed—through repentance, self-examination, and divine grace—can one see with clarity, discerning both their own path and how to truly aid another.

This teaching reflects a universal mystical truth: the journey inward precedes the journey outward. In the *Sermon on the Mount*, Jesus commands, *"Blessed are the pure in heart, for they shall see God"* (Matthew 5:8). The unpurified heart sees through a veil, mistaking shadows for substance, judging others while failing to perceive its own shortcomings.

The great mystics understood this saying not only as a moral teaching but as a spiritual process. The Desert Fathers spoke of the *eye of the soul*, which must be cleansed before it can truly perceive divine light. The Eastern tradition echoes this in the concept of *avidya*—spiritual ignorance—as the root of suffering. In order to attain wisdom, one must first remove the beam of delusion, of ego, of self-righteousness.

Christ's words also point to the nature of divine sight. When one removes the beam, they do not merely see others' faults—they see others with love, mercy, and truth. They see not the speck, but the whole person, as God sees them. To judge rightly is not to condemn but to restore. This is the vision of the healed soul, one that reflects the Light of the world.

Thus, saying 26 calls the seeker to humility, introspection, and transformation. The way to heal the world begins with healing oneself. Only then does one become a true servant of light, guiding others not with blindness but with the clear vision of love.

Bhagavad Gita 16.2-3: "Humility, self-restraint, and freedom from hypocrisy..."

༄ ❀ ༄

Saying 27: Fasting from the World and Observing the Sabbath

"Jesus said: 'If you do not fast from the world, you will not find the Kingdom. If you do not observe the Sabbath as a Sabbath, you will not see the Father.'" (27)

In this powerful saying, Jesus calls his disciples to a profound spiritual discipline—a call to detachment from the temporal world and a deeper union with the divine through the sacred observance of the Sabbath. These two teachings are not merely external actions but profound invitations to transform the inner life, to set aside distractions and worldly attachments in order to enter the full experience of the Kingdom and behold the Father.

Fasting from the World

The first part of the saying—"If you do not fast from the world, you will not find the Kingdom"—addresses the need for inner purity and detachment. It is not just a physical fast but a spiritual one, a fasting from the distractions and entanglements of the material world that draw the soul away from the divine. The "world" here is the realm of temporary pleasures, ego-driven desires, and the noise of everyday life. To "fast from the world" is to cultivate a state of inward stillness, free from the grasp of worldly attachments, so that the soul can turn toward God with undivided attention.

This fasting is akin to the practice of asceticism in many mystical traditions, where a conscious effort is made to detach from anything that draws the soul away from God. It resonates with the words of the Apostle Paul, who wrote: *"Do not conform to the pattern of this world, but be transformed by the renewing of your mind"* (Romans 12:2). The fasting Jesus speaks of is not about abstaining from food or drink alone, but about abstaining from everything that keeps us spiritually blind or distracted, so that we may fully encounter the Kingdom of Heaven.

Observing the Sabbath as a Sabbath

The second part of the saying—"If you do not observe the Sabbath as a Sabbath, you will not see the Father"—emphasizes the sanctity of rest and divine communion. While the outward observance of the Sabbath in Jewish tradition is a day of rest from physical labor, Jesus speaks of a deeper, spiritual Sabbath, a time of communion with God. Observing the Sabbath "as a Sabbath" means to enter into a space of sacred rest where the soul can be still and receptive to God's presence.

The Sabbath is a sign of God's creative and redemptive work. In Genesis, God rested on the seventh day after creating the world, not because He was tired, but to set a pattern for humanity, a rhythm of work and rest that points to the ultimate rest in God. Jesus teaches that this deeper rest is essential for spiritual transformation. In observing the Sabbath, one enters a deeper relationship with the Father, ceasing from the busyness of life and opening the heart to divine presence and love.

In the New Testament, Jesus challenges conventional understandings of the Sabbath by teaching that the Sabbath is made for humanity, not humanity for the Sabbath (Mark 2:27). True observance of the Sabbath is not merely about external rituals, but about entering into the rest of God, aligning oneself with the divine rhythm of creation.

The Spiritual Invitation

Taken together, these two teachings point to the necessity of inner discipline for those who seek to truly know God. To fast from the world is to deny the ego and worldly distractions, to create space within for God's presence to fill. To observe the Sabbath as a Sabbath is to embrace a deeper rest in God, where the soul can be restored and renewed, prepared for a direct encounter with the Father.

These teachings reflect the invitation of Jesus to live with purpose, focus, and divine awareness. The Kingdom is not a far-off reality, but a present reality for those who are willing to detach from the world and enter into the sacred rest of God's presence. In this way, we truly see the Father—not as an abstract concept, but as a living, intimate presence in our lives.

To follow this path requires the courage to step away from the distractions of the world, to make space for God, and to embrace the deeper rhythms of divine communion. By fasting from worldly entanglements and observing the Sabbath in its fullest spiritual sense, we move closer to the heart of God and the experience of His Kingdom.

⅋❧❦❧

Saying 28: The Drunkenness of the Soul

"Jesus said: 'I took my stand in the midst of the world, and in flesh I appeared to them. I found them all drunk, and I found none among them thirsty. My soul ached for the children of humanity, because they are blind in their hearts and do not see. For they came into the world empty, and they seek to depart from the world empty. But now they are drunk—when they shake off their wine, then they will repent.'" (28)

This saying is a profound reflection on the spiritual condition of humanity, one that speaks to the blindness of the heart, the emptiness of worldly pursuits, and the deep yearning for spiritual awakening. In this message, Jesus stands as both a witness and a compassionate observer of the human condition, a condition in which most are "drunk" with worldly desires, unaware of the deeper truth that calls them.

Drunkenness as a Metaphor for Spiritual Blindness

When Jesus says, *"I found them all drunk, and I found none among them thirsty,"* he is describing a state of spiritual intoxication. The "drunkenness" here symbolizes a loss of clarity and awareness, where the soul is numbed by the distractions and pleasures of the world. Just as alcohol dulls the senses and impairs judgment, so do the excesses of worldly desires dull the heart's ability to perceive the deeper, spiritual truths. People are caught up in their desires, consumed by the things of the world, yet they are not spiritually "thirsty"—they do not long for the Living Water that can truly satisfy the soul.

The metaphor of drunkenness also highlights the nature of human pride and self-deception. In our intoxicated state, we may feel satisfied or content with what the world offers, but in truth, we are spiritually empty, unaware of the greater depths of existence that await us. As St. Augustine once said, *"Our hearts are restless until they rest in Thee,"* indicating that without the knowledge of God, human beings remain thirsty, even when they do not realize it.

The Ache of the Soul for Humanity

Jesus expresses deep sorrow when he says, *"My soul ached for the children of humanity, because they are blind in their hearts and do not see."* Here, we see the heart of Jesus—a heart full of compassion for the state of humanity. He recognizes the blindness that afflicts the human soul, a blindness that prevents people from seeing the truth of their divine origin and the love that surrounds them. The "blindness" is not physical, but spiritual—a lack of awareness of the divine presence that permeates all things. It is a blindness that keeps humanity from realizing their potential for union with God, their true nature as children of the Divine.

This ache for humanity's blindness resonates with many of the prophets of the Old Testament who lamented the spiritual condition of Israel. The prophet Hosea, for example, mourns, *"My people are destroyed for lack of knowledge"* (Hosea 4:6). Jesus, in his compassion, sees beyond the external distractions and senses the deep spiritual hunger that lies beneath the surface of human striving.

Emptiness in Birth and Death

Jesus further observes, *"For they came into the world empty, and they seek to depart from the world empty."* This speaks to the inherent emptiness of human existence when it is disconnected from God. We enter the world without spiritual awareness, and unless we are awakened to the truth of our divine nature, we leave the world empty, having missed the opportunity to live in full communion with the Divine. Life, in this sense, becomes a cycle of searching for meaning in transient things, only to discover that true fulfillment cannot be found in the world itself.

The emptiness Jesus speaks of is a metaphor for the soul's longing for fulfillment, for purpose beyond the material realm. It echoes the ancient teaching of the Buddha, who spoke of the suffering (dukkha) inherent in life due to the insatiable desires that bind us to the cycle of birth and death. Yet, in both the Christian and Buddhist traditions, there is the promise of a way out of this suffering—through awakening, through union with God.

Repentance as the Key to Awakening

Finally, Jesus states, *"But now they are drunk—when they shake off their wine, then they will repent."* This is a moment of hope amidst the sorrow. The drunken state, though it may seem hopeless, is not permanent. There is the possibility of awakening, of shaking off the spiritual intoxication that clouds the soul's vision. Repentance, in this sense, is not merely a sorrowful turning away from sin, but a profound shift in perception—a turning toward the light of God, away from the darkness of ignorance.

In Christian mysticism, repentance is often seen as a spiritual rebirth, a return to the original state of union with God. It is not merely about regret for wrong actions but about a transformation of the heart, a rediscovery of the true self. As St. John of the Cross wrote in his *Dark Night of the Soul*, the journey of the soul is often one of disillusionment and awakening—a process in which the soul gradually sheds its illusions and is brought into the presence of divine truth.

The Call to Awakening

Saying 28 is a profound call to spiritual awakening. It challenges us to examine our own spiritual condition: Are we drunk with the world, distracted by fleeting desires and material pursuits? Are we blind to the divine presence that surrounds us, seeking fulfillment in things that can never truly satisfy? The message of this saying is not one of condemnation, but of compassionate invitation—an invitation to awaken from our spiritual stupor and turn toward the divine light.

In the Christian tradition, this awakening is symbolized by the *coming of the Holy Spirit*—the Paraclete who brings clarity to the mind and peace to the heart. In the mystical teachings of the saints, the process of awakening is often described as a journey of purification, where the soul gradually becomes free from the illusions of the world and enters into the deeper knowledge of God.

Thus, the journey from drunkenness to awakening is one of spiritual transformation. The soul that was once blind and spiritually intoxicated can, through repentance and divine grace, awaken to the truth and live in the fullness of the Kingdom.

When you come to know yourself, you will be at peace, for in knowing who you truly are, you awaken to the truth of all existence. You will see the Divine in every form, and no longer seek outside yourself for what has always been within.

> **Bhagavad Gita 2.69**: *"What is night for all beings, the self-controlled one is awake to. What is day for all beings, is night for the sage."*

Saying 29: The Wonder of the Spirit and Flesh

"Jesus said: 'If the flesh came into being because of the spirit, it is a wonder. But if the spirit came into being because of the body, it is a wonder of wonders. Yet I marvel at how this great wealth has taken up residence in this poverty." (29)

This saying delves into the mystery of the relationship between spirit and body, exploring the paradox of divine presence and human limitation. It presents a profound meditation on the nature of creation, the soul, and the embodiment of divine wealth in human poverty.

The Spirit and Flesh: The Wonder of Creation

In the first part of the saying, *"If the flesh came into being because of the spirit, it is a wonder."* Here, Jesus acknowledges the miracle of human life. The flesh, or physical body, is seen as the outward manifestation of the spirit, a temporary vessel that comes into being because of the divine breath. This speaks to the biblical idea that humanity is created in the image of God, with the *spirit* as the essential life force behind the body. The wonder in this is the fact that the physical realm, including human bodies, reflects the divine reality—spirit manifesting in form. It echoes the teaching of the Apostle Paul, who writes in 1 Corinthians 15:44, *"It is sown a natural body, it is raised a spiritual body."*

The wonder of spirit giving rise to the body is rooted in the concept of creation as a divine act, where the unseen (spirit) becomes visible through the seen (body). The human body, in this light, is a reflection of the spiritual world, containing within it the spark of the divine. The physical world, as expressed in the body, carries the weight of the spiritual, pointing back to the Creator.

The Spirit and Body: The Wonder of Wonders

The second part of the saying presents an even greater marvel: *"But if the spirit came into being because of the body, it is a wonder of wonders."* This phrase introduces a profound mystery—one that challenges conventional thinking about the relationship between body and spirit. It suggests that the spirit, the immaterial and eternal aspect of human beings, can also be born out of the body, the material and temporal. This idea speaks to the wonder of the Incarnation, where the eternal Word (the Spirit) became flesh in the person of Jesus Christ. The "wonder of wonders" is the fact that the divine Spirit took on human form, allowing for the infinite to dwell within the finite, for the eternal to become bound by time and space.

This concept echoes the mystical idea that divine truth is hidden within the material world, that the body itself, despite its apparent impermanence, contains the potential for divine revelation. It also touches on the idea of *theosis*—the process by which humans are united with God. In the Christian mystical tradition, this union of spirit and body, heaven and earth, is considered the ultimate mystery and the goal of salvation.

The Great Wealth in Human Poverty

Finally, Jesus says, *"Yet I marvel at how this great wealth has taken up residence in this poverty."* This line reflects the paradox of the divine presence within the human form. The "great wealth" refers to the divine Spirit—God's infinite love, wisdom, and creative power—while "poverty" refers to the humble, limited nature of the human body. The marvel here is the fact that the boundless richness of the divine has chosen to inhabit the finite and fragile human form.

This statement mirrors the central mystery of the Christian faith—the Incarnation of Christ. The Word, which existed before time and through whom all things were made, took on the poverty of human nature, entering into the limitations of the flesh. Jesus, who was fully divine, chose to live within the poverty of the human condition. As Paul writes in 2 Corinthians 8:9, *"For you know the grace of our Lord Jesus Christ, that though he was rich, yet for your sake he became poor, so that you through his poverty might become rich."*

This mystery of the divine taking up residence in human poverty is at the heart of Christian mysticism. It speaks to the humility of God, who chooses not to remain distant and aloof from creation but enters into it fully, embracing the frailty and suffering of human life. The "wealth" of the divine is made manifest in the poverty of the human body, offering an extraordinary gift to humanity—the possibility of union with God.

The Spiritual Paradox: Union of Spirit and Flesh

Saying 29 offers a profound paradox about the nature of existence and the relationship between the material and the spiritual. The spirit, which is pure and uncontainable, is both the source of the body and the one that is contained within it. The body, which is finite and perishable, is also the dwelling place of the infinite and eternal. This paradox invites contemplation on the nature of God's presence in the world and the mystery of the Incarnation.

For the mystic, this saying offers a deep reflection on the union of the divine with humanity, the meeting point of the eternal and the temporal. It emphasizes the radical humility of God, who comes to dwell in human form, and challenges the seeker to see beyond the surface of the body to the hidden spiritual wealth that resides within.

Implications for the Mystical Path

The mystical implications of this saying are profound. It calls the seeker to see the divine in the human body—not merely as a physical structure but as a vessel for spiritual transformation. It invites the soul to recognize the presence of God within the self, within the body, and within all of creation. It is a call to reverence the body as the temple of the spirit and to see all material things as containing the potential for divine revelation.

This saying encourages the seeker to reflect on the mystery of incarnation, not only in Christ but in every human being. It challenges the believer to honor the dignity of the human body and to seek the divine presence within all things, seeing beyond the poverty of external appearances to the great wealth of the Spirit within.

The temple is not made with hands. It is the body joined to Christ—not as an idea, but as bone of His bone.

> *Genesis 2:7: "Then the Lord God formed a man from the dust of the ground and breathed into his nostrils the breath of life, and the man became a living being."*
>
> *"But if the spirit came into being because of the body, it is a wonder of wonders." This challenges materialist thinking—if consciousness were merely a product of the body, it would be even more astonishing.*
>
> *"Yet I marvel at how this great wealth has taken up residence in this poverty." "Great wealth" refers to the spirit, the divine spark or higher consciousness within.*
>
> *Plato's Allegory of the Cave: The soul is trapped in the material world but belongs to a higher, eternal realm.*

The idea of the Trinity is one of the most profound and challenging teachings in Christianity. How can God be three and yet one at the same time? This is a mystery that challenges our logical minds. Today, we will dive into this mystery and explore how it can transform our understanding of God's nature.

Each person of the Trinity is fully God, sharing the same divine nature, while also having distinct roles and relationships with the Godhead. The Father is seen as the source and originator, the Son (Jesus Christ) is the manifestation of God in human form, and the Holy Spirit is the active presence of God in the world and in the lives of believers. The understanding of God as both an action and a personal manifestation is reconciled within the framework of the Trinity. God is the ultimate source of all action and happening, while also being capable of revealing Himself personally through the Son and the Holy Spirit. The Trinity offers a way to understand the multifaceted nature of God's engagement with creation, encompassing both the transcendent and immanent aspects of God's presence and activity.

God Beyond Form: The Father as Energy, Mind, and Unity

In my visionary experience, the Heavenly Father is not a physical entity but an energetic mind, a realm of thoughts and intentions. This aligns with the concept of God as the eternal Source and the "mind" behind all creation. The Father, as the Mind of the Universe, is the consciousness that pervades all of existence, constantly creating and observing the unfolding of reality. This aspect embodies divine wisdom and intelligence, and it is through this divine mind that the universe and its intricate laws are orchestrated.

Saying 30 from the Gospel of Thomas—"Where there are three gods, they are gods. Where there are two or one, I am with him"—speaks to the profound unity of the Trinity. Whether the divine is experienced as three, two, or one, Jesus assures us that He is with us. This emphasizes that God's presence is not bound by number but is always present, intimate, and engaged with creation. It affirms that the Father, Son, and Holy Spirit are not separate, distant entities but are united in purpose and essence, always available to the believer.

In Job 37:15-16, the Father's presence is described as a force in nature—clouds and lightning represent His power, which is beyond human comprehension. These descriptions reflect God's energetic and dynamic nature, not a tangible, human form. The Father's role as the mind or energy of creation speaks to His position as the origin of all things, providing the initial spark or idea that becomes manifest through the Son and the Spirit. Ultimately, whether in the fullness of the Trinity or in the intimate presence of Christ, God's unity and presence remain constant, drawing us ever closer into divine communion.

What are the attributes of God?

In considering the attributes of God, we encounter a multifaceted understanding of divine nature that encompasses both relational and metaphysical qualities. God is often seen as pure love, embodying an unconditional and self-giving nature that transcends human understanding. This love is intrinsically tied to self-awareness, where God possesses full consciousness of self and existence. As the originator and source of all creation, God is the foundational being from which everything flows, embodying the essence of wholeness and completeness.

Alongside these qualities, God is regarded as mind, representing intellect, reason, and purpose. Divine attributes also include kindness and compassion, illustrating God's deep care and empathy toward creation. God's almightiness points to the infinite power and sovereignty over all things, while consciousness reveals a profound awareness of reality and existence. God is not static but infinite, constantly becoming—a dynamic being whose nature and involvement in the world are ongoing. God's active presence in the world is seen in His continuous shaping and transforming of creation according to divine will.

God as the Body: The Manifestation of Creation and the Incarnation of the Word

Body: Symbolizes God as the material world, the manifestation of creation. Everything that exists physically, from the smallest atom to the largest galaxy, is part of the divine body of

God. This allows God to be present and active within all matter, interconnected through divine presence. Jesus can be seen as the incarnate aspect of God in the material world.

Jesus Christ: The Unique Incarnation of the Word

In the beginning was the Word, and the Word was with God, and the Word was God (John 1:1). This profound and eternal truth echoes across time and space—God, in His infinite love, chose to speak Himself into being. The Word is not a mere utterance, a fleeting sound, or an idea; it is the very essence of God, the divine Logos, the perfect expression of the Father's heart. This Word, as eternal and unchangeable as God Himself, entered into time and history in the person of Jesus Christ, revealing the depths of the divine, and offering the world the ultimate invitation to know the true nature of God.

In Jesus, the Word of God became flesh and dwelt among us (John 1:14). This is the ultimate mystery, the revelation of a God who does not remain distant, aloof, or unknowable, but a God who chooses to enter into creation, to become one with us, to bridge the gap between the eternal and the temporal. In the person of Jesus, the Word of God became visible, touchable, and tangible. No longer abstract or hidden in the heavens, the Word clothed itself in human flesh and walked the earth. In every word spoken, in every miracle performed, in every act of love and compassion, the Word of God was made manifest, revealing to us not just a truth, but the truth of God Himself.

Jesus Christ is not merely a prophet or teacher; He is the living embodiment of the Word—the Logos of God, the final revelation of the divine will. He is the Truth that cannot be contested or surpassed, the perfect expression of God's infinite wisdom, beauty, and love. The Word of God is not something distant or impersonal; it is the very person of Christ. He is the one who reveals God to us, and through Him, we are able to see the face of the invisible God: *"The Son is the image of the invisible God, the firstborn over all creation"* (Colossians 1:15, NIV). As Jesus Himself said, *"Believe me when I say that I am in the Father and the Father is in me; or at least believe on the evidence of the works themselves"* (John 14:11, NIV).

The Word that was with God from the beginning, through whom all things were made, entered into the world, not in grandeur or power, but in humility—in a manger, in a life of simplicity, and ultimately in suffering. The Word was not content to remain in the realm of theory, philosophy, or distant theological concepts. Instead, the Word entered the very heart of human experience: the pain, the joy, the temptation, the tears, and the sacrifice. He revealed Himself as the divine love incarnate, a love that suffered with us, rejoiced with us, and understood our deepest struggles.

This is where the divine Word becomes the most personal, most passionate, and most transformative message ever given to humanity. Jesus is the Word made flesh not only to show us God's love, but to invite us into the very life of God, to offer us a share in the eternal union of the Father, Son, and Holy Spirit. In Jesus, we are invited to hear the Word, to see the Word, and to live the Word. The Word does not just speak; the Word becomes. The Word becomes love in action, grace in the flesh, truth that redeems, light that transforms.

As Jesus Himself taught, **"Jesus replied, 'Anyone who loves me will obey my teaching. My Father will love them, and we will come to them and make our home with them.'"** (John 14:23, NIV) The Word of God is not something to be kept at arm's length; it is meant to dwell within us, to become part of who we are. The living presence of the Word calls us into an intimate relationship—a relationship where the divine comes to abide with us, to transform our hearts, to make His home in us.

Every word Jesus spoke was not merely a message—it was the expression of the Father's will, delivered with a love that could not be contained. His teachings were not abstract propositions, but the living truth that cuts through the lies of the world and pierces the hearts of those who hear with faith. In His presence, the Word of God was no longer distant or unknowable—it was close, it was near, it was with us. God is not far off, He is near, as near as the breath we breathe, as near as the love we feel.

Through Jesus, the Word shows us what it means to be fully human and fully divine. He is the true reflection of God's nature, the perfect image of the invisible God (Colossians 1:15). His life is the Word in action: the love of God poured out for humanity, the truth of God made tangible, the glory of God revealed. Jesus is the fullness of the divine expression— the Word of God, who shows us who God is and who we are meant to be.

To know Jesus is to know the Word, to know the truth of God. He is *"the way and the truth and the life"* (John 14:6, NIV). He is the divine revelation of the Father, the One who calls us into relationship—into union with the divine. In Him, we are invited to participate in the eternal communion of God, to know and be known by the One who is the source of all life, all love, all truth. As Jesus promised, *"And I will do whatever you ask in my name, so that the Father may be glorified in the Son. You may ask me for anything in my name, and I will do it"* (John 14:13–14, NIV).

Jesus Christ, the unique Incarnation of the Word, is not just a teacher, not just a prophet, not just a figure in history—He is the living Word of God, the divine Truth made flesh, the face of God revealed to the world. Through Him, we are brought into the eternal love of God, transformed by the divine truth He embodies, and invited to become co-creators with Him in His great work of love and revelation.

In the end, all things find their meaning in Him—the Word who was with God, who is God, and who made all things. The Word has spoken, and in His voice, we hear the call to come, to know, to live in Him, and to live in the truth of His divine love.

Jesus said, "I am the light that is over all things. I am all: from me all has come forth, and to me all has reached. Split a piece of wood; I am there. Lift up the stone, and you will find me there." Gospel of Thomas, Saying 77

The true Light who gives light to every man was coming into the world. The true Light who enlightens every man has come into our world. John 1:9

"Just as a body, though one, has many parts, but all its many parts form one body, so it is with Christ. For we were all baptized by one Spirit so as to form one body— whether Jews or Gentiles, slave or free—and we were all given the one Spirit to drink." 1 Corinthians 12:12-27

"My prayer is not for them alone. I pray also for those who will believe in me through their message, that all of them may be one, Father, just as you are in me and I am in you. May they also be in us so that the world may believe that you have sent me." John 17:20-21

We, too, are made as a three-part being made of mind, body, and spirit. This harmonious connection between our mind, body, and spirit allows us to access the divine essence that resides within us.

Jesus' mission was to rescue humanity from ignorance and the lack of self-realization. He aimed to demonstrate what each individual can ultimately become, igniting a spark of divine consciousness within us. The Kingdom of God resides within us.

Invisible Threads: The Metaphysics of the Holy Spirit

The Holy Spirit represents God's transcendent essence, existing beyond the physical world. It is eternal, beyond space and time, and the source of the inner peace and light that guides humanity. The Spirit connects all beings through invisible threads of love and energy, allowing us to experience unity with the Divine. In John 14:16-17, Jesus promises the coming of the Holy Spirit to guide believers, particularly in times of waiting or difficulty: "And I will ask the Father, and he will give you another Advocate to help you and be with you forever—the Spirit of truth." This passage highlights the Holy Spirit's role as an enduring presence that supports and sustains believers through their journey.

Metaphysically, the Holy Spirit can be understood as a conscious, formless energy that transcends all physical limitations. Unlike Jesus, who embodied a human form, the Holy Spirit is both immanent—present within creation—and transcendent—existing beyond creation. It permeates all things without being confined by them, existing everywhere simultaneously, unaffected by space, form, or time. The Holy Spirit is a timeless, eternal current of divine energy that flows beyond the constraints of time, always present in the state of "now," unchanging and without decay. This energy behaves similarly to electromagnetic waves, which can spread through space and influence matter. Just as electromagnetic waves are a form of energy traveling through space, the Holy Spirit is a dynamic force of divine energy and consciousness that moves through and interacts with all of creation.

The Holy Spirit, in its boundless grace, radiates joy and love, smiling upon us with magnificent glory. It is a presence so pure and vibrant that it fills every corner of existence with warmth and light. The smile of the Holy Spirit is not merely an expression but a reflection of the divine joy that flows from the heart of God—an affirmation of life, creation, and the unbreakable connection between the Creator and all creation. In its glory, the Holy Spirit envelops us, lifting our spirits with a love that transcends all understanding. This love is transformative, healing, renewing, and empowering us to share in the beauty of eternal joy. In the smile of the Holy Spirit, we glimpse the divine truth: that love and joy are the very essence of the universe. Through this grace, we are continually embraced by the glory of God.

❧❦❧

Saying 30: The Unity of Divine Presence

"Jesus said: 'Where there are three gods, they are gods. Where there are two or one, I am with him.'" (30)

This saying touches on the mystical understanding of God's presence and the nature of divine unity, offering both a theological and spiritual insight into the dynamics of the divine and human relationship.

"Paternity of Our Lord Icon (c.1880), Nevyansk School, Russia"

Three Gods – The Plurality of Divinity

The first part of the saying, *"Where there are three gods, they are gods,"* could be interpreted as a reflection on the plurality of divinity. It may reference a kind of polytheistic concept where each of the three figures is considered a god in its own right. However, when viewed through a Christian lens, this can also be seen as a cryptic reference to the **Holy Trinity**— Father, Son, and Holy Spirit—where each of the three persons is distinct, yet they are fully and equally God. In traditional Christian theology, the concept of the Trinity does not imply three separate gods, but rather one God in three persons, united in essence and divine nature.

In some Gnostic interpretations, the notion of "three gods" could reflect different divine emanations or the various levels of spiritual beings. This saying might be understood as affirming the reality of divine plurality, but with the assertion that the divine presence is not limited to this specific number, as suggested in the second half of the saying.

The Unity of God's Presence in Two or One

The second part, *"Where there are two or one, I am with him,"* speaks to the profound unity of Christ with the believer. It implies that regardless of the apparent number of persons or spiritual beings, the essential presence of God is manifested wherever two or one person are gathered in communion. This reflects the intimate relationship between Christ and the faithful, echoing passages such as Matthew 18:20: *"For where two or three are gathered in my name, there am I with them."* In this sense, the saying affirms the divine presence with the individual or small group, emphasizing that God's manifestation is not dependent on numerical significance but on the presence of the faithful.

This also suggests that God is not confined to human categories or limitations. Whether in the context of a community of believers (even if small) or a single soul, the essence of God is present in a direct, personal way. The emphasis on "I am with him" reveals the closeness of Jesus to those who seek him, regardless of external circumstances or numbers.

The Mystical Implication – God Beyond Numbers

The deeper mystical implication of this saying is the transcendence of divine presence over human concepts of quantity and separation. The saying subtly challenges our understanding of the divine as something bound by earthly concepts of numbers. In a mystical sense, the "three gods" could also allude to the divine manifestations or archetypes (Father, Son, and Holy Spirit) as distinct yet ultimately united in essence. But the true essence of the divine is not confined to these three; God's presence transcends these categories and manifests in all situations, whether in community or solitude.

This saying also alludes to the *unity of being*—a core idea in nondual philosophy, where the ultimate reality is indivisible, regardless of the apparent multiplicity we encounter in the world. The three may represent the ultimate divine diversity, but the two or one reflects the singularity of God's presence in all aspects of creation. Whether in the plurality of divine persons or in the solitary heart of an individual, the divine is present in fullness.

Theological Reflection on Christ's Presence

In Christian terms, this saying also aligns with the concept of the *Immanuel*—"God with us." Jesus, as the incarnate Word, promises to be with his followers, regardless of their number. This highlights the significance of the personal relationship between Christ and the believer. It is not the external circumstances that matter, but the inner truth that Christ is with the believer, abiding in them.

This idea is central to the Christian mysticism that emphasizes direct communion with the divine. It is through the indwelling presence of God, whether perceived in the small gathering of two or in the solitude of one, that the believer experiences the fullness of divine life.

Where names dissolve and gods are counted no more, the Holy One waits—not in the multitude, but in the stillness of union. For when the two become one, the I AM whispers through the veil.

The Unity of God in the Mystical Path

For the mystic, this saying invites the seeker to look beyond superficial distinctions between the divine persons or external forms of worship. The essence of the divine is not constrained by numbers or structures. The true presence of God is revealed in the union of the soul with the Divine, and this union transcends external appearances.

The saying teaches that the divine is equally present whether in a grand gathering of many or in the quiet solitude of the soul, and that this presence is available to all who seek it with sincerity. This reinforces the mystical principle that union with the divine is not dependent on external factors but is a matter of inner awakening and communion with God.

In summary, saying 30 in the *Gospel of Thomas* offers a profound meditation on the unity and presence of God in the life of the believer. It reflects both the plurality of divine manifestations (as seen in the Christian Trinity) and the intimate, personal presence of Christ with each individual, whether in the context of a large community or in the quiet solitude of one. The saying emphasizes that the true nature of divine presence transcends external conditions and is accessible to all who open themselves to it.

While I wouldn't call myself a prophet, I do see myself as a messenger of artistic vision—a witness to divine beauty, entrusted with revealing glimpses of God's glory through visionary experience. Yet I've struggled to express the ancestral imagery we all share—a sacred inheritance often hidden beneath the routines of everyday life. When I tried to share what I had seen, many dismissed it. After the revelation, I underwent a profound transformation that took time to understand and integrate. At the time, I knew little of scripture. In search of meaning and spiritual community, I returned to the Catholic Church for a season, sensing deep within that I had become a vessel of the Church itself—a living temple of the Spirit. I joined the RCIA program at Saint Joseph's in Blende, Colorado, hoping to deepen my understanding of scripture and receive the sacrament of Holy Communion. I even shared my vision with the parish priest, the bishop, and wrote a letter to Pope Francis. In my innocence, I believed such a miraculous event could not be ignored—how could anyone hide a light under a bushel basket? But ecstatic revelation is often met not with awe, but with silence. Though the Church teaches that miracles should be investigated, my testimony fell on deaf ears. It was too wondrous—too strange—for those who stand at the threshold of the Church.

A farmer knows when the fruit is ripe—at its peak of nourishment and beauty. In the same way, there is a call for spiritual laborers to awaken, teach, and guide the human flock we all belong to. When seeds of wonder and awareness begin to sprout, we each share a responsibility to nurture understanding in those around us. In my journey, there was a ripening within—a stirring of the Holy Spirit. It felt like an invitation to open the door to all that is. The Spirit moved gently, yet purposefully, nudging me to seek the deeper nature of my being. This awakening became a calling. Many have walked the paths of wisdom before us, each offering a pearl that enriches the collective soul. But the harvest requires devotion. There is a season—a window of grace—to gather the fruits of the Spirit into a basket of understanding. This takes reverence, reflection, and connection. We are not meant to walk alone. Our purpose is fulfilled in relationship with others alongside us, helping to carry and share the fruit of the Spirit.

Chapter 5

The Unity of the Divine (Sayings 31-40)

Saying 31: The Rejection of the Prophet and the Doctor's Challenge

"Jesus said: 'No prophet is accepted in his own village; a doctor does not heal those who know him.'" (31)

This saying speaks to the common themes of rejection, familiarity, and the challenge of healing in the presence of pre-existing expectations or biases. It highlights two key ideas: the prophet's struggle to be recognized in their own community and the difficulty of offering healing to those who are too familiar with the healer to receive true help.

The Prophet's Rejection in His Own Village

The first part of the saying, *"No prophet is accepted in his own village,"* draws on the common biblical theme of a prophet being dismissed by those who are closest to them. This idea is echoed in the Gospels, particularly in Luke 4:24, where Jesus himself states, *"Truly I tell you, no prophet is accepted in his hometown."* The statement underscores the challenge faced by individuals who attempt to bring transformative messages to those who know them best, whether as family members, childhood friends, or fellow townspeople.

There is a deep irony here: the closer one is to a prophet, the more likely they are to dismiss the prophetic message. This can happen because of familiarity—those who grew up with the prophet may struggle to see beyond the person's earthly origins or past to recognize their divine calling. In Jesus' case, the people of Nazareth had trouble seeing beyond the carpenter's son, failing to grasp his divine nature and mission.

This theme of rejection is not just about the personal experiences of the prophet, but also speaks to a broader spiritual principle: sometimes, those who are closest to us, or who share our everyday context, may be the last to understand or accept the deeper, transformative truths we seek to convey. In a spiritual sense, this saying points to the difficulty of transcending ordinary, worldly perceptions in order to see the deeper, divine reality.

The Doctor's Challenge: Healing Beyond Familiarity

The second part of the saying, *"A doctor does not heal those who know him,"* extends the same theme of rejection to the realm of healing. A doctor, symbolizing a healer or spiritual guide, may face difficulty in offering true healing to those who already have preconceived notions of them. These notions, grounded in past experiences or familiarity, may block the recognition of the healer's true authority or ability to bring about change.

This metaphor also points to the challenge of healing or transformation in the context of relationships where the healer is too familiar. In psychological or spiritual healing, this dynamic is often seen when someone who is deeply embedded in a community or family struggles to bring about change because others are too familiar with their flaws or past mistakes. The healing process requires a certain degree of openness and willingness to receive the healer's aid, which is difficult when the individual is not seen with the right perspective.

The healer must often move beyond these boundaries to truly help. In the context of the spiritual life, this can be seen as an allegory for the way in which a seeker must sometimes break free from old patterns of thought and being in order to experience divine transformation. It's also a reminder that spiritual healing requires a certain receptivity and humility, both on the part of the one who seeks healing and the one who offers it.

A Deeper Reflection on Familiarity and Spiritual Transformation

On a deeper level, this saying highlights a spiritual paradox: true transformation often comes from the most unexpected or humble sources. Just as a prophet is not accepted in his own village, the healing power of the divine often enters into our lives in ways that challenge our preconceived notions of what healing or transformation should look like. Familiarity can become a barrier to perceiving the divine work in our lives, and it takes a certain level of spiritual openness to recognize that healing can come from unexpected places or people.

The saying also touches on the human tendency to resist change, especially when it is introduced by someone we know well. There is comfort in the known and familiar, even if it means remaining in a state of dis-ease. The challenge for both the healer and the one in need of healing is to move beyond the surface level of familiarity and embrace the deeper, more transformative process that may require surrender and trust in the unseen.

The Mystical Implication

Mystically, this saying also points to the deeper, inner work of the soul. Often, those who are closest to us are unable to see the true divine work being done within us. Similarly, we may struggle to recognize the divine presence and work in our own lives because we are too familiar with our personal struggles, limitations, and past wounds. Yet, just as a prophet is rejected in their hometown, divine grace is often unseen by those who are too immersed in the ordinary world, lacking the spiritual vision to perceive the miraculous.

The doctor in this saying symbolizes not just physical healing, but also spiritual transformation. The doctor's struggle to heal those who know him reflects the challenge of overcoming the limitations of the human ego and conditioning. True spiritual healing often requires breaking through these barriers, which may involve a change in perspective, a shift in how we see ourselves and others, or a breaking away from familiar yet limiting patterns of behavior.

Conclusion: No Prophet Among Their Own: The Cost of Transformation

Saying 31 emphasizes the difficulties of both offering and receiving transformation in the face of familiarity, expectation, and preconceived notions. It speaks to the challenges faced by prophets, healers, and spiritual teachers in delivering their messages and bringing about healing in contexts where the participants are not open to the new or the unfamiliar. The message is one of openness, transcendence of old patterns, and a reminder that true healing often requires stepping beyond the confines of what is known and comfortable.

> *"The prophet is a man who is not content with the world as it is. He feels the brokenness of the world and yearns for the wholeness that ought to be. He is a man who is disturbed by the way things are, who cannot tolerate the status quo, and who speaks for the sake of redemption."* — Abraham Joshua Heschel, *The Prophets*

Saying 32: The Unshakeable City: Unshakable Truth

"Jesus said, 'A city built on a high hill and fortified cannot fall, nor can it be hidden.'" (32)

This saying presents a powerful metaphor for spiritual strength and resilience. The city on a high hill represents a soul that is firmly rooted in divine truth, elevated above the distractions of the world. Just as a fortified city stands strong against external forces, a heart grounded in divine love and wisdom cannot be easily swayed or hidden. It is a light that cannot be extinguished, a beacon of hope for all who seek shelter.

In this context, the "high hill" is reminiscent of the idea of spiritual ascent. The Psalms speak of the "mountain of the Lord" where God's presence is fully realized (Psalm 24:3).

Similarly, in the teachings of Jesus, the kingdom of heaven is portrayed as a kingdom of light, truth, and strength, where those who seek it will find refuge and security.

The city also speaks to the community of believers—those who come together in unity and faith, fortified by shared purpose and devotion to God's will. As Paul writes to the Corinthians, the church is the "temple of God" (1 Corinthians 3:16), a sacred and secure space that embodies God's presence.

Thus, saying 32 invites reflection on the strength of spiritual foundations—both individual and communal—and the unshakeable nature of divine truth that neither time nor adversity can overcome.

༺❀❀❀༻

Saying 33: The Light of Revelation

"Jesus said, 'What you hear with your ears, you must proclaim from your rooftops. For no one lights a lamp and puts it under a basket, nor does one put it in a hidden place. Rather, one puts it on a lampstand so that all who come and go will see its light.'" (33)

In this saying, Jesus speaks to the urgency and responsibility of sharing divine truth. The image of a lamp placed on a stand reflects the idea that wisdom and spiritual insight are not meant to be hidden or hoarded but shared freely with the world. The lamp represents the light of understanding, the revelation of God's presence, and the inner knowing that illuminates the soul. It is a divine gift that, once received, compels the believer to spread that light to others.

Jesus's call to "proclaim from your rooftops" is an invitation to live boldly in the truth of God's love and presence, to make one's faith visible and known to all. The rooftop is a place of prominence and visibility, symbolizing the courage required to let one's inner transformation be seen by others. This also echoes the words of the Apostle Paul, who encouraged believers to "shine like stars in the universe" (Philippians 2:15), making known the light of Christ to the world.

In this context, the lamp on a stand also recalls the symbolism of Christ himself as the "Light of the world" (John 8:12). As the ultimate Light, He calls his followers to reflect that light in the world, not hiding it under fear or shame, but allowing it to shine for all to see. The faithful are not to live in spiritual secrecy, but in a way that others may be drawn to the divine light shining through them.

In a mystical sense, this saying speaks to the illumination of the soul. When a person awakens to the divine presence within, their spirit becomes like a lamp, shining with God's glory, capable of transforming the darkness of the world into light. Just as the light of a lamp dispels physical darkness, the light of spiritual truth dispels ignorance and sin, bringing clarity and understanding.

Saying 33 is a call to action, urging believers to step into the fullness of their divine calling, to live out their faith boldly, and to share the revelation they have received. It is a message of proclamation and witness, urging believers to be visible beacons of the divine light in a world that longs for hope and truth.

⇌❧❧⇋

Saying 34: The Blind Leading the Blind

"Jesus said, 'If a blind man leads a blind man, they will both fall into a pit.'" (34)

This saying contains a powerful warning about the importance of spiritual insight and discernment. It speaks to the danger of following someone who is spiritually blind, someone who lacks true understanding or revelation of the divine. Just as physical blindness leads to danger and confusion, spiritual blindness causes individuals to lead others astray, resulting in a fall into darkness or destruction.

In the context of the Gospel, Jesus often criticized the spiritual leaders of his time, particularly the Pharisees, for their inability to see the truth despite their positions of authority. They were blind to the deeper spiritual truths of God's kingdom, and, in their blindness, they misled others. This saying calls attention to the necessity of spiritual clarity and insight, emphasizing that only those who have truly seen the truth of God can lead others into it.

On a mystical level, the "blind" represent those who are disconnected from the divine source, who have not yet awakened to their true nature. The "pit" symbolizes the consequences of spiritual ignorance—disillusionment, suffering, and separation from the divine. Without illumination, the path is unclear, and one may unknowingly lead others into the same darkness.

However, the saying also points toward the importance of spiritual guidance. To avoid falling into the pit, one must be guided by those who possess true vision, those who have encountered the divine and have the wisdom to lead others toward the light. This guidance is not just about intellectual knowledge but spiritual awakening, where the heart and soul are aligned with the truth of God's kingdom.

This saying also connects with the theme of discernment found throughout the Gospels, where Jesus encourages his followers to seek the truth and to test the spirits. It is not enough to follow blindly; one must actively cultivate the inner vision that allows one to see the path clearly. As Jesus often said, "Blessed are the pure in heart, for they shall see God" (Matthew 5:8).

In the end, this teaching calls for personal responsibility in the spiritual journey: to not follow blindly, but to seek true insight and to recognize when others, too, are spiritually blind. Only through illumination can one avoid the pit and find the true path to the kingdom of God.

ஜ⁂ஜ

Saying 35: Binding the Strong Man: Overcoming Inner Resistance

Jesus said, "It is not possible for anyone to enter the house of a strong man and take it by force unless he binds his hands. Then he will be able to ransack his house." (35)

This saying echoes a parable also found in the Synoptic Gospels (Mark 3:27, Matthew 12:29, Luke 11:21–22), where Jesus speaks about binding the "strong man" to plunder his house — often interpreted in the context of Christ overcoming the power of evil (or Satan) in order to liberate those held captive.

In Mark 3:23–27, Jesus responds to accusations that He is casting out demons by the power of Satan. Rather than engaging in theological speculation, He answers with a striking parable: "How can Satan drive out Satan? If a kingdom is divided against itself, it cannot stand." Traditionally, this is read as a statement about the incoherence of demonic self-opposition. But if we suspend belief in a literal Satan, this teaching can be seen as a profound reflection on inner division—on the way the ego, fear, and fragmentation undermine any attempt at real transformation.

Seen through this symbolic lens, "Satan" becomes a metaphor for the self-destructive patterns and divided will of the human soul. A mind torn by inner conflict cannot heal itself using the very forces that create the division. Hatred cannot expel hatred. The ego cannot liberate itself. A house divided—whether an individual psyche or a social order—collapses under the weight of its contradictions. Jesus' words then shift from being a commentary on supernatural conflict to a powerful insight into the process of interior reconciliation and psychological integration.

This teaching climaxes with a powerful image: "No one can enter a strong man's house and plunder his possessions unless he first ties up the strong man." Here, the "strong man" is no longer just a demonic figure, but the entrenched ego, the false self, the inner authority that guards one's attachments, illusions, and wounds. The "house" represents the soul, the inner life, or the structure of consciousness. To liberate what is held within—to access wisdom, healing, or the divine spark—one must first bind that which resists change. The ego must be confronted, disarmed, and quieted. Only then can the deeper treasure of the self be unveiled.

This same metaphor appears in Saying 35 of the Gospel of Thomas:

Jesus said, "It is not possible for anyone to enter the house of a strong man and take it by force unless he binds his hands. Then he will be able to ransack his house."

In Thomas, a text often interpreted through mystical or esoteric frameworks, the saying takes on a distinctly inner meaning. The "strong man" becomes a symbol of ego, ignorance, or worldly fixation—the internal resistance that guards the threshold of awakening. Binding his hands implies restraining the forces of distraction, pride, and fear that prevent access to the soul's hidden treasure. Only through this interior work, this symbolic "binding," can one ransack the house—not to steal, but to reclaim what has been lost or hidden: the divine image, the sacred knowledge, the true self.

Thus, both in the Synoptics and in Thomas, this parable points to a deeper truth: the path to liberation begins with the binding of that which binds us. The enemy is not external but internal. The real "plundering" is the recovery of one's own soul from the grip of the false self. Jesus' wisdom here is not about war with darkness, but about the inner conquest of illusion—so that the light within might be revealed.

Saying 36: The True Disciple

Jesus said: "Do not worry from morning to evening and from evening to morning about what you will wear." (36)

This saying speaks to the spiritual importance of detachment from material concerns, particularly those centered around outward appearances and worldly anxieties. Jesus encourages his followers to focus on spiritual matters rather than being consumed by daily, superficial worries.

Jesus is pointing out that material concerns, like clothing, are temporary and secondary to spiritual life. By advising not to worry about such matters, Jesus is reminding his followers to focus on eternal truths rather than the fleeting worries of daily life. This reflects the importance of trusting in divine providence and not being bound by materialism.

> *"Therefore I tell you, do not worry about your life, what you will eat or drink; or about your body, what you will wear. Is not life more than food, and the body more than clothes? (Matthew 6:25)*

Saying 37: Unveiling the Hidden Christ: A Path to Divine Vision and Transformation

"His disciples said: On what day will you be revealed to us, and on what day shall we see you? Jesus said: When you unclothe yourselves and are not ashamed, and take your garments and lay them beneath your feet like the little children (and) trample on them, then [you will see] the Son of the Living One, and you will not be afraid." (37)

In this stark and arresting saying, Jesus answers the disciples' longing for divine revelation with a call to radical vulnerability and childlike freedom. The unveiling of the divine presence is not bound to a future event or external sign—it is a *present unveiling* that requires the stripping away of illusion, identity, and shame.

The act of "unclothing oneself" is not merely metaphorical; it gestures toward a complete *undoing of egoic coverings*—the social, religious, and psychological garments that conceal our true nature. To *unclothe and not be ashamed* recalls the innocence of Adam and Eve before the fall, before shame entered human consciousness. Jesus invites a return to that primordial nakedness, not of the body alone but of the soul, unmasked and unafraid.

The instruction to *lay garments beneath your feet like children and trample them* is especially potent. It suggests not only discarding false identities, but *rejoicing in their undoing.* Children do not yet wear the heavy garments of ego, status, or reputation. To trample the garments is to *treat these external identities as dust*—to playfully, innocently reject the masks that keep us from seeing.

Only then, Jesus says, will you see "the Son of the Living One"—a title that evokes the *living Christ*, the radiant presence of divine life. This vision is not external; it is an *inner unveiling*, a direct and fearless encounter with the Christ within. To see the Son is to awaken to your own divine nature, freed from the illusions that once obscured it.

This echoes John 8:12: *"I am the light of the world. Whoever follows me will never walk in darkness, but will have the light of life."* But in Thomas, the path is not to follow outwardly, but to descend inwardly—to become like children again, clothed in nothing but the light of being.

This theme resonates deeply with mystical traditions across time. In Kabbalah, the soul must remove its "garments" to reunite with the divine source. In Sufism, the lover of God strips away all veils until only the Beloved remains. And in Christian mysticism, particularly among the Desert Fathers and Mothers, the path to divine vision is marked by the relinquishing of all attachments, including the self-image.

Ultimately, this saying is not about asceticism, but about *transparency before God.* It is a call to vulnerability as strength, and to inner nakedness as the condition for divine sight.

When we cast off what we thought defined us and become unashamed in our divine origin, *we behold the Living One—not as other, but as the unveiled radiance within.*

There is no fear in this seeing, for the vision does not come to destroy, but to unite. It is a recognition: *"The one who sees me sees the one who sent me."* (John 12:45). In that moment, fear dissolves, and only light remains.

> *"He who plants is not separate from the seed, nor is the sower from the harvest. We are part of the divine planting."*—The unity of Being and Becoming is revealed when all garments fall away.

৯৪৬৫

Saying 38: The Longing for Understanding

"Jesus said, 'Many times have I desired to tell you the things which are in my heart, but you do not inquire about them. There are some who will come in the future who will search, and they will find it." (38)

This saying expresses Jesus' deep longing to share divine wisdom, yet he encounters a lack of inquiry among his immediate audience. It echoes his lament in the canonical Gospels: *"O Jerusalem, Jerusalem… how often I have longed to gather your children together, as a hen gathers her chicks under her wings, and you were not willing"* (Matthew 23:37). The divine teacher stands ready to reveal truth, but revelation requires a seeking heart.

The second part of the saying introduces a prophetic vision—there will come seekers in the future who, with genuine longing, will uncover these hidden truths. This speaks to the timeless nature of spiritual wisdom, which is not bound to one moment in history but continually unfolds for those who earnestly seek it. It parallels Jeremiah's promise: *"You will seek me and find me when you seek me with all your heart"* (Jeremiah 29:13).

Mystics and sages throughout history have affirmed that divine wisdom is ever-present but requires an active pursuit. St. Augustine reflected this when he wrote, *"Late have I loved you, O Beauty ever ancient, ever new. Late have I loved you! You were within me, but I was outside."* The human soul must turn inward to discover the treasures Christ longed to reveal.

Saying 38 invites the reader to become one of those future seekers—to ask, to knock, to search, and ultimately, to find.

৯৪৬৫

Saying 39: The Keys of Knowledge

"Jesus said, 'The Pharisees and the scholars have taken the keys of knowledge and hidden them. They themselves have not entered, nor have they allowed those who want to enter to go in. You, however, be as wise as serpents and innocent as doves." (39)

This saying critiques those in religious authority who, rather than illuminating the path to divine wisdom, obscure it. Jesus' rebuke recalls Matthew 23:13: *"Woe to you, teachers of the law and Pharisees, you hypocrites! You shut the door of the kingdom of heaven in people's faces. You yourselves do not enter, nor will you let those enter who are trying to."* The imagery of the 'keys of knowledge' suggests a responsibility entrusted to religious leaders—one they have failed to fulfill.

Instead, Jesus instructs his followers to embody both wisdom and innocence. The serpent, in ancient thought, symbolizes shrewdness and awareness, while the dove represents purity and divine presence. The balance of these qualities—wisdom without corruption, innocence without naivety—is essential for navigating a world where truth is often hidden.

The Jewish mystic Abraham Joshua Heschel echoes this sentiment: *"The search for reason ends at the known; on the immense expanse beyond it, only the sense of the ineffable can glide."* True wisdom is not about hoarding knowledge but about guiding others to divine truth with humility and grace.

Woe to the Pharisees, Then and Now

Sayings 34, 39, 89, and 102 all echo a common warning—one that rings as true today as it did two thousand years ago. The spirit of the Pharisee is not a relic of the past. It is alive and well, taking many forms in our modern world.

> *It is the learned scholar, steeped in scripture, who speaks with confidence and authority:*
> *"This is the way. The texts are clear. Walk this path."*
> *Clothed in certainty, they stand firm in doctrine and righteousness, pointing to their interpretation as the only truth.*

> *Paradoxically, it is also the scholar who unravels the scriptures—who questions, dissects, and deconstructs:*
> *"This doesn't add up. These stories contradict. The history is suspect."*
> *They chip away at belief not with malice, but with reason, leaving many to drift between skepticism and despair.*

It is the atheist who, after grappling deeply with biblical accounts, abandons all belief—not out of apathy, but exhaustion.

It is the preacher who proclaims:
"You are unworthy. You are fallen. Repent, or be lost."
Still echoing the old refrain of sin and salvation, shaping hearts through fear and guilt.
It is the faithful apologist, with sincere love for Christ, who leads others to the cross—
offering Jesus as the only way, as written, as believed, as inherited.

It is the institution—the many arms of organized religion—each proclaiming,
"Our way is right. Yours is flawed."
Endlessly debating, clinging to righteousness, viewing truth through narrow lenses.

How do we find our way out of this conundrum?

I often wonder.
So many are labeled heretics, called blasphemers—though it all depends on where you stand, and whose truth you follow.

In this vast sea of modern-day Pharisees, I've come to learn that the only way forward is inward.
To seek the still voice within.
To listen with the heart.

During my awakening, I conversed often with the Almighty. In those moments of divine nearness, I was confronted by the collective mind of our age—its doubts, divisions, and endless debates. Will humanity ever agree on who or what God truly is? I'm not sure we will. We live in a universe of paradox, a kaleidoscope of lenses and layered perspectives, each shaped by a personal path. But one truth remains unwavering in my soul: **God is Pure Love.**

And I—like you—am made in the image and likeness of that radiant Love. Nature herself has shown me this, in light and wind and wonder.

Jesus, my beloved brother, whom I hold close to my heart, whispered to me that I am a co-creator with the Divine. That this universe is not something we merely observe but something we participate in—actively, consciously, beautifully. That I am a child of the Divine, as he is.

The Gospel of Thomas tells us that once we come to know who we truly are, *"we will be troubled"*— for the burden of remembering our origin is both heavy and liberating. We carry a pearl within us, a treasure buried in the field of our being. To discover it is to awaken. To awaken is to become responsible for the light we carry.

Bhagavad Gita 9.32 –
"O son of Kunti, those who are not deluded by the three modes of material nature, who are situated in the transcendental position, worship Me with determination."

This verse reflects the idea of divine knowledge being hidden from those who are caught in the material world. True understanding of God is reserved for those who are not entrapped by illusion or dogma, similar to how the Pharisees and scholars were seen as withholding true knowledge from others.

Rig Veda 1.164.39 –
"Truth is one, but the sages call it by many names."

This verse highlights the universal nature of truth, which is often obscured or divided by human institutions or those who guard spiritual knowledge. It resonates with Jesus' criticism of the Pharisees, who took the knowledge and hid it, not allowing others to enter the true understanding of the divine.

Saying 40: The Vine and the Father's Garden

"Jesus said, 'A grapevine has been planted outside of the Father. But since it is not strong, it will be pulled up by the roots and will die. Whoever has ears to hear, let him hear.'" (40)

This parable speaks of a vine that exists apart from the Father's domain—a plant that lacks the vitality of divine nourishment and, therefore, withers. The imagery of the vine evokes deep biblical and mystical symbolism. In John 15:1-2, Jesus proclaims: *"I am the true vine, and my Father is the gardener. He cuts off every branch in me that bears no fruit."* The metaphor emphasizes that only in divine union can one bear lasting fruit.

Mystics often describe the soul as a seed or tree planted in sacred soil. The *Zohar* speaks of the divine as the *Tree of Life*, from which all existence flows. Likewise, Meister Eckhart writes, *"The seed of God is in us. Given an intelligent and diligent farmer, it will thrive and grow into God, whose fruit is God."* The vine planted outside the Father's presence, then, represents a life disconnected from its true Source—a soul attempting to flourish apart from divine grace.

Nature itself mirrors this truth. A tree with shallow roots cannot withstand storms; a seed that falls on barren ground cannot bear fruit. The Gospel of Thomas frequently returns to themes of divine planting, hidden seeds, and harvests of light. The Father's garden is the domain of eternity, where all who are rooted in divine love grow into the fullness of life. But those who remain unanchored in this spiritual reality will, like the uprooted vine, fade away.

This parable speaks of a vine that exists apart from the Father's domain—a plant that lacks the vitality of divine nourishment and, therefore, withers. The vine planted outside the Father's presence represents a life disconnected from its true Source—a soul that has yet to realize the divine reality from which it originates. Not knowing its true nature, it cannot flourish.

Chapter 6

Transformation of the Self (Sayings 41-50)

Saying 41: The Paradox of Abundance and Lack

"Jesus said, 'Whoever has something in hand will be given more, and whoever has nothing will be deprived of even the little they have.'" (41)

This saying reveals the mystical law of spiritual abundance, a principle that transcends material wealth and speaks to the inner life of the soul. It reflects the dynamic of spiritual growth and the consequences of spiritual poverty. The one who has something, even if it is but a spark of awareness, will be graced with further illumination, while the one who possesses nothing, lacking the awareness of their own divine nature, will find even their meager understanding slipping away.

This paradox reflects the nature of spiritual receptivity. In the Gospel of Thomas, as in the broader biblical tradition, those who are open to the mysteries of God, who seek with sincere hearts, are given more—*seek, and you will find* (Matthew 7:7). Yet, those who are blind to the divine, who are attached to their own ignorance or pride, find themselves in spiritual poverty, for *to those who have, more will be given; and from those who do not have, even what they have will be taken away* (Mark 4:25).

In mystical terms, this saying speaks to the state of the soul's attunement to the divine. It suggests that the more one aligns with the divine Source, the more the soul is filled with grace and understanding. This mirrors the biblical concept of abundance: *God is able to bless you abundantly, so that in all things at all times, having all that you need, you will abound in every good work* (2 Corinthians 9:8). Abundance, in this sense, is not a mere material phenomenon but a reflection of the soul's capacity to receive and radiate divine love.

The *having* and *not having* also evoke the contrast between spiritual fullness and spiritual emptiness. To have something in hand is to possess the awareness of the divine presence in one's life, to live in constant communion with the Source. It is the beginning of mystical realization—the realization that one's true identity is not separate from God. To have nothing is to live in a state of forgetfulness, disconnected from the wellspring of life, unaware of one's true nature and origin.

The Eastern wisdom traditions, too, speak of this principle. The *Bhagavad Gita* suggests that the one who possesses wisdom becomes ever more enlightened, while the ignorant soul remains bound by illusion: *"The one who is free from all attachments, whose mind is unaffected by pleasure or pain, is truly wise"* (Bhagavad Gita 2:13). In this light, the soul that is anchored in divine knowledge receives an ever-greater outpouring of spiritual wealth, while the soul detached from this knowledge remains in a state of spiritual poverty.

Thus, Jesus' words call us to spiritual awareness. They urge us to realize the divine presence already within, to recognize the gifts of grace that we carry, and to cultivate these gifts so that we may receive more. When we embrace our connection to the divine Source, we open ourselves to an inexhaustible flow of spiritual riches.

This teaching also encourages us to release our attachment to the fleeting things of this world, for they are like dust compared to the divine treasure within. The seeker of truth must learn to hold lightly to worldly concerns, trusting that true fulfillment comes only from spiritual awakening and union with the Divine.

Finally, this saying calls us to reflect on the state of our own hearts. Do we live in spiritual abundance, fully aware of the divine presence in our lives? Or do we remain spiritually impoverished, unaware of the treasures we already possess? By cultivating the awareness of God's ever-present love, we can receive an ever-deepening revelation of His grace, moving ever closer to the Kingdom within.

Saying 42: The Call to Be Passers-By

"Jesus said, 'Become passers-by.'" (42)

This brief yet profound saying invites the seeker to embrace a life of detachment and spiritual freedom. To "become passers-by" is to acknowledge the transient nature of worldly existence and to approach life with a sense of impermanence. It is a call to recognize that the things of this world—pleasure, pain, success, and failure—are fleeting. They do not define the soul, nor do they hold ultimate meaning. Instead, one is to move through life without becoming overly attached to any particular moment, identity, or material possession.

In a mystical context, being a *passer-by* suggests living with a sense of detachment from the ego and worldly concerns. The ego tends to cling to experiences, identities, and desires, yet Jesus calls the seeker to rise above this attachment, to move through life like a traveler on a journey. This state of mind encourages the seeker to remain open and fluid, to not become overly entrenched in the roles and labels of the world, for they are temporary and impermanent.

The concept of being a *passer-by* echoes the teachings found in both Christian and Eastern traditions. In Christianity, Jesus often speaks of being in the world but not of the world (John 17:16). The apostle Paul echoes this in his letters, urging believers to live as *strangers and pilgrims* on the earth (1 Peter 2:11), knowing that their true home lies in the eternal. The soul's journey is not about becoming rooted in the temporary world, but rather about seeking a higher, spiritual reality.

In Eastern wisdom traditions, the idea of impermanence is central. The *Bhagavad Gita* teaches that all things in the material world are temporary, and that attachment to them leads to suffering. The sage is one who sees beyond the fleeting appearances of life, recognizing that all phenomena are transitory and that true fulfillment lies in the eternal nature of the Self (Atman). As the Buddha also taught, attachment to the world leads to suffering, while liberation comes from detaching from the transient.

The call to become *passers-by* is a spiritual invitation to free oneself from the false sense of permanence that binds us to the world. It asks us to live with the awareness that everything in life is in constant flux and that the only true constant is the divine presence within. By adopting the perspective of a *passer-by*, we learn to move through the world without becoming weighed down by it, to embrace each moment without clinging to it, and to allow the divine to guide our journey.

This saying also hints at the importance of mindfulness. To be a *passer-by* is to engage in the present moment with full awareness, yet without attachment. It is to recognize the divine presence in each fleeting experience, knowing that it is but a passing glimpse of the eternal reality. As the Psalmist writes, *"For I am a stranger with You, a sojourner, as all my fathers were"* (Psalm 39:12).

Ultimately, Jesus' words challenge us to view life from a spiritual perspective—one that sees beyond the illusion of permanence and embraces the deeper reality of the eternal journey. Life is a passing moment, a sacred pilgrimage, and we are called to walk it with the awareness of divine presence, knowing that our true home is in the heart of the Creator.

Saying 43: The Tree and Its Fruit

"His disciples said to him, 'Who are you, that you should say these things to us?' Jesus said, 'Do you not recognize who I am from what I say to you? But you have become like the Jews, for they love the tree but hate its fruit, or they love the fruit but hate the tree.'" (43)

In this saying, Jesus addresses a fundamental misunderstanding of his disciples regarding the nature of his teachings and identity. The disciples, despite hearing his words, do not yet perceive the fullness of who he is. Jesus challenges them to recognize him not just through external appearances, but through the substance and fruit of his teachings. His message is not merely an intellectual exercise or a collection of wise sayings; it is the embodiment of divine truth and wisdom that must be recognized in its fullness.

The metaphor of the tree and its fruit speaks to the inseparable nature of truth and its expression. The tree symbolizes the source—be it the teachings of Jesus or the divine wisdom that gives rise to them. The fruit represents the manifestation of those teachings in action, in life, and in the spiritual transformation they bring about. To love only one and not the other is to misunderstand the nature of the divine message.

Jesus' reference to the Jews in this context is not a blanket condemnation but rather a reflection on a spiritual tendency. It is a critique of those who admire the outward form, whether the law, tradition, or ritual—yet fail to recognize the deeper truth that those forms are meant to point toward. As the prophets often warned, religious rituals and laws without the inner transformation and love that they are meant to inspire are empty. In the Gospels, Jesus repeatedly challenges the Pharisees and religious leaders for their focus on the letter of the law while neglecting its spirit (Matthew 23:23-24).

In this saying, Jesus urges his disciples to perceive him not merely as an external figure to be admired, but as the embodiment of divine truth. His words and actions are intertwined, and to truly understand him, one must recognize that the tree and its fruit are inseparable. The fruit is the expression of the tree's life force, just as his teachings are the fruit of divine wisdom. As it is written in Matthew 7:16-20, *"By their fruits, you will recognize them."*

This saying also echoes the ancient mystical idea that wisdom, once received, must be lived out. In both the Christian and Eastern traditions, true wisdom is not merely intellectual knowledge, but a lived experience that transforms the soul. In the *Bhagavad Gita*, Krishna teaches that wisdom must be embodied in action (Bhagavad Gita 3:16). Similarly, in the Gospel of James, it is written that faith without works is dead (James 2:26). Thus, the tree and its fruit are intimately connected: true understanding of the tree (the divine wisdom) must result in the fruit of righteous action.

Moreover, this saying calls us to reflect on our own relationship with spiritual teachings. Do we merely admire the form—whether it is the scriptures, the rituals, or the symbols—or do we recognize their deeper meaning and live according to them? To love only the tree and not its fruit, or vice versa, is to miss the point entirely. The fruit is a natural expression of the tree's life, and similarly, true spiritual understanding manifests in love, compassion, and transformative action.

Finally, in a mystical sense, Jesus points to the divine unity of form and essence. The tree and the fruit are one—just as he and his teachings are one. Recognizing this unity is essential for understanding the fullness of divine truth. In the words of Meister Eckhart, *"The eye with which I see God is the same eye with which God sees me."* To love both the tree and its fruit is to recognize the divine essence in all things—both in the external world and within ourselves. It is a call to transcend dualities and see the interconnectedness of all that is divine.

In sum, saying 43 is a profound reflection on spiritual understanding: it challenges us to see beyond external forms and to recognize the divine truth in both the teachings and the actions that arise from them. It reminds us that the tree and the fruit are inseparable, and true spiritual wisdom is not merely admired but lived.

John 8:25 – "Who are you?" they asked. "Just what I have been telling you from the beginning," Jesus replied.

John 10:25-26 – "Jesus answered, 'I did tell you, but you do not believe. The works I do in my Father's name testify about me, but you do not believe because you are not my sheep.'"

Matthew 7:16-20 – "By their fruit, you will recognize them... A good tree cannot bear bad fruit, and a bad tree cannot bear good fruit."

Plato's Allegory of the Cave (Republic, Book VII): Just as prisoners in the cave struggle to recognize the true light of the sun, so too do the disciples fail to recognize Jesus' divine nature.

Hindu Advaita Vedanta: The concept of Maya (illusion) suggests that people mistake the external world for the ultimate reality, much like how Jesus' disciples fail to grasp his divine essence beyond his physical form.

Saying 44: Blasphemy Against the Holy Spirit

"Jesus said, 'Whoever blasphemes against the Father will be forgiven, and whoever blasphemes against the Son will be forgiven, but whoever blasphemes against the Holy Spirit will not be forgiven, either on earth or in heaven.'" (44)

This saying offers a deeply paradoxical and profound teaching about divine forgiveness and the nature of sin. On the surface, it seems to emphasize the unforgivable nature of blasphemy against the Holy Spirit, while also suggesting a more merciful posture toward offenses against the Father and the Son. However, when delved into more deeply, this saying reveals not just theological boundaries, but also a deeper spiritual truth about the nature of divine presence, grace, and transformation.

The Context of Forgiveness

Jesus' words affirm that forgiveness is a central theme in his teachings, as seen throughout the Gospel narratives. The forgiveness of sins, especially for those who repent, is presented as one of the key facets of Jesus' mission on Earth. He offers forgiveness not just for sins against the Father or himself (the Son) but, in his extraordinary grace, also extends the possibility of forgiveness for even the most grievous sins. The Parable of the Prodigal Son (Luke 15:11-32), for instance, exemplifies God's willingness to forgive those who return to Him, regardless of their transgressions.

However, Jesus introduces a critical distinction here: blasphemy against the Holy Spirit is portrayed as an unforgivable offense. To understand this, we must first consider the nature of the Holy Spirit in Christian theology, which is often regarded as the very breath of God—the divine presence that dwells in and among believers. The Spirit is the comforter, the guide, and the one who reveals the truth to humanity. Blasphemy against the Holy Spirit, then, represents more than a verbal insult; it is a rejection of the very transformative, illuminating force that makes reconciliation with God possible.

The Unforgivable Sin

Blasphemy against the Holy Spirit is often interpreted as the act of rejecting God's grace and refusing the means of spiritual transformation. It is not simply an offense against the Spirit in a trivial sense, but a conscious and persistent refusal to accept the invitation to repentance, healing, and enlightenment. As Jesus teaches in the Gospels, the Holy Spirit plays an essential role in revealing the truth of God to the human heart. The Spirit's work is to illuminate the soul, to call it back to its source, and to lead it toward salvation.

In this light, blasphemy against the Holy Spirit is seen as the deliberate and final rejection of the divine light and love that could lead to spiritual renewal. This is a rejection of the very grace that offers forgiveness and healing. By refusing the Holy Spirit's work, one closes oneself off to the very possibility of transformation and reconciliation with the divine. This rejection becomes unforgivable, not because God refuses to forgive, but because the person has chosen to remain in a state of spiritual blindness and hardness of heart, unwilling to accept the gift of grace.

Mystical and Symbolic Interpretations

In mystical traditions, the Holy Spirit is often symbolized as the divine breath or wind, the very presence of God that sustains and vivifies all creation. To blaspheme against the Holy Spirit, in this context, can be understood as rejecting the essential life force that animates the soul and all living beings. It is akin to rejecting the breath of life itself. The soul, in such a state, becomes spiritually deadened, incapable of perceiving divine presence or receiving spiritual guidance.

Furthermore, the Holy Spirit is frequently seen as the agent of the deep inner work of transformation—transforming the heart, mind, and soul. To reject the Holy Spirit is to refuse this inner alchemical process, where the soul is purified and made one with the divine. As Meister Eckhart, the great Christian mystic, put it, *"The soul is a place where God is born, and where God is born in the soul, the soul is made new."* To reject this inner work is to remain in a state of spiritual stagnation.

In a broader mystical context, blasphemy against the Holy Spirit can be seen as rejecting the very nature of divine love that permeates the universe. The Holy Spirit is often understood as the link between the Father and the Son, the unifying force that draws all things back into divine unity. To deny this force is to deny the interconnectedness of all creation, to refuse the reality that everything in the cosmos is imbued with divine presence and purpose.

Conclusion: The Holy Invitation: Saying Yes to the Spirit's Call

Saying 44 of the *Gospel of Thomas* calls us to a deeper understanding of forgiveness, grace, and the transformative power of the Holy Spirit. It reminds us that while all sins are forgivable, there is one sin that leads to spiritual death: the rejection of the divine presence that guides and heals. The challenge, then, is to remain open to the work of the Spirit, to continually seek divine truth, and to allow the Spirit's transformative power to lead us to spiritual renewal. This saying urges us to recognize the sacredness of the Holy Spirit as the life-giving force in our journey toward unity with God.

Saying 45: Uprooting Falsehood: The Power of Inner Strength

"Jesus said, 'Grapes are not harvested from thorns, nor are figs gathered from thistles. They do not produce fruit in my Father's kingdom. For truly, they are like the evil one who is the father of all who practice evil." (45)

In this saying, Jesus speaks of the natural order, where thorns and thistles, though they grow abundantly, do not bear the fruit of the vine or the fig. This simple image draws us into a profound mystical reflection on the nature of spiritual fruitfulness and the inner workings of divine love.

"Christ on a Vine by Leos Moskos"

The Garden of the Kingdom

The Kingdom of God is often likened to a garden in the sacred texts, a fertile, sacred space where the divine presence grows within the hearts of those who are open to it. The parables of the vine and the fruit are familiar throughout Scripture, representing the way in which the soul must be cultivated and nourished to bear fruit that is pleasing to the Father. Grapes, symbols of divine sweetness, and figs, symbols of spiritual richness, are the fruits of a soul in communion with the divine.

Yet thorns and thistles, though they too grow in the garden, are not meant to bear fruit of the Kingdom. Their growth is a result of the corruption and brokenness in the natural world, mirroring the spiritual barrenness that comes from aligning oneself with forces that are contrary to divine love. The thorns and thistles, though alive, symbolize hearts hardened by self-interest and pride, like the evil one who sowed them in the garden of humanity.

The Path of the Thorns

In the mystic's journey, the path is often one that requires shedding thorns, both external and internal. St. John of the Cross, in his *Dark Night of the Soul*, speaks of the soul's passage through desolation and dryness before it is able to experience the fullness of divine union. The thorns represent those inner obstacles—attachments, pride, and sin—that prevent the soul from receiving the true fruit of God's kingdom. These thorns are not inherently evil, but rather they are the natural result of a soul in need of purification. Just as a vine must be pruned to bear good fruit, so too must the soul go through the painful process of self-emptying and surrender.

But the thistles, like the evil one, represent something more insidious. They are not merely obstacles to be cleared away; they are the manifestations of forces that intentionally lead the soul away from the Father's love. They draw nourishment from the soul's misguided desires, twisting it into something harmful, just as the evil one seeks to sow seeds of hatred and division.

The Fruit of the Spirit

In contrast to the thorns and thistles, the fruit of the Kingdom is born of the divine seed that takes root in the soil of a humble and open heart. The soul that aligns itself with divine will, like a tree planted by the river, will bear fruit that nourishes not only itself but also those around it. The fruit of the Spirit—love, joy, peace, patience, kindness, goodness, faithfulness, gentleness, and self-control (Galatians 5:22-23)—grows naturally in a heart that remains open to the Father's love, just as figs ripen in the warmth of the sun and grapes swell under the tender care of the vine dresser.

Jesus' warning here is not one of condemnation but of discernment. The thorns and thistles represent the forces of division, hatred, and selfishness that poison the garden of the soul. They grow where love and mercy are not cultivated, where the soil is not tended to with care. The heart that yields such fruit is far from the Kingdom, and it is in need of healing, of turning back to the Father who is the true Gardener.

The Evil One as the Thorn in the Garden

The "evil one" who is described as the father of those who practice evil is not merely an external figure but an internal force that leads the soul astray. In the mystic tradition, evil is not simply an opposition to good; it is a distortion of the good, a perversion of love. The evil one plants seeds of discord, hatred, and fear in the hearts of humanity, causing them to become like thorns and thistles—barren and incapable of bearing the fruit of divine love. These souls, rooted in selfishness and pride, are disconnected from the flow of divine grace and cannot partake in the harvest of the Kingdom.

The evil one, as the force of separation, isolates the soul from the communion of divine love. This isolation is likened to the thorns and thistles that grow up amidst the true fruit-bearing plants—causing harm to those who seek to grow in the garden of the soul. Yet, even the thorns are not beyond redemption, for through the transformative power of divine grace, they can be uprooted and replaced with the fruits of love and peace.

The Harvest of Heaven

Ultimately, the Kingdom of God is a place of divine communion, where only the fruit of love can grow and be harvested. In this harvest, the vine and the fig are gathered into the Father's storehouse, representing the souls that have been transformed through divine love. The thorns and thistles, however, are left behind, for they do not carry the essence of the Kingdom. But even in their barrenness, there is hope for redemption, for the Father's grace is ever-flowing, and the soul that turns back to Him can be transformed from thorn to fruit.

As the mystics have often said, *"The soul that loves is like a garden that bears fruit for the Father's kingdom."* The soul must cultivate its inner garden, tending to the soil with humility, patience, and love. It is only when the heart is free from the corruption of selfish desires—free from the thorns—that it can bear the true fruit of the Kingdom, the fruit that nourishes both the soul and the world around it.

Thus, the invitation of this saying is not one of judgment, but of a call to spiritual discernment. The thorns may be present, but they need not be the defining feature of the soul's garden. With the grace of the Father, even the thorns can be uprooted, and the fruit of the Kingdom can grow.

Matthew 7:16-20 –

"By their fruit, you will recognize them. Do people pick grapes from thornbushes, or figs from thistles? Likewise, every good tree bears good fruit, but a bad tree bears bad fruit."

Bhagavad Gita 16.24 –

"Those who are free from pride and arrogance, who have conquered desire and anger, who are free from attachment and possess a pure heart, attain liberation."

༺❦❦❦༻

Saying 46: The Greatness of John and the Childlike Soul

"Jesus said, 'From Adam to John the Baptist, among those born of women, there is none greater than John the Baptist, so that his eyes should not be averted. But I have said: Whoever among you becomes a child will know the kingdom and will become greater than John." (46)

The nature of John the Baptist has quite a mystical tone in biblical scripture. From his miraculous birth to his role as the forerunner of the Messiah, and even his connection to Elijah. John the Baptist is a threshold figure—a **gateway** between the old world and the inbreaking Kingdom of Heaven. He *decreases* so that **Christ may increase** (John 3:30). A powerful model of humility, purpose, and divine calling.

The Angel Gabriel appeared to Zechariah while he was serving in the Temple and announced that Elizabeth would bear a son named John. Zechariah doubted and was rendered mute until the child's birth. When John was born, Zechariah's voice returned, and he prophesied in the *Benedictus* (Luke 1:68–79) that his son would be the prophet of the Most High.

"The Hidden Christ Meets the Hidden Prophet"

John was a kin of Jesus, perhaps a second cousin. When Jesus' mother, Mary, visited Elizabeth during their pregnancies, John leaped in the womb at the presence of Jesus (still in Mary's womb). Elizabeth was filled with the Holy Spirit and recognized Mary as "the mother of my Lord" (Luke 1:41-45). It's a deeply mystical moment, almost a pre-natal recognition of the Messiah.

John's ministry did not arise in a vacuum. He emerged from the wilderness, clothed in camel's hair and eating locusts and wild honey—a figure both prophetic and ascetic, reminiscent of Elijah. His voice echoed through the Judean countryside: *"Repent, for the Kingdom of Heaven is at hand"* (Matthew 3:2). But John did not merely preach repentance— he enacted it through a baptism of water, a ritual both symbolic and preparatory. This act of immersion was not merely for purification, but for readiness—for the One who was coming after him.

John's baptism marked a threshold between what was and what was to come. And fittingly, it was there—in the waters of the Jordan—that Jesus appeared. The moment is a convergence of earthly humility and heavenly affirmation. Jesus, though sinless, steps into the waters of repentance to be baptized by John. And as he rises from the water, the heavens are opened.

The Holy Spirit descends in bodily form **like a dove**, and a voice from heaven declares: *"You are my beloved Son; with you I am well pleased"* (Luke 3:22). This theophany—the appearance of the Triune God—is both majestic and intimate: the Son in the water, the Spirit descending gently, and the voice of the Father affirming divine sonship. The dove, a symbol of peace, purity, and the Spirit's creative presence, hovers over the waters, echoing the Spirit's movement over the deep in Genesis 1:2. It is a new creation moment.

John's role is complete here, but not diminished. He is the baptizer of the Messiah, the voice preparing the way, and the one who recognizes Jesus as *"the Lamb of God, who takes away the sin of the world"* (John 1:29). He steps aside not out of weakness, but out of deep awareness of his purpose. In this, John embodies a spiritual posture of release—of making space for the greater light to shine.

Despite the crowds who flocked to him, John the Baptist never exalted himself. His ministry always pointed beyond himself. One of his most striking declarations was: *"After me comes one who is mightier than I, the strap of whose sandal I am not worthy to untie."*

"Baptism of Christ"

John baptized with water, a symbol of cleansing and preparation. Jesus, he says, will baptize *"with the Holy Spirit and with fire"* (Luke 3:16; Matthew 3:11). This contrast is profound. Water washes the outside; fire transforms from within.

Fire, in biblical imagery, is often a sign of divine presence—think of the burning bush (Exodus 3:2), the pillar of fire guiding Israel (Exodus 13:21), or the tongues of fire at Pentecost (Acts 2:3). To be baptized with fire is to undergo a purification that penetrates the soul—a refining that consumes what is impure and ignites the divine spark within. It is a baptism of awakening, of divine indwelling, of transfiguration.

Jesus does not merely call for repentance; He **imparts the Spirit** that makes new life possible. John knew his own baptism could prepare hearts, but only Christ could fulfill them. His words resonate with awe and prophetic vision—he saw the coming of a divine fire that would not only cleanse, but illuminate and empower.

Thus, the sandal and the fire are symbols intertwined: the former expressing the **lowliness of the forerunner**, and the latter, the **glory of the One to come**. The Messiah carries within Him the fire of God's presence—the Spirit who hovers, descends, indwells, and refines.

The sacredness of baptism is far more than a rite of passage or a symbolic cleansing—it is a **mystical union** with the divine. To be baptized is to be *christened*—anointed into the life of Christ—and drawn into the eternal communion of the **Triune God**. In this sacred act, heaven and earth touch; the soul is awakened to its origin and destiny in divine love.

The **waters of baptism** carry deep symbolism. In one sense, **water represents the Father**—the Source, the wellspring of life from whom all things flow. Just as the Spirit hovered over the face of the deep in Genesis, so the waters of baptism speak of **primordial creation**, the Father's generative love, and the womb of new birth.

Jesus, the Son, represents the **fire**—the consuming and illuminating flame of divine presence. He is the one who baptizes with the Holy Spirit and fire, igniting the soul with divine love and transforming it from within. As the eternal Logos made flesh, He enters the waters not to be cleansed, but to **sanctify** them, turning them into a gateway of divine union.

And in this sacred moment, the **Holy Spirit** descends—often symbolized as a dove—gently, yet powerfully sealing the soul with divine indwelling. The Spirit is the bond of love between Father and Son, now poured out upon the baptized to dwell within them as guide, comforter, and sanctifier.

Thus, in baptism, one is immersed not only in water, but in the life of the Trinity:

- **The Father** is the fountain of life and grace.
- **The Son** is the flame of divine love and the one who makes the way.
- **The Spirit** is the breath and presence that completes the union.

To be baptized is to pass through the waters of origin, be kindled by the fire of transformation, and be filled with the Spirit of divine communion. It is the beginning of a new creation—where the image of God is not only restored, but united with the very being of God.

In this contrast, Jesus does not diminish John but reveals a more hidden path—one that transcends greatness in the eyes of the world or even prophetic stature. The child, uncluttered by ambition or pretense, becomes the vessel through which the Kingdom flows. It is not through striving but through surrender, not through knowledge alone but through wonder, that one enters divine union. To step into this mystery, we must return to the primal sanctuary of the heart and the world around us—where trees whisper ancient truths, rivers carry the memory of Eden, and every breeze speaks of the Spirit's nearness. Here, in the silence of nature and the innocence of a child's gaze, the voice of the Living One is still speaking.

In this saying, Jesus contrasts two spiritual paths—one exemplified by John the Baptist, the other by those who come to the Kingdom through the humility and simplicity of a child's heart. To fully grasp the depths of this teaching, we must enter into the sacred space of nature and the childlike soul, where the profound mysteries of divine wisdom can be found.

"Saint John the Baptist and Forerunner of the Lord"

The Greatness of John the Baptist

John the Baptist, a solitary figure in the wilderness, stands as the epitome of prophetic zeal and righteousness. His calling was to prepare the way for the Messiah, and his life was one marked by radical devotion to God. Among those born of women, he is described as the greatest—a mighty force who called for repentance, who baptized with water, and who boldly declared the coming of the Lamb of God.

John was a voice crying out in the wilderness, a burning light that pointed to the coming Kingdom. His life was one of purification, fire, and fervent witness. He stood as a bridge between the Old Covenant and the New, embodying the spirit of the prophets while preparing the way for the fulfillment of God's promise through Christ.

Yet, Jesus, in his divine wisdom, reveals a deeper mystery. John's greatness, though unparalleled among men, is not the ultimate measure of greatness in the Kingdom. For the Kingdom of God, unlike earthly kingdoms, does not follow the patterns of power, might, and recognition as we understand them. In the Kingdom, greatness is not defined by outward strength or righteousness but by a profound, inward humility.

The Child and the Kingdom

Jesus turns the traditional idea of greatness on its head by inviting his followers to become like children. The image of the child, pure and open to the world, represents a soul free from pride, free from the complex entanglements of ego, and free from the distortions of worldly ambition. The child is a symbol of innocence, trust, and receptivity—the qualities that are required to enter the Kingdom of God.

In the natural world, children are the first to receive the gift of wonder. Their eyes behold the world as a mystery, filled with beauty and awe. They are untouched by the cynicism and disillusionment that often accompany adulthood. In their simplicity, children reflect the unspoiled nature of creation itself. To become like a child is to return to the garden before the fall, before the complexities of knowledge, self-consciousness, and desire distorted the soul's perception of reality.

In mystical traditions, the child is not merely an innocent bystander but a teacher in their own right. The child's heart is open to the sacred mysteries that adults often overlook. The Kingdom of Heaven, Jesus teaches, is not to be found in intellectual achievement or religious asceticism alone but in the pure, untainted heart—a heart that is open, trusting, and deeply attuned to the presence of God in all things.

Greater Than John

The invitation to become like children is not a call to immaturity, but to spiritual maturity in the most paradoxical of ways. The mystics have often said that the path to enlightenment is one of unlearning. We must unlearn the ways of pride, the ways of self-sufficiency, the ways of separateness, and return to a state of divine childlikeness. In this state, the soul is able to see the Kingdom of God in its fullness—able to behold the divine presence in all creation, as the child sees the beauty and wonder of the world around them.

Jesus' proclamation that those who become like children will be greater than John reveals the profound shift that occurs in the heart of one who accepts this invitation. It is not the loud voice of the prophet, nor the boldness of the ascetic that defines greatness in the Kingdom, but the quiet, humble receptivity of the child who sees with eyes unclouded by the world's distractions. In this receptivity, the soul is able to commune with God in the deepest, most intimate way.

Nature's Wisdom and the Child's Heart

Nature, in its infinite cycles and mysteries, reflects the purity and simplicity of the child's soul. Consider the infant bird, who instinctively spreads its wings and trusts the air to carry it. Or the child who, upon seeing the beauty of a flower or the shimmer of a stream, finds joy and wonder in its mere existence. These moments are not grasped by intellectual effort but are received with the innocence of the heart.

The child sees the divine in the simple acts of life, the same way a mystic beholds the presence of God in the stars, the river, and the wind. There is no need for grand theological explanations or complex rituals in these moments—only pure, untainted experience of the divine presence that surrounds all things. The child does not seek to possess or control; they simply receive, trusting that what is given is enough.

The Kingdom Revealed in the Child's Heart

To be a child in the Kingdom is to live in this openness, to embrace the mystery of divine love and grace with a heart unguarded. It is to let go of the need for control, to release the self-reliance that often limits us, and to allow the divine to move within us like the wind through the trees.

The Kingdom of God is not a distant place but a living reality within the heart of every child who can still see with the eyes of wonder, who can still hear with the ears of innocence. It is in this childlike state that the soul enters the Kingdom, for it is not through wisdom or strength but through the simplicity of heart that the mysteries of God are revealed.

As we walk through the garden of life, let us learn from the child who marvels at the beauty of each moment, who sees in every leaf and every stone the fingerprints of the divine. For in this wonder, we touch the very heart of the Kingdom, and in this simplicity, we become greater than the mightiest of prophets, greater than John the Baptist himself.

Matthew 11:11 – "Truly I tell you, among those born of women there has not risen anyone greater than John the Baptist; yet whoever is least in the kingdom of heaven is greater than he."

Mark 10:15 – "Truly I tell you, anyone who will not receive the kingdom of God like a little child will never enter it."

Tao Te Ching 55 – "One who is filled with virtue is like a newborn child. Poisonous insects will not sting him; wild beasts will not seize him; birds of prey will not strike him." (Laozi speaks of the enlightened being returning to a childlike state.)

Saying 47: The Unity of Purpose and the Dangers of Division

"Jesus said, 'A person cannot mount two horses or bend two bows. And a servant cannot serve two masters. If that person is a slave to the one, they will be opposed to the other. No one drinks aged wine and immediately desires to drink new wine. One does not pour old wine into new wineskins, or they will burst. An old patch is not suitable for a new garment, because a new patch will tear away from the old, and the tear will be worse.'" (47)

In this saying, Jesus speaks of the impossibility of divided loyalty, urging a decisive choice in one's spiritual life. Through vivid metaphors, he brings attention to the inherent tension between old and new, the past and the present, and the dual callings that often pull the soul in different directions. These teachings invite us into a deeper understanding of what it means to live fully in the present moment, without clinging to the past or dividing our hearts.

The Rider and the Two Horses

The first image Jesus offers is of a person who cannot ride two horses. Imagine a rider perched awkwardly, with one foot in each stirrup, struggling to maintain balance. The tension is palpable, and the danger of falling is inevitable. To ride two horses is to split one's attention and energy, which leads to confusion and chaos. A person who tries to serve two masters, Jesus warns, will find themselves pulled in opposing directions—torn between two forces that cannot coexist peacefully.

In nature, we see this reflected in the dualities of life: day and night, earth and sky, light and shadow. To try to hold onto both at once—saying "yes" to both—dilutes the power of each. Just as the sun cannot shine brightly at midnight, we, too, cannot give our full allegiance to two competing forces. The soul, when divided, becomes restless and unstable.

The rider of two horses must choose: either focus on one path or risk being lost in the wilderness of indecision. Similarly, the person divided between two masters will ultimately serve neither, for no one can sustain true devotion to opposing forces.

The Slave and the Two Masters

In the second metaphor, Jesus refers to the servant who cannot serve two masters. This is an image of spiritual servitude, where the heart is bound to one will, one purpose. A person who is bound to two conflicting desires will find their life torn apart, unable to give themselves fully to either. The soul is a vessel that can only truly serve one guiding force. When divided, it fragments, unable to experience the fullness of any calling.

The natural world, with its cycles of life and death, reveals the same truth: the seasons serve one rhythm, one cycle of growth and decay. If the earth were divided in its devotion— half blooming, half withering—chaos would ensue. The harmony of nature requires that each season, each force, remain true to its nature.

In this teaching, Jesus calls for undivided devotion. A single, clear purpose allows the soul to align with divine intention, and in that alignment, the deepest peace is found. To serve two masters is to court spiritual confusion, for the soul cannot be fully nourished by two opposing sources.

The Aged Wine and the New Wine

The third image Jesus uses is the contrast between old wine and new wine. A person who has tasted the depth and richness of aged wine would not immediately desire the fresh, unfermented flavor of new wine. This speaks not just of taste, but of spiritual experience. The soul that has matured in the wisdom of the past may find it difficult to leap into the unfamiliar newness of an entirely different experience or worldview.

Aged wine represents the depth of spiritual insight gained through time, trial, and reflection. It is the wisdom that comes from having walked a long path, from having encountered suffering and joy in equal measure. New wine, on the other hand, represents a fresh, unspoiled vision—a new revelation, a new phase of spiritual growth that calls for openness and receptivity.

The key point here is that both the old wine and the new wine have their place. However, they cannot be hastily mixed. Just as new wine requires new wineskins—those that are flexible enough to expand as the wine ferments—so too must our hearts be open to new experiences, even as they honor and integrate the wisdom of the past.

The Old Patch and the New Garment

The final image Jesus offers is of an old garment with a new patch. To place a new patch on an old, worn garment would only cause greater harm. The patch would tear away from the fabric, making the tear worse. This speaks to the way in which old structures, old ways of thinking, cannot easily accommodate the new growth of the spirit. The garment represents the old self, the worn-out patterns of behavior and thought that may no longer serve us in our new spiritual understanding.

In nature, the leaf that has withered and fallen cannot bear new fruit. The soil must be prepared, the root system must be nurtured, before new growth can emerge. Similarly, the soul must be made ready for new wisdom—old patterns must be shed, or they will hinder the blossoming of new life.

This teaching reminds us that true transformation cannot simply be patched onto old ways of thinking or being. The new garment of spiritual renewal requires a deep cleansing, a shedding of the old self, so that we can truly embrace the new, untainted by the old limitations.

The Spiritual Path: Unity and Devotion

Ultimately, Jesus is urging us to focus our devotion and energy on a singular path. The spiritual journey is not about splitting our attention, nor is it about holding onto old wisdom while refusing to embrace the new. Rather, it is about walking the path with integrity, allowing each step to be a full expression of our soul's deepest desire. Just as the earth cycles through the seasons with perfect alignment, so must we align our hearts with the divine will, choosing the path of simplicity, clarity, and undivided loyalty.

In the natural world, a tree cannot grow two trunks, nor can the river flow in two directions. Similarly, the soul must choose its direction, for only in full devotion can we experience the fullness of life, of love, and of the divine mystery that calls us forward.

Thus, Jesus calls us to examine where we place our hearts and minds. Are we divided, torn between conflicting desires, or are we ready to surrender to the singular path that leads us home?

Matthew 6:24 –
"No one can serve two masters. Either you will hate the one and love the other, or you will be devoted to the one and despise the other."

Dhammapada, Verse 210: "Let go of attachment to pleasure and to suffering. The mind that is not attached to these things is the peaceful mind."

Taittiriya Upanishad, 1.11: "The one who is established in truth, whose mind is firm, becomes free from all conflict."

Saying 48: The Power of Unity

"Jesus said, 'If two make peace with each other in this one house, they will say to the mountain, 'Move away,' and it will move.'" (48)

In this saying, Jesus speaks of the power of peace and unity between two individuals. When two people come together in harmony, their combined strength is so potent that it can command even the mountain itself to move. The mountain here symbolizes the seemingly insurmountable obstacles and challenges of life. With mutual understanding and unity, even the most formidable of challenges can be overcome.

This is not just a physical act of commanding nature but a profound spiritual truth. True peace, rooted in love and mutual respect, has the power to transcend the limitations of the material world. When two hearts are aligned in peace, they possess an inner strength that is far greater than any external force. Together, they can achieve what would be impossible alone.

A House Divided

The power of unity is echoed in the wisdom of many cultures. The Chinese proverb "If a house is divided against itself, it cannot stand" serves as a profound reminder of the fragility of any structure built on division. Just as a house that is split in its foundations cannot endure the storm, so too will a heart divided against itself fail to remain firm when faced with trials.

When there is discord in the home, when there is conflict and division between its members, the whole structure weakens. The house—the foundation of love, trust, and shared purpose—becomes fragile, and any external pressure can cause it to collapse. This is not only true for the physical home but for the inner life as well. A soul divided against itself is unstable and lacks the strength to confront the challenges it encounters.

The Mountain of Obstacles

The mountain in this teaching represents the obstacles that stand before us. These obstacles can take many forms: personal struggles, challenges in relationships, or societal pressures. When two individuals—whether in a family, community, or partnership—work together in peace and understanding, they can face these challenges with greater resilience. The unity between them creates an energetic force that is capable of transforming the reality around them.

Unity brings about a state of harmony that aligns the heart with the greater flow of the universe. Just as the water flows effortlessly around obstacles, so too does peace allow us to navigate life's challenges with grace and ease. A house that is united is like a tree with strong roots, able to bend with the wind but never break.

The Spiritual Path of Harmony

On the spiritual journey, peace between individuals is essential not only for personal well-being but for the collective growth of all. In relationships, whether familial, romantic, or spiritual, peace creates a fertile ground for love, wisdom, and growth. The unity between hearts forms a sacred foundation from which transformation can occur. The mountains we face—whether in our own hearts or in the world around us—are not insurmountable when we are united in purpose and love.

This teaching invites us to reflect on where division may exist in our lives and hearts. Do we harbor conflict with others, or are we open to reconciliation? Are we divided within ourselves, torn between different desires and beliefs? In cultivating peace, we unlock the ability to move mountains—both within and around us.

When we choose unity, when we make peace, we align ourselves with the deeper truths of the universe. The house—our hearts, our families, our communities—will stand firm, and the mountains that once seemed immovable will yield to the power of love and harmony.

> *Matthew 17:20 –*
> *"He replied, 'Because you have so little faith. Truly I tell you, if you have faith as small as a mustard seed, you can say to this mountain, 'Move from here to there,' and it will move. Nothing will be impossible for you.'"*

> *Bhagavad Gita 18.63 –*
> *"Thus, I have explained to you this knowledge that is more secret than all secrets. Ponder over it deeply, and then do as you wish."*

Saying 49: The Blessed Solitary and the Kingdom

"Jesus said, 'Blessed are the solitary and the elect, for you will find the Kingdom. For you have come from it, and you are going to it.'" (49)

In this saying, Jesus pronounces a blessing upon those who walk the path of solitude and inner election—those who seek the Kingdom of Heaven within themselves. The solitary, though they may appear alone in their journey, are blessed because they recognize the deeper truth: that the Kingdom of God is not found in external circumstances, but within their own hearts. The "elect" refers to those chosen by divine grace, who have been awakened to the spiritual reality that transcends worldly distractions.

The Solitary Path

Solitude, in the mystical tradition, is not a state of isolation but one of profound connection with the Divine. In solitude, the seeker is able to quiet the noise of the world, turning inward to discover the eternal truth that resides within. The journey of the solitary soul is a path of introspection, contemplation, and prayer. It is in the stillness, away from external distractions, that the soul can hear the subtle whisper of the Divine.

The solitary find the Kingdom because they seek it not in the ephemeral things of the world but in the depths of their own being. They understand that the Kingdom is within them, as Jesus often taught—*"The Kingdom of God is within you"* (Luke 17:21). The solitary soul is not alone but in communion with the Divine, and through this communion, they find the presence of the Kingdom everywhere they go.

Coming From and Going To the Kingdom

Jesus speaks of the Kingdom as both a place of origin and destination. "For you have come from it" suggests that the soul's true nature originates from the Divine Kingdom—the place of perfect peace, love, and unity. The soul, in its essence, is not bound by the physical world but is a spark of divine light that transcends time and space. It comes from the Kingdom, from the eternal truth of God's presence.

"Going to it" speaks of the return to this divine source, the final reunification of the soul with the Creator. The journey is not one of discovery but of remembrance. The seeker does not need to find the Kingdom as though it were lost, but to realize that they have always been a part of it. As the mystic Rumi once said, *"You were born with wings, why prefer to crawl through life?"* The return to the Kingdom is the soul's awakening to its true nature, free from the illusions of separation and limitation.

The Elect: Chosen for the Kingdom

The "elect" are those chosen not by the world's standards, but by the divine call to remember their true self. These are the ones who, through grace, awaken to the knowledge of the Kingdom within. They are chosen not for their outward achievements but for their inner recognition of the Divine.

The mystical tradition often speaks of this divine election as an awakening to one's true identity. The soul is chosen by God not in the sense of being picked out of a crowd, but in the sense of being called to remember its divine origin and ultimate return. The elect are those who recognize the Kingdom within, who hear the call to reunite with their Source.

The Eternal Kingdom

The Kingdom that Jesus speaks of is not a distant place but an eternal presence that transcends time and space. It is the realm of divine truth, love, and unity. In the Kingdom, there is no separation between the Creator and the created; all are one in the Divine. It is the state of being where the soul is fully awakened to the truth of its existence.

In this sense, the Kingdom is not something to be attained in the future, but a reality to be realized in the present. The solitary and the elect are those who have realized that the Kingdom is within them, and they walk the path of remembrance, returning to it with each step.

A Call to Inner Awakening

This saying calls us to look inward, to seek the Kingdom not in the external world but in the depths of our own being. It reminds us that the Kingdom is not a place to be found in time, but a state of being that transcends time. The solitary and the elect are blessed because they remember this truth, and in their remembering, they are united with the eternal presence of the Divine. The journey to the Kingdom is not one of separation, but one of realization—of coming to know that we have always come from it, and always will return to it.

> *Luke 17:21 –"The kingdom of God is within you."*
>
> *Matthew 13:44 –"The kingdom of heaven is like treasure hidden in a field. When a man found it, he hid it again, and then in his joy went and sold all he had and bought that field."*
>
> *Bhagavad Gita 15.7: "The living entities in this conditioned world are My eternal fragments. Due to conditioned life, they are struggling with the six senses, which include the mind."*

Saying 50: The Light of the Kingdom

"Jesus said, 'If they say to you, "Where did you come from?" say to them, "We came from the light, the place where the light came into being of its own accord, and established itself and became manifest through their image." If they say to you, "Who are you?" say, "We are its children, and

we are the elect of the living Father." If they ask you, "What is the sign of your Father in you?" say to them, "It is a movement and a rest." (50)

This passage affirms a fundamental truth: We are *children of the light and children of the day* (1 Thessalonians 5:5). Jesus speaks of a preexistent reality, a place where divine light generated itself, bringing forth the elect. This evokes the prologue of John's Gospel: *In the beginning was the Word, and the Word was with God, and the Word was God... In Him was life, and that life was the light of all mankind* (John 1:1-4).

The phrase *a movement and a rest* suggests the dual nature of existence: the dynamic unfolding of creation and the stillness of divine presence. In Eastern Christian thought, hesychasm—the practice of inner stillness—mirrors this divine balance. As St. Gregory Palamas teaches, *The divine light moves in us, yet is beyond all motion*. This echoes the Psalmist's words: *Be still, and know that I am God* (Psalm 46:10). Saying 50 ultimately reveals that to be children of the light is to embody both the cosmic dance of creation and the deep, silent presence of the Father's eternal being.

Imagine a seeker standing at the threshold of divine knowledge, peering into the vast expanse of existence, asking, *"Who are you?"* and *"Where do you come from?"* The question is not merely one of identity but of essence—of origins stretching beyond flesh and bone, beyond time itself.

Jesus' answer in Saying 50 is not one of earthly descent or lineage but of light:

"We came from the light, the place where the light came into being of its own accord, and established itself and became manifest through their image."

To the unawakened mind, this answer may seem like a riddle. But to those with eyes to see, it is the unveiling of a great truth. We are not merely beings of dust and matter—we are children of the light, emanations of the divine radiance that was before the world began. This echoes the Gospel of John:

"In the beginning was the Word... In Him was life, and that life was the light of all mankind. The light shines in the darkness, and the darkness has not overcome it." (John 1:1-5)

This saying calls us to remember—to look within and recognize the uncreated light that moves through us, the luminous thread binding all things together. As the outsider listens, they may ask again, *"But how do I know? What is the sign of your Father in you?"*

Jesus responds:

"It is a movement and a rest."

These words, though simple, contain the rhythm of all existence—the pulse of the cosmos, the breath of God. The divine dance of creation moves forward ceaselessly, yet within it, there is stillness. In Eastern traditions, this balance is found in the Tao, the harmony between action and non-action. In Christian mysticism, it is the paradox of contemplation and love—Martha's labor and Mary's quiet devotion (Luke 10:38-42).

The stillness is not emptiness but fullness. The movement is not chaos but divine order. St. Isaac of Nineveh writes, *"Love is the kingdom; hidden within it is the fullness of joy. Enter into it, and you will find rest."*

To stand before these words is to feel the heart quicken, to sense a revelation hovering just beyond understanding. We are called not only to know this truth but to embody it. If we are truly children of the light, then we must shine—not as mere reflections, but as bearers of the very radiance from which we came.

Jesus' words are not an abstraction; they are a summons. The one who hears them is no longer just an outsider asking questions but a soul standing on the threshold of awakening. The light from which we came is not distant—it is within. It is the fire of being, the stillness in movement, the movement in rest. It is the answer to the question, *Who are you?*

You are light. You are the elect of the living Father. You have always been.

Chandogya Upanishad 3.14.1: "The self is in the light of the sun, in the light of the moon, in the fire, in the wind, in the stars. It is all-pervading and omnipotent. From it, all things are born."

Chapter 7

Duality and the Mystery of Life (Sayings 51-60)

Saying 51: The Hidden Resurrection

His disciples said to him: On what day will the rest of the dead come into being, and on what day will the new world come? He said to them: What you await has come, but you do not know it. (51)

This saying presents a profound challenge to conventional expectations about time, death, and the arrival of a new world. The disciples ask Jesus a question grounded in apocalyptic anticipation: *"On what day will the rest of the dead come into being, and on what day will the new world come?"* Their question reflects a future-oriented hope—a longing for resurrection and renewal, imagined as an event yet to occur.

But Jesus' response dismantles their framework: *"What you await has come, but you do not know it."* This is a radical inversion of eschatology. The resurrection is not some distant miracle. The new world is not a horizon event. Both are already present. The problem is not delay but perception. The disciples are waiting for what is already here.

This teaching calls the seeker to awaken to a present-tense reality hidden beneath the veil of ordinary consciousness. The "rest of the dead" may refer not only to the physically deceased but to those spiritually asleep—living in forgetfulness, unaware of their divine origin. The "coming into being" is not future resurrection but present awakening. Similarly, the "new world" is not a future cosmos but a transformed way of seeing—the Kingdom of God already in the midst of us (Luke 17:21), invisible to the unawakened eye.

In this light, Jesus is not predicting the future but revealing the now. The eternal has broken into time. The world has already been made new, but the mind clings to its old patterns, waiting for what can only be seen through the eye of the heart. This is not a denial of resurrection—it is its reinterpretation. Resurrection is not the reanimation of corpses, but the reawakening of the soul. The new world is not coming *to us*, it is *within us*, awaiting recognition.

Like many sayings in *Thomas*, this one invites a shift in consciousness. It is not a riddle to solve, but a veil to lift. The living presence of the Kingdom is not elsewhere—it is here.

The dead are raised when they remember. The world is made new when it is seen rightly. The time is not later. The time is now.

I can attest to this hidden nearness through my own experience. On that sacred day, I encountered the Resurrected Christ not as a memory or figure of the past, but as an eternal, infinite reality—shining with light, unveiling himself as the Triune Being: the Father, the Son, and the Holy Spirit. This was not a vision locked in time, but a revelation of what always *is*. Two thousand years after his resurrection, Christ appeared to me not as someone returning, but as someone who had never left.

In that moment, it became clear that the "new world" is not a future event. It is the unveiled reality beneath this one. The light Christ shines is not foreign to us—we are part of that light. We are participants in the divine radiance, never separate from Source, though we often forget who we truly are. What he revealed to me was not just himself, but ourselves—as reflections of the divine nature, each of us a unique ray from the same eternal Light.

Thus, this saying in *Thomas* is not merely a teaching. It is a mirror. The resurrection is now. The Kingdom is here. The dead awaken not by waiting, but by remembering. The veil between heaven and earth is thinner than breath. We are already home—we need only recognize it.

Saying 52: The Living One Before You

"His disciples said to him, 'Twenty-four prophets spoke in Israel, and they all spoke of you.' He said to them, 'You have disregarded the one living before you and have spoken of the dead.'" (52)

There is a moment when the seeker must stop looking to the past for answers. We often find ourselves reaching for the wisdom of those who came before us, looking for prophets and sages to point the way. We honor the voices of history, from the ancient prophets of Israel to the mystics of every tradition, as they echo through the corridors of time. But in this search, we often miss the living presence that is right before us.

Jesus, in his wisdom, calls us to see what is living right now, what is present in this very moment. The past prophets spoke of a truth, yes, but it is the living truth, the presence here and now, that demands our attention. There is a danger in revering the past too much—it can cause us to overlook the truth that is unfolding before our eyes.

There is a divine presence that moves through all things, not confined to the words of prophets or the records of ancient history, but in the very air we breathe, the soil we tread, and the hearts we open. The past has its place, but the present is where the Kingdom is found.

His words are eternal, but to truly see, we must not look to the dead, but to the living. And in that moment of recognition, we too become prophets, speaking not of things that have passed, but of the living truth that is here, now, before us.

The real is not far. It is the breath behind your breath, the silence between your thoughts.

"For the word of God is living and active, sharper than any two-edged sword, piercing to the division of soul and of spirit, of joints and of marrow, and discerning the thoughts and intentions of the heart." (Hebrews 4:12)

The Seed That Remembers

"Where there is one, I am with him."
"Become passers-by."

You are still in the world—but no longer of it.
You move through like a traveler, light-footed, carrying nothing but the Pearl.
It's enough. It is everything.

You became the seed dropped in good soil.
And the fruit, unseen, will bloom in others when the time is right.

Saying 53: The True Circumcision: Spiritual Transformation Beyond the Flesh

"His disciples said to him, 'Is circumcision useful or not?' He said to them, 'If it were useful, their father would have begotten them already circumcised from their mother. But the true circumcision in spirit has become profitable in every respect." (53)

Saying 53 from the Gospel of Thomas addresses a theological and ritualistic concept that was particularly relevant to the early Jewish and Christian communities. Circumcision, a physical sign of the covenant between God and the people of Israel, was considered a fundamental ritual of Jewish identity. The disciples' question about its usefulness suggests that they are still grappling with the relationship between the old Jewish law (which required circumcision) and the new spiritual teachings that Jesus was offering.

In his response, Jesus goes beyond the physical ritual of circumcision and points to a deeper, spiritual transformation. He suggests that physical circumcision is not the key to entering the Kingdom of God. Instead, he emphasizes the "circumcision in spirit"—a metaphor for the purification and transformation of the heart and mind.

This reflects the idea that true spiritual identity comes from inner change rather than outward rituals.

Jesus' teaching here challenges the traditional view that external rituals are what make someone righteous. He is calling for a deeper, internal transformation, one that transcends mere physical actions or cultural identity markers. This aligns with many of his teachings about inner purity, humility, and the need for a personal, transformative relationship with God.

> *Romans 2:28-29 (NIV): "A person is not a Jew who is one only outwardly, nor is circumcision merely outward and physical. No, a person is a Jew who is one inwardly; and circumcision is circumcision of the heart, by the Spirit, not by the written code. Such a person's praise is not from other people, but from God."*

This passage from Paul's letter to the Romans closely mirrors the message in Saying 53. Paul makes a clear distinction between outward religious observance and inner spiritual transformation. Just as Jesus in the Gospel of Thomas teaches about the "circumcision of the spirit," Paul highlights the importance of internal change rather than external rituals.

> *Colossians 3:11: "Here there is no Greek or Jew, circumcised or uncircumcised, barbarian, Scythian, slave or free, but Christ is all, and is in all."*

> *Bhagavad Gita 4.36: "No one can purify himself by merely performing external rituals. One must purify the heart and mind. True purity is found within."*

Summary: Heart Before Ritual: The True Sign of the Covenant

Saying 53 from the Gospel of Thomas addresses the concept of circumcision, a key ritual in Jewish tradition, and reinterprets it in a spiritual context. Jesus teaches that physical circumcision is not necessary for entering the Kingdom of God; rather, the true circumcision is one of the heart and spirit. This teaching shifts the focus from outward rituals to inward transformation and purity. It resonates with the Apostle Paul's letters and is also reflected in Eastern spiritual traditions, which emphasize inner transformation over external rites. The message is clear: true spiritual growth and connection with God are not achieved through physical markers or rituals, but through the purification of the heart and mind.

Saying 54: The Blessed Poverty of the Kingdom

"Jesus said, 'Blessed are the poor, for yours is the Kingdom of God.'" (54)

In these few words, Jesus reveals a paradox: those who have little in the world are the ones who will inherit everything in the divine realm. This is not simply a material statement, nor is it solely about economic poverty—it is a mystical truth about the soul's emptiness before God, the state of openness that allows one to receive the fullness of the Kingdom.

The Poverty That Makes One Rich

To be *poor* in the sense Jesus describes is not merely to lack possessions but to be free from attachment to the material world. It is a poverty of spirit, a humility that recognizes our dependence on the Divine. The rich often hold onto their wealth, status, and self-sufficiency, but the poor in spirit know that all things come from God. In surrendering their reliance on the transient, they open themselves to the eternal.

This echoes the Beatitudes in the Gospel of Matthew: *"Blessed are the poor in spirit, for theirs is the Kingdom of Heaven" (Matthew 5:3).* The poor in spirit are those who have emptied themselves of ego, pride, and attachment to the illusions of the world. In that emptiness, they make space for divine abundance.

The Kingdom Belongs to the Empty-Handed

The Kingdom of God is not obtained by force, nor is it earned through earthly riches or power. Instead, it is given freely to those who have nothing to cling to, those who approach God with empty hands and open hearts. This is the great reversal of the Gospel—the first will be last, the last will be first, the humble will be exalted, and the rich will be sent away empty.

The mystic Meister Eckhart once said, *"God is not found in the soul by adding anything but by a process of subtraction."* This is the heart of Jesus' teaching on blessed poverty: when we strip away the distractions, illusions, and burdens of the world, we discover that the Kingdom is already within us.

The Sacred Emptiness of the Soul

Nature itself teaches us the wisdom of this saying. The river flows because it is hollowed out; the sky holds the light because it is vast and empty; the seed must be buried in darkness before it grows into a tree. So too, the soul must be made empty so that it can be filled with the presence of God.

To be *poor* is to be receptive—to recognize that we own nothing and yet, in God, we possess everything. It is the state of childlike trust, the return to the simplicity of being, where nothing is hoarded, and everything is received as a gift.

Thus, blessed are the poor, for they stand at the threshold of divine abundance. The Kingdom of God is not distant—it is already theirs, already unfolding in the hearts of those who have made room for its light.

Heaven does not shout. It appears in stillness, in clouds, in the soft hoofbeats of deer at dawn.

> *Bhagavad Gita 18.20 –*
> *"There is no one who is richer than a man of wisdom. There is no greater wealth than knowledge."*

> *Katha Upanishad 2.1.1 –*
> *"The Self is not a subject for knowledge in the way that objects are. It is to be perceived by the wise alone.*

Saying 55: The Path of the Cross and the Burning Love of God

"Jesus said, 'Whoever does not hate father and mother as I do cannot be a disciple of mine, and whoever does not hate brothers and sisters and bear the cross as I do will not be worthy of me.'" (55)

These words are a fire that purifies, a sword that divides. To the unawakened ear, they sound harsh—how could the Master, whose essence is love, speak of hatred toward father, mother, and kin? But those who walk the path of divine wisdom hear a different call: this is not the hatred of malice, but the holy detachment that frees the soul to love with the love of God.

The Cost of the Path

Mystics throughout the ages have spoken of the great renunciation, the moment when the soul must leave behind all that binds it to the world. The call of Christ is not a mere invitation to admiration—it is a call to *transfiguration*. The disciple is summoned to a love so all-consuming that it makes all earthly ties secondary.

To "hate" in this sense is to loosen the grip of lesser loves so that the soul may be seized by the Absolute. It is the burning away of attachments, not out of disdain, but so that one may love rightly, not as the world loves, but as God loves.

As Meister Eckhart wrote, *"He who would be serene and pure needs but one thing, detachment."* This is the detachment that Christ demands—not abandonment of love, but a refining of it, so that no human bond holds us back from the eternal embrace.

Bearing the Cross: The Mark of the Disciple

Christ does not merely call his followers to let go—he calls them to *take up the cross*. The way of divine union is not a path of comfort, but of surrender. To follow him is to die to the small self, to let the ego be crucified so that the radiant self, made in God's image, may rise.

The mystic St. John of the Cross spoke of the "dark night," where the soul is stripped of all falsehood and plunged into divine longing. This is the cross that Christ bore—the surrender of all things for the sake of the Highest.

The cross is the great paradox: it is suffering, yet it is joy. It is loss, yet it is gain. It is death, yet it is the threshold of eternal life.

The Fire of Divine Love

The one who takes up the cross is not left in the darkness; they are set ablaze with love. The love of Christ is not a half-measure—it is total, consuming, like a burning star. Those who cling to the world as it is cannot walk this path, for the world is passing away. But those who surrender all things, even their closest earthly bonds, will find that they have lost nothing and gained *everything*.

For when all else falls away, what remains is God alone. And God is *Love*.

Avatamsaka Sutra, Chapter 30: "The bodhisattva who has awakened to the truth does not cling to worldly attachments, including family ties. They embrace the interconnectedness of all things and transcend the distinctions that bind them to the world of suffering."

❧❧❧

Saying 56: The World as a Passing Shadow

"Jesus said, 'Whoever has come to know the world has discovered a corpse, and whoever has discovered a corpse, of him the world is not worthy.'" (56)

The world, in all its brilliance and seeming life, is but a passing shadow. To the eyes that are veiled, it appears full of motion, desire, and ambition. But to the one who has awakened—to the one whose vision has been opened—the world is seen for what it truly is: *a fading dream, a husk without life, a corpse awaiting its burial.*

The Illusion of the World

What is this world that Jesus speaks of? Not the beauty of creation, not the heavens that declare the glory of God, nor the earth that sings with divine harmony. Rather, it is the world of illusion—the world of grasping hands and restless minds, the world that seeks permanence in what is perishing. It is the realm of fleeting riches, power built on dust, and pleasures that vanish like mist in the morning sun.

To *know* this world is to see through its veil. It is to recognize that what men call greatness is but dust on the wind. It is to stand amidst the revelry and hear the silence beneath it, to walk through the marketplace and feel the weight of impermanence pressing upon it.

The One Who Sees Beyond

And what of the one who has discovered the corpse? This is the soul who has *pierced the illusion*, who has seen that all things born of time must fall to time. To this one, the world offers nothing, for they no longer hunger for its bread nor thirst for its wine. They have tasted of something higher, something eternal.

And because they belong to eternity, the world—caught in its illusions—does not know what to do with them. It rejects them, casts them aside, calls them mad or foolish. The prophets, the saints, the mystics—they walked as strangers in the world, for they saw beyond it.

The Hidden Invitation

But beneath these words of Christ lies an invitation: *Come, step beyond the corpse, and walk into life.* See the world for what it is, and in doing so, become free of its chains. For the one who is no longer bound by the world is the one who can truly *live*—not in the world's way, but in the way of the Kingdom.

"For what does it profit a man to gain the whole world and forfeit his soul?" (Mark 8:36)

The world passes away, but the one who walks with God *will never taste death.*

> *Matthew 6:19-21 –*
> *"Do not store up for yourselves treasures on earth, where moths and vermin destroy, and where thieves break in and steal. But store up for yourselves treasures in heaven, where moths and vermin do not destroy, and where thieves do not break in and steal."*
>
> *Bhagavad Gita, Chapter 15, Verse 10: "The ignorant do not understand the soul's transcendence over the body. But the wise one sees that the soul is eternal and indestructible, beyond the material world."*
>
> *Dhammapada, Verse 184: "All conditioned things are impermanent—when one sees this with wisdom, one turns away from suffering. This is the path to purification."*
>
> *Avatamsaka Sutra, Chapter 39: "The enlightened one sees beyond the world of appearances, understanding the true nature of all things. In this way, one is freed from attachment to the fleeting and illusory nature of the world."*

৯৪৯৫৯

Saying 57: The Field of Discernment

Jesus said: "The kingdom of the Father is like a man who had [good] seed. His enemy came by night and sowed weeds among the good seed. The man did not allow them to be pulled up. He said to them: Lest you go and pull up the weeds, (and) pull up the wheat with it. For on the day of the harvest the weeds will be manifest; they will be pulled up and burned." (57)

This saying closely parallels the Parable of the Weeds (also known as the Parable of the Wheat and the Tares) found in Matthew 13:24–30. In both versions, Jesus speaks of a man who sows good seed, but an enemy secretly plants weeds among the crop. When the servants ask whether they should pull out the weeds immediately, the master refuses, concerned that doing so will harm the wheat. Instead, he instructs them to wait until the harvest, when the separation can be made clearly.

In the *Gospel of Thomas*, this parable can be understood not as a literal prediction of final judgment, but as a metaphor for spiritual discernment and inner transformation. The field may represent the human soul or the world itself, where light and shadow grow together. The good seed symbolizes divine awareness or awakened truth, while the weeds reflect ignorance, ego, or illusion—disruptive elements that arise from within, rooted in the fragmented or unconscious aspects of the self.

The master's wisdom is in recognizing the danger of premature judgment. Attempting to eliminate the "weeds" too soon may damage the authentic growth. This reflects the need for patience in spiritual development. We are not called to violently uproot every imperfection in ourselves or others, but to let the truth mature—knowing that, in time, clarity will come.

In light of mystical interpretation, the "harvest" may refer to a moment of awakening, when what is false is naturally burned away by the light of presence. The fire, rather than a symbol of punishment, becomes a purifying force—the consuming brilliance of the divine, revealing what is real.

᠁᠁᠁

Saying 58: The Suffering That Births Life

"Jesus said, 'Blessed is the man who has suffered and found life.'" (58)

The Refining Fire of Suffering

In the silence of suffering, the soul is tested, the heart is broken open, and the spirit is refined like gold in fire. To suffer is to be stripped of illusion, to stand naked before the mystery of existence. Yet, it is precisely in this breaking that life is found—not the life the world offers, fleeting and fragile, but the life that is eternal, luminous, and whole.

The Wound That Opens the Way

"The wound is where the light enters you." – Rumi

Blessed is the one who has walked through the valley of shadows and emerged into the dawn. The one who has wept and yet still believes, who has been pierced but not forsaken. For in the wound, the light enters. In the breaking, the veil is lifted.

There is no resurrection without the cross, no dawn without the night, no true life without passing through the death of the self that clings to the perishable. The seed must fall into the earth and die before it can rise and bear fruit.

The Secret of the Kingdom

The world sees suffering as loss, but the kingdom sees it as birth. The man who suffers and finds life has glimpsed what is hidden, has touched what is real. He no longer fears death, for he has already died to what is false and been reborn into what is true.

Blessed is the one who has suffered, for he has passed through fire and become light.

Romans 5:3-4 –
"Not only so, but we also glory in our sufferings, because we know that suffering produces perseverance; perseverance, character; and character, hope."

Saying 59: While You Live, See the Living One

Jesus said: Look upon the Living One so long as you live, that you may not die and seek to see him, and be unable to see him. (59)

This saying urges a profound immediacy in our spiritual vision. It is not merely about seeing with the eyes, but about awakening the inner eye—the heart's awareness—to perceive the Living One, the ever-present source of life, while we are still in the body and able to connect with the divine through personal relationship.

The "Living One" here can be understood as Christ, not as a distant figure in history, but as the eternal Logos—the light that animates all being. To look upon him "while you live" is to awaken to divine reality in the present moment, to pierce through the veil of illusion and recognize that the sacred is not elsewhere or in another time—it is here, now.

The warning is subtle but sobering: if we do not cultivate this spiritual sight while embodied, we risk missing the presence of the divine even after death. It suggests that heaven is not simply a place one enters, but a reality one must learn to perceive. The veil is not external; it is the condition of an unawakened heart.

Mystically, this resonates with teachings across traditions: that the true seeing is an inward seeing, and the greatest tragedy is not physical death but spiritual blindness. Life is the opportunity to awaken to what is always already here—the Living One who is also our own true nature.

Saying 60: Seek Your Rest Before the Feast

<They saw> a Samaritan carrying a lamb, who was going to Judaea. He said to his disciples: (What will) this man (do) with the lamb? They said to him: Kill it and eat it. He said to them: While it is alive

he will not eat it, but (only) when he kills it (and) it becomes a corpse. They said to him: Otherwise he cannot do it. He said to them: You also, seek a place for yourselves in rest, that you may not become a corpse and be eaten. (60)

In this vivid and symbolically rich passage, Jesus observes a Samaritan carrying a lamb on the road to Judea. He turns to his disciples and asks a seemingly simple question: *"What will this man do with the lamb?"* They respond in practical terms: *"Kill it and eat it."* Jesus affirms this logic—but then pivots sharply, using it to deliver a deeper teaching about spiritual life and death.

He says, *"While it is alive, he will not eat it, but only when he kills it and it becomes a corpse."* The disciples agree: the lamb must first die before it can be consumed. Jesus then delivers the parable's piercing conclusion: *"You also, seek a place for yourselves in rest, that you may not become a corpse and be eaten."*

Here, the lamb is more than an animal—it becomes a metaphor for the soul, or for the self caught in the world's demands. The act of being eaten represents what happens when one becomes spiritually unconscious: consumed by external forces, devoured by distraction, ego, or illusion. The world, like the man with the lamb, will consume whatever is not awake.

The phrase *"seek a place for yourselves in rest"* is key. This "rest" is not physical sleep, but spiritual refuge—an awakened state of being in communion with the divine. In several sayings of Thomas, rest is associated with wholeness, return to Source, and recognition of one's true nature. To rest is to abide in the Living One, the light of Christ, and to escape the cycle of death and consumption.

In this way, Jesus warns that without inner transformation—without a conscious seeking of divine rest—we risk becoming spiritual carcasses, subject to the world's consumption.

The Feast of the World and the Rest of the Soul

The world consumes all that is lifeless, all that has lost the breath of the divine. Just as the lamb is only eaten once it has become a corpse, so too does the world prey upon those who have fallen from the light—those who have surrendered to the ways of decay.

But what of those who remain alive in the Spirit? They are beyond the reach of corruption, beyond the grasp of the devourer.

The Resting Place of the Living

To "seek a place of rest" is not merely to withdraw from the world but to abide in the stillness of the Eternal. It is to find refuge in the living breath of God, where neither death nor darkness can consume you.

Those who walk the path of wisdom do not let themselves be slain by the desires of the world. They do not become as corpses, fit for consumption by the hunger of the earth. Instead, they remain living, breathing the light of the Kingdom, unclaimed by the feast of corruption.

"But seek first his kingdom and his righteousness, and all these things will be given to you as well." (Matthew 6:33)

John 6:35: Jesus calls himself the bread of life, the sustenance for those who seek spiritual rest in him. This could relate to the lamb in the saying—while the lamb is a symbol of death, Jesus represents spiritual nourishment and life.

"I am the bread of life. Whoever comes to me will never go hungry, and whoever believes in me will never be thirsty." (John 6:35)

Chapter 8

The Role of the Disciple (Sayings 61-70)

Saying 61: From the One Who Is Equal

Jesus said: Two will rest upon a bed; one will die, the other live. Salome said: Who are you, man, whose son? You have mounted my bed and eaten from my table. Jesus said to her: I am he who comes forth from the one who is equal; I was given of the things of my Father. ‹Salome said:› I am your disciple. ‹Jesus said to her:› Therefore I say: If he is equal, he is full of light, but if he is divided, he will be full of darkness. (61)

This deeply enigmatic saying blends intimate imagery with metaphysical insight. It begins with Jesus declaring, *"Two will rest upon a bed; one will die, the other live,"* echoing apocalyptic motifs from the Synoptic Gospels (Luke 17:34) where two are side by side, yet only one is taken or awakened. But in Thomas, this distinction is not about future judgment—it's about present awareness. The "bed" becomes a symbol of shared human condition or even physical intimacy, yet only one attains life—the life that is true, conscious, and eternal.

Salome, a rare female voice in the Gospel of Thomas, enters boldly: *"Who are you, man? Whose son are you? You have mounted my bed and eaten from my table."* Her words, though provocative, carry symbolic weight. She questions Jesus' identity not in shame but in mystery: who is this being who communes so freely, even intimately, and yet claims divine origin?

Jesus responds with a cryptic affirmation: *"I am he who comes forth from the One who is equal."* This "One" is the undivided Source, the fullness of being. He adds, *"I was given of the things of my Father,"* affirming that his authority and identity flow from unity with the divine—he is not separate but emanates from perfect equality, the fullness of light.

Salome declares herself his disciple, and Jesus responds with a profound spiritual principle: *"If he is equal, he is full of light, but if he is divided, he will be full of darkness."* This is not merely about God—it's about the human condition. **To be "equal" is to be whole, undivided, integrated in spirit, body, and soul.** Division—between ego and essence, between the false self and the true—breeds darkness. Unity brings illumination.

The saying, taken as a whole, affirms that the divine presence is not distant or reserved for the elite. It is accessible—even shockingly close. But only those who recognize the undivided nature of the divine (and of themselves) will "live." The rest, unaware and fragmented, remain in spiritual death.

꤮

Saying 62: Hidden Mysteries for the Worthy

Jesus said: I speak my mysteries to those [who are worthy of my] mysteries. What your right hand does, let not your left hand know what it does. (62)

In Saying 62, Jesus declares, *"I speak my mysteries to those [who are worthy of my] mysteries."* This reflects the Gospel of Thomas's overarching emphasis on hidden knowledge—gnosis— not as secretive elitism, but as the inner unveiling of truth for those prepared to receive it. The word "worthy" here is not moralistic; it suggests spiritual readiness, the capacity to comprehend what is beyond surface understanding.

Mysteries, in this context, refer not merely to doctrines or teachings, but to direct revelations of divine reality—truths about the soul, the Kingdom, and the unity with the Source. Jesus does not broadcast these to the unready; they are given intimately, experientially, and inwardly.

The second part—*"What your right hand does, let not your left hand know what it does"*— though echoed in Matthew 6:3, takes on a different tone in Thomas. Rather than being solely a call for humility in charitable deeds, it may point toward non-duality, inner integrity, and the discipline of spiritual secrecy. The "right" and "left" hands could symbolize the dual nature of the self—action and awareness, the conscious and unconscious. Jesus invites a kind of mystical silence and wholeness, where even one's own ego does not interfere with the sacred flow of divine activity.

This saying challenges us to cultivate inward receptivity, to become vessels of hidden wisdom, and to live in such a way that the most sacred movements of the Spirit are not paraded, but preserved. The mystery of the Kingdom is not a spectacle—it is a seed planted in secret, growing in silence, and bearing fruit in stillness.

This enigmatic saying invites the seeker into the concealed wisdom of the Kingdom. Mysteries are not given to all but are disclosed only to those prepared to receive them. This echoes Matthew 13:11, where Jesus tells his disciples, *"To you it has been given to know the mysteries of the kingdom of heaven, but to them, it has not been given."* The divine is not revealed through intellectual grasping but through spiritual readiness, an openness of the heart and soul.

The mystic path has long spoken of the necessity of inner silence and stillness to perceive divine mysteries. The anonymous author of *The Cloud of Unknowing* writes, *"God can well be loved, but he cannot be thought. By love, he can be grasped and held, but by thought, never."* Similarly, Rumi declares, *"Silence is the language of God, all else is poor translation."* The knowledge of the soul is not something to be grasped but something to be received in stillness and surrender. Thus, Saying 62 invites the seeker into the quiet depths where the soul's mystery is unveiled through divine grace.

Saying 63: A Harvest Never Gathered

Jesus said: There was a rich man who had many possessions. He said: I will use my possessions to sow and reap and plant, to fill my barns with fruit, that I may have need of nothing. Those were his thoughts in his heart; and in that night he died. He who has ears, let him hear. (63)

In Saying 63, Jesus offers a parable of a rich man absorbed in his own self-sufficiency. The man plans expansively—to sow, reap, build, and store, believing his wealth will secure his future. Yet, death arrives unexpectedly, revealing the fragility of his plans and the futility of hoarding. This echoes a similar parable in Luke 12:16–21, but the Gospel of Thomas frames it more starkly as a cautionary tale against the illusion of control and the seduction of material security.

The saying challenges the listener to recognize the ephemeral nature of earthly attachments. The rich man's internal monologue reveals a closed loop—his vision is entirely turned inward, disconnected from community, spirit, or source. His heart is set not on God or awakening, but on permanence in the impermanent.

Jesus concludes with a familiar admonition: *"He who has ears, let him hear."* This signals a deeper layer of meaning—this is not merely a warning about death, but a call to awaken before it's too late. The "rich man" symbolizes the egoic self that invests all energy in building a lasting identity in the material world, only to find that true life was always elsewhere—in the eternal present, in the Living One, in the treasure not subject to decay.

This saying invites the reader to consider: What barns am I building? What harvest am I seeking? And do I hear the deeper call before the night comes?

The Illusion of Abundance

The rich man, trusting in the wealth of the earth, believed his storehouses would shield him from lack, that his barns of grain would be his security. But what is the harvest of the body if the soul remains barren? The fullness of his hands concealed the emptiness of his spirit.

The True Inheritance

The world calls the rich man blessed, yet his riches will pass like dust in the wind. He is full, yet he will hunger. The poor man is forgotten, yet he will be remembered. He thirsts now, yet he will drink from the rivers of life.

To be poor is not merely to lack possessions but to hunger for the eternal. To be rich is not merely to have wealth but to be weighed down by the fleeting.

The storehouses of the world crumble, but the treasure of heaven remains. The question is not how much you own, but how free you are to inherit the Kingdom.

> *Matthew 6:19-21 –*
> *"Do not store up for yourselves treasures on earth, where moth and rust destroy, and where thieves break in and steal. But store up for yourselves treasures in heaven, where moths and rust do not destroy, and where thieves do not break in and steal. For where your treasure is, there your heart will be also."*

Saying 64: The Parable of the Banquet and the Rejected Invitation

Jesus said, "A man was receiving guests. When he had prepared the dinner, he sent his servant to invite the guests.

The servant went to the first and said, "My master invites you." The man replied, "I have claims against some merchants. They owe me money. They are coming to me this evening. I must go and give them instructions. Please excuse me from dinner."

The servant went to another and said, "My master invites you." This man replied, "I have just bought a house, and I am needed there for the day. I will not have time."

The servant went to another and said, "My master invites you." This man replied, "My friend is going to be married, and I must prepare the banquet. I cannot come. Please excuse me."

The servant went to another and said, "My master invites you." This man replied, "I have bought a farm. I am on my way to collect the rent. I cannot come. Please excuse me."

The servant returned and said to his master, "Those whom you invited have asked to be excused."

The master said to his servant, "Go to the roads outside and bring back whoever you find, so that they may have dinner. Businessmen and merchants will not enter the places of my Father." (64)

The Call and the Excuses

The invitation of the Kingdom comes like the wind through the trees, stirring those who are listening. Yet the ears of the world are filled with the clamor of possessions, of business, of obligations that tether the soul to the earth.

Each one had their reason, their justification, their pressing concern. Yet what is wealth when the eternal feast is prepared? What is a house when the Father's dwelling is open? What is a banquet when the table of God is set?

The Kingdom is not for those who hesitate, but for those whose hands are too full to receive what is freely given.

The Guests of the Feast

And so, the invitation is extended beyond the gates, beyond the halls of privilege. The roads and pathways are filled with those who have no business to attend to, no fields to manage, no debts to collect. They come as they are, with empty hands and open hearts.

The rich pass by the table they were too busy to approach. The humble enter and feast.

For the banquet of God is not for those who seek their own gain but for those who have nothing—so that they may receive everything.

Matthew 19:24: "It is easier for a camel to go through the eye of a needle than for a rich person to enter the kingdom of God."

Buddhism (Dhammapada 75): "The wise who renounce the world and seek the highest truth will enter the eternal joy, but the one who clings to riches is like a bird trapped in a golden cage."

Hinduism (Bhagavad Gita 18:66): "*Abandon all varieties of duty and surrender unto Me. I shall deliver you from all sinful reactions. Do not fear.*"

This aligns with Jesus' call to forsake worldly attachments and accept divine grace.

"*The Parable of Sower, 14th Century Manuscript, Trnovo, Bulgaria*"

⁂

Saying 65: The Rejected Heir and the Vineyard

He said, "A good man owned a vineyard. He gave it to tenant farmers so they would work it and he could collect its fruit from them. He sent his servant so the tenants would give him the fruit of the vineyard. They seized his servant, beat him, and nearly killed him. The servant went back and told his master. The master said, 'Perhaps they didn't recognize him.' So he sent another servant. The tenants beat this one as well. Then the master sent his son and said, 'Perhaps they will show respect to my son.' Since those tenants knew that he was the heir of the vineyard, they seized him and killed him. Anyone who has ears should listen." (65)

The parable from the *Gospel of Thomas* (65) speaks to the rejection and betrayal of divine messengers, ultimately pointing to the rejection of the Son, the heir to the vineyard. In this story, the vineyard can be seen as a symbol of the world or the kingdom of God, entrusted to humanity to cultivate and nurture. The master represents the divine Creator, who has entrusted human beings with the responsibility of caring for creation and bearing fruit that aligns with divine will.

The repeated rejection of the servants sent by the master illustrates humanity's historical resistance to God's messengers, including the prophets and spiritual guides who have come to guide people toward righteousness. The severe mistreatment of these servants represents the human tendency to dismiss or harm those who bear divine truth, often out of fear, pride, or misunderstanding. When the master finally sends his son, hoping for respect and reverence, it highlights the culmination of God's patience and trust. However, the decision of the cultivators to seize and kill the son signifies the ultimate rejection of God's most direct and intimate revelation—Jesus Christ, who is not merely a servant but the heir, the divine Son.

The parable serves as a profound warning about the consequences of rejecting the divine message. The phrase "He who has ears, let him hear" suggests that the lesson is not merely intellectual but requires deep, spiritual listening and understanding. It calls us to recognize the sacredness of divine revelation and the importance of responding to it with respect, humility, and faith. Just as the vineyard is meant to bear fruit for the master, our lives are meant to bear the fruit of righteousness, and the rejection of God's invitation can lead to spiritual desolation. The parable is a reflection on the relationship between humanity and God, urging individuals to recognize the sacredness of the divine calling and to heed the message of the Son.

Saying 66: The Rejected Stone Becomes the Cornerstone

Jesus said, "Show me the stone which the builders have rejected. That one is the cornerstone." (66)

The Rejected Cornerstone

In this brief but profound saying, Jesus points to an ancient truth about value and worth, especially as it relates to the Kingdom of God. The "stone which the builders have rejected" signifies what the world, with its worldly wisdom and criteria, often overlooks or dismisses.

The builders are those who assess and judge, who make decisions about what fits and what does not, what is acceptable and what is not. In their eyes, the stone—perhaps humble, unassuming, or misunderstood—was seen as unworthy of the foundation.

But Jesus reveals that this very stone, rejected by men, is the cornerstone of God's Kingdom. The cornerstone is the essential piece upon which the entire structure rests. It is the most important, the foundation of the new creation. The stone that was overlooked, cast aside, or deemed insignificant becomes the very pillar of divine truth.

The Mystical Meaning

This saying evokes the theme of spiritual paradox—the first shall be last, the weak shall be made strong, the humble shall be exalted. It points to Christ himself, rejected by those who could not see the fullness of the divine in his humble form. Yet, it is through his rejection, his suffering, and his resurrection that the world is transformed.

In a mystical sense, the saying also invites us to look within. What parts of ourselves have we rejected, overlooked, or dismissed as unworthy? In doing so, we may be rejecting the very thing that holds the key to our spiritual growth and our connection with the divine. The rejected stone may be the part of our own soul that, when embraced, becomes the cornerstone of our inner transformation.

The Call to Embrace the Rejected

Jesus challenges us not to be deceived by the outward appearances or the judgments of the world. What is often rejected or scorned may be the very thing that holds the deepest wisdom, the purest love, and the most essential truth. Just as Christ, the rejected stone, became the cornerstone of salvation, so too can the rejected and marginalized parts of our own lives be the source of our greatest spiritual awakening.

Matthew 21:42 –
"Jesus said to them, 'Have you never read in the Scriptures: The stone the builders rejected has become the cornerstone; the Lord has done this, and it is marvelous in our eyes?'"

Psalm 118:22 –
"The stone the builders rejected has become the cornerstone."

Saying 67: The Poverty of Empty Knowledge

Jesus said, "One who knows all but lacks within is utterly lacking." (67)

The Knowledge Beyond the Surface

In this simple yet piercing saying, Jesus speaks to the gap between external knowledge and internal transformation. Knowledge, in this sense, is not just information, facts, ideas, or intellectual understanding. It is the knowledge of the soul, the wisdom that arises from deep within, from the heart, and from union with the Divine.

"One who knows all but lacks within" refers to the person who has accumulated vast amounts of worldly wisdom, understanding, and knowledge, yet still remains spiritually empty. The mind may be full of facts, and one might be able to articulate profound truths, but without inner wisdom, without love, compassion, and spiritual insight, such knowledge remains incomplete.

The Call for Inner Fulfillment

Jesus is inviting us to look beyond the surface, to seek a deeper kind of knowing—one that is rooted in the heart and spirit. Knowledge without depth, without love, without inner harmony, is like a vessel that is full on the outside but hollow on the inside. Such a vessel cannot hold the fullness of life.

The true wisdom that Jesus calls us to is not the accumulation of intellectual knowledge, but the cultivation of inner peace, love, humility, and an intimate connection with the Divine. This wisdom is transformative. It is a knowledge that is lived, not just learned.

The Mystical Meaning

Mystically, this saying echoes the idea that the journey inward is as important as the journey outward. External accomplishments, achievements, and recognitions are meaningless if they do not reflect an inner transformation. One can gather the world's knowledge, but without love, compassion, and spiritual growth, it remains as dust. True fulfillment comes from within, from aligning the mind, heart, and soul with the Divine.

In essence, this saying invites us to seek wholeness, to integrate the knowledge we acquire with the wisdom of the heart. It reminds us that true knowledge is not just about knowing—it is about becoming. Becoming whole, becoming one with the Divine, and allowing this truth to shape how we live and how we relate to the world.

The Inner Journey

In mystical traditions, the soul's journey is often described as one of awakening the inner knowing—the deep, intuitive wisdom that comes from a connection with the Divine. Jesus here reminds us that it is not enough to know about the Divine; one must also experience the Divine within. When we know the Divine within, the knowledge of the external world aligns with our true purpose, and we are no longer lacking.

Thus, the saying urges us to seek not only the world's wisdom but also the transformative wisdom that arises from deep within our souls, where God's presence dwells. Without this internal depth, all the knowledge in the world is but a shadow of the truth that is meant to fill our lives with peace, love, and meaning.

Matthew 16:26 "What good will it be for someone to gain the whole world, yet forfeit their soul?"

1 Corinthians 13:2 "If I have the gift of prophecy and can fathom all mysteries and all knowledge, and if I have a faith that can move mountains, but do not have love, I am nothing."

⁂

Saying 68: The Blessing of Persecution

Jesus said: Blessed are you when you are hated and persecuted, and they will find no place where you have been persecuted. (68)

In this profound saying, Jesus speaks of a paradox that resounds throughout mystical traditions: that suffering, rejection, and persecution are not signs of failure, but invitations to enter deeper into the mystery of the Divine. Mystics across the ages have echoed this truth in their writings, seeing suffering as both the crucible and the gateway to spiritual transformation.

"Blessed are you when you are hated and persecuted…" Jesus' words resonate with the call to embrace the cross, the great symbol of self-sacrifice, humility, and divine love. In the mystic's journey, persecution is not to be avoided or feared, but rather, understood as the means through which one's attachment to the ego and worldly desires is stripped away, leaving the soul open to the Divine.

The voices of mystics like Saint John of the Cross, who spoke of the dark night of the soul, and Meister Eckhart, who referred to the necessity of detachment from all that is not God, find their resonance in this saying. Suffering, to the mystic, becomes a path of purgation—a means of being transformed into the image of the Divine. As the body undergoes pain, the soul is purified, and the ego is diminished, creating space for the light of the Divine to shine through.

The Divine in the Wilderness

Saint Teresa of Ávila, in her mystical writings, often spoke of the soul's journey through adversity as akin to a journey through the wilderness, where the soul encounters trials and temptations, yet through these experiences, it finds God in ways that cannot be attained in comfort and ease. She said, "God has to make you perfect in the crucible of pain." The persecutions and hatred described in this saying are, therefore, not signs of abandonment but of a deeper calling, leading to a greater union with the Divine.

In the words of Rumi, the beloved Sufi poet, "Don't grieve. Anything you lose comes round in new form." Rumi reminds us that the apparent loss we experience through persecution is often the doorway to a higher state of consciousness, where our old selves die, only to be reborn in the light of God's presence.

The Kingdom of God as Inner Transformation

To the mystics, the Kingdom of God is not just a future promise but a present reality—the realm of divine union and inner peace, where the soul is at one with God. The Kingdom is where the soul finds its true home, transcending the limitations of the material world. The trials and tribulations that the mystics undergo are not punishment, but purification—purifying the soul to enter the Kingdom of God.

The Hesychast monks of the Eastern Orthodox tradition, who practiced the Jesus Prayer for decades, often spoke of the suffering one endures as a means of purifying the heart. For them, persecution and the pain of spiritual trials were the very fire that forged the purity of heart required to see God, much like the refining of gold through fire. The greatest blessings, they understood, come through the surrendering of the self, the crucifixion of the ego, and the eventual emergence into the full light of God's presence.

Rebirth in the Face of Adversity

The words of Simone Weil, a mystic and philosopher, resonate here as well. She wrote, "The most important part of our work in this world is to learn how to suffer… It is through suffering that we encounter God." In this way, Jesus' words point toward the profound mystery that the soul finds its way to the Kingdom of God through the very struggles and persecutions that seem to separate us from joy. The struggle itself becomes the fertile ground for spiritual awakening.

In the mystical tradition, the cross is the symbol of ultimate transformation. The persecution faced by the soul is not a defeat, but a prelude to rebirth—a crossing over into new life. The soul, when it is stripped of pride, of illusion, and of attachment to the world, enters into a deeper union with the Divine, where all suffering becomes a sacred vessel for spiritual growth.

The Hidden Blessing in Persecution

Thus, when Jesus says, *"You will be the ones to inherit the kingdom of God,"* He is inviting us to see beyond the external suffering and understand that within every trial lies the seed of spiritual victory. Mystics like Julian of Norwich, who endured long periods of physical suffering, famously said, "All shall be well, and all shall be well, and all manner of thing shall be well." For her, suffering was not something to be feared, but a path leading to union with the Divine. In persecution, the soul is invited to transcend all worldly concerns and to seek the eternal peace of God's presence.

Conclusion: The Kingdom of God Within

Ultimately, the blessing of persecution is the call to live from a deeper place within the heart—a place where the ego no longer controls, but the soul is fully attuned to the Divine. It is an invitation to surrender the small self and to emerge, like the phoenix from the ashes, into the fullness of the Divine Kingdom, where peace, love, and unity reign. This inner kingdom, once found, is where true fulfillment lies, regardless of external circumstances.

In the words of Thomas Merton, "The greatest freedom is to be free of the self." When we surrender to the Divine through trials and persecution, we are, in truth, coming home to the Kingdom that is within us all along.

> *Matthew 5:10-12 –*
> *"Blessed are those who are persecuted because of righteousness, for theirs is the kingdom of heaven. Blessed are you when people insult you, persecute you and falsely say all kinds of evil against you because of me. Rejoice and be glad, because great is your reward in heaven, for in the same way they persecuted the prophets who were before you."*

> *Luke 6:22-23 –*
> *"Blessed are you when people hate you, when they exclude you and insult you and reject your name as evil, because of the Son of Man. Rejoice in that day and leap for joy, because great is your reward in heaven. For that is how their ancestors treated the prophets."*

Saying 69: The Persecution of the Heart

Jesus said: Blessed are those who have been persecuted in their heart; these are they who have known the Father in truth. Blessed are the hungry, for the belly of him who desires will be filled. (69)

In this powerful saying, Jesus invites us to reflect on the deeper, spiritual aspect of persecution: the internal conflict between our lower nature and the Divine calling. It is not the external forces of the world that shape the soul, but the internal battles that reveal true spiritual depth. The mystical path often speaks of this kind of inner struggle, where the heart, torn between the worldly and the spiritual, is purified in the fire of divine love.

"Blessed are those who have been persecuted in their hearts."

The mystics tell us that this internal persecution is the soul's refinement process. Simone Weil, the French philosopher and mystic, once remarked, "The love of our neighbor in all its fullness simply means being able to say, 'What are you going through?'" Here, she touches on the idea that our suffering, especially the suffering of the heart, connects us to the divine compassion that runs through all things. It is a deep empathy with the Divine and with all creation that arises from enduring inner tribulation. We come to know God through this suffering—through the painful, purifying transformation that draws us closer to Him.

The Mystical Process of Purification

The spiritual path often involves an inner purification, which is frequently likened to fire or a refining furnace. Khalil Gibran, the Lebanese poet and mystic, writes in his work *The Prophet*: *"Your pain is the breaking of the shell that encloses your understanding."* This profound insight reflects the idea that, just as a seed must break open to give birth to the new life within it, the soul must undergo a form of destruction to make room for divine light. The heart that suffers and endures, that embraces the divine purification, is the one that will emerge with a deeper understanding of the Father.

"King David Playing the Harp"

In Christian mysticism, this idea finds resonance in the writings of Hildegard of Bingen, who spoke of divine purification as necessary for spiritual awakening: *"The soul is like a harp, which only sings when it is stretched tight. Therefore, it is necessary to feel the tension of the struggle in order to know the peace of union with the Divine."* Hildegard's words show that the tension created in the heart during this internal struggle is a means of attuning the soul to God, leading to a greater union with Him.

The Knowledge of the Father Through Suffering

Jesus tells us that those who have experienced this internal persecution come to know the Father. It is through the suffering of the heart that we come to understand God not as an abstract figure, but as a real, living presence in our lives. Thomas Merton, an American Trappist monk and mystic, stated, *"The deepest of our emotions, the secret center of our feelings, is the place where God is closest to us."* Merton's teaching reflects the truth that the inner afflictions of the heart are the very place where the Divine touches the soul. In this sacred space, God reveals Himself most intimately.

The knowledge that comes from suffering is not intellectual, but experiential. Meister Eckhart, the German mystic, wrote: *"The soul's desire is God's desire for it. What the soul desires, God desires to be."* Through this paradoxical suffering, the soul becomes a vessel for divine love, a reflection of God's true nature. The suffering of the heart draws the soul nearer to the Father, leading it to a deeper, more intimate knowledge of God.

The Kingdom of God as a Gift for the Pure in Heart

Jesus promises that those who undergo this inner persecution will enter the Kingdom of God. The Kingdom is not a distant place, but a present reality for those who purify their hearts. The soul's purification allows it to experience the fullness of God's presence. Rainer Maria Rilke, the Bohemian poet, expressed this understanding beautifully in his letters: *"The kingdom of heaven is within you, but you must not look for it with the eyes of the body. You will see it with your soul."* Rilke emphasizes the inward nature of the Kingdom—it is a state of being, a deep spiritual presence, found within the purified heart.

The Paradox of the Kingdom: Persecution as a Blessing

Jesus' words present a spiritual paradox: the suffering of the heart is not a curse, but a blessing that leads to the Kingdom of God. Carl Jung, the Swiss psychiatrist and mystic, pointed out, *"The privilege of a lifetime is to become who you truly are."* This becoming, this spiritual evolution, often involves discomfort and pain as the ego dies away and the true self, aligned with the divine, emerges.

In the writings of Saint Augustine, we find a similar thought: *"God is always trying to give good things to us, but our hands are too full to receive them."* The persecution of the heart empties our hands, making space for the gifts of God. This purification process, painful as it may be, creates the conditions for divine grace to fill the soul.

Conclusion: The Heart's Union with the Divine

Ultimately, the persecution of the heart is not a meaningless suffering, but a profound process of transformation. Through it, the soul comes to know God in a way that is deeper than intellectual understanding. As Rabia al-Adawiyya, the Islamic mystic, beautifully stated, *"I am the slave of the One who loves me, and I am free from everything except the One who loves me."* The true Kingdom of God is found in that place of complete surrender, where the heart is emptied and filled with divine love. It is through the suffering of the heart that the soul finally finds its resting place in God's eternal embrace.

> *"Many are saying of me, 'God will not deliver him.' But you, Lord, are a shield around me, my glory, the One who lifts my head high."*—Psalm 3:2–3

> *"Create in me a clean heart, O God, and renew a right spirit within me."*—Psalm 51:10

Saying 70: The Power Within

Jesus said, "If you bring forth what is within you, what you have will save you. If you do not bring forth what is within you, what you do not have will kill you." (70)

This profound saying of Jesus speaks to the transformative power of self-realization and the necessity of drawing upon the divine essence that resides within each of us. The inner light—often described in mystical traditions as the divine spark, the soul, or the higher self—must be brought forth for our spiritual liberation. If we keep it hidden, if we suppress our true nature, we risk spiritual death.

In mystical literature, this is echoed by the concept of the *inner light* or *divine presence* that is always there, waiting to be acknowledged and manifested. The poet Rumi speaks of this light: *"Don't be satisfied with stories, how things have gone with others. Unfold your own myth."* Rumi's call to "unfold your own myth" aligns closely with Jesus' teaching here—he encourages the individual to give life to the divine potential within.

The Inner Light as a Path to Salvation

When Jesus says, **"what you have will save you,"** he points to the latent spiritual power each person possesses. This is not a salvation through outward actions alone, but through the recognition and expression of our divine essence. Thomas Merton, the mystic and monk, understood this power as being rooted in the soul's direct connection with God: *"The greatest temptation is to settle for too little. The answer to the problem of life is not to ask for less, but to demand more—much more, the very essence of life, which is the divine life of the soul."* In other words, our deepest essence is nothing less than the divine life, and our salvation lies in recognizing and bringing forth this divine essence.

The process of bringing forth what is within is often one of inner realization—of seeing beyond the superficial to the spiritual core that connects us to the Divine. This inner unveiling can take the form of mystical awakening, or moments of profound realization when we finally access the depths of our being. The great mystic Meister Eckhart writes: *"The more a soul is united with God, the more it enters into its own being."* This union with God through the inner self is the very path to salvation.

The Dangers of Suppressing the Inner Self

On the flip side, Jesus warns that failing to bring forth what is within will lead to spiritual death. This death is not a physical one, but a disconnection from the divine essence that gives life. The mystical tradition consistently warns against living in ignorance of one's divine nature. Khalil Gibran, the Lebanese mystic and poet, captures this beautifully: *"You give but little when you give of your possessions. It is when you give of yourself that you truly give."* If we do not give of ourselves—our truest essence—then we are left with an empty shell, disconnected from the source of life.

Carl Jung, the famous psychologist and mystic, also spoke to this idea when he said, *"The privilege of a lifetime is to become who you truly are."* Suppressing the inner self, refusing to recognize or live according to one's divine nature, results in a life that is not fully lived. It is like a person walking through life asleep, unaware of their inner potential and the divine light within. Jung emphasizes that *becoming who you truly are*—by manifesting that inner light—is not only essential for psychological health, but also for spiritual awakening.

The Path to Inner Wholeness

This saying of Jesus invites us to step into the fullness of our spiritual potential. It calls us to embrace our truest self and to manifest the divine qualities that are embedded deep within. This is the mystical path—the journey of becoming more fully alive by realizing and embodying our connection with the Divine. Rabia al-Adawiyya, the Islamic mystic, expressed this beautifully: *"I am not my own. I am the Beloved's, and He is mine."* When we recognize that the essence within us is not merely personal but divine, our life becomes an expression of the Divine itself.

The mystics speak of this realization as the soul's return to its source. As Hildegard of Bingen wrote: *"The soul is like a bird in a cage; it must break free to fly toward God."* The cage is often made of the illusions and attachments of this world—the things we cling to out of fear or ignorance. When we bring forth what is within us, the cage is broken, and the soul is free to soar into union with the Divine.

The Mystical Invitation to Self-Realization

To "bring forth what is within" is an invitation to self-realization, to uncover the deep wellspring of divinity that exists in every person. Sri Aurobindo, the Indian philosopher and mystic, put it this way: *"The divine life is not a life withdrawn from the world, it is a life that is awakened within the world."* This awakening happens not by retreating from the world but by bringing our inner divinity to life in every action, thought, and moment. This is the path to salvation, as Jesus teaches: through the discovery and manifestation of our inner, divine nature.

Conclusion: The Inner Kingdom

Ultimately, what Jesus is offering in this saying is a vision of salvation that is not distant or external, but very much rooted in the soul's recognition of its divine essence. When we bring forth what is within, we enter into the kingdom of God, not as a far-off future event, but as a present reality. This kingdom is already within us, and our task is simply to recognize it, manifest it, and live from it.

As Blaise Pascal, the French mathematician and mystic, said: *"All human beings are born with a God-shaped void in their hearts."* The fullness of this void is filled when we allow what is within to be brought forth, and in doing so, we come to know the truth of who we are: beings in union with the Divine. In this realization, we find the salvation that Jesus speaks of—one that is not earned, but uncovered and lived.

Chapter 9

The Hidden God and the Kingdom Within (Sayings 71-80)

Saying 71: The Destruction of the House

Jesus said, "I will destroy this house, and no one will be able to build it again." (71)

In the sacred union of humanity with Christ, we understand Jesus as the embodiment of the divine, the temple through which all creation is connected to its Creator. Just as the cornerstone is the foundational element of a structure, Christ is the cornerstone of our spiritual journey, holding together the divine plan and guiding us toward unity with the Father.

We are not separate from the divine; we are individuations of that pure love and light, reflecting the divine spark that resides in all things. Just as a puzzle piece finds its place in the larger picture, we too are essential elements of the divine master plan, linked to the whole through the love that Jesus exemplifies.

This connection, through the temple of Christ, is the bridge between the human and the divine. It is in Him that we find our true identity—joined in the body of Christ, inseparable from the divine essence that sustains us. The divinity we embody cannot be destroyed, for it is eternal, woven into the very fabric of creation. As we recognize our place in this divine tapestry, we understand that the love and light of God are within us, guiding us home to the Kingdom.

A Mystical Reflection: The Fall of the Egoic Temple

This enigmatic saying speaks of the dissolution of the old structures—the external and internal edifices—that we build to protect and define ourselves. In the mystical tradition, this "house" can be understood as the ego, the false self that seeks to control and categorize our experience of the Divine. The ego builds a "house" that is disconnected from the true self, a house of illusion that keeps us from fully realizing the Kingdom within.

Thomas Merton, the Trappist monk and mystic, spoke of this when he wrote: *"The first step to the salvation of the soul is to realize its own condition, and its separation from God."* The ego, like a house, creates a false sense of separation from the Divine. Jesus' pronouncement of destroying this house is a call for the ego to fall, for the illusion of separation to be shattered. In mystical terms, this is the dissolution of the false self that keeps us trapped in suffering.

The Mystical Death of the False Self

In mysticism, the concept of "destroying the house" resonates with the idea of spiritual death and rebirth. Rumi touches on this when he says: *"The wound is the place where the Light enters you."* The destruction of the ego or false self is often painful, yet it is through this breaking down that the soul is able to connect more deeply with the Divine presence. This destruction is not an end, but a necessary step in the journey toward spiritual enlightenment.

Meister Eckhart, the German mystic, reflects on this process: *"The soul must be so free of all attachment to the world that it can be said that it has nothing. When the soul is free, then God can fully enter it."* The house of ego—the attachment to worldly identity—must be destroyed for the soul to be emptied of distractions and be filled with the Divine. This "house" no longer serves its purpose once it no longer reflects the truth of who we are: Divine beings experiencing a temporary illusion of separation.

The Impossibility of Rebuilding the House

When Jesus says, **"no one will be able to build it again,"** he refers to the irrevocable nature of the destruction of the false self. Once the ego has been dismantled by the realization of its own illusion, it cannot be rebuilt. The truth of the self, as a part of the Divine, transcends all false structures.

The individual can no longer build the false houses of identity or attachment, for they have awakened to the deeper truth of their nature. Sri Aurobindo states: *"The self, knowing its own identity, cannot return to ignorance."* When we have seen the truth of our being, we cannot unsee it. The old "house" that was built upon illusion has crumbled and cannot be rebuilt because it no longer holds the truth of who we are.

The Sacred House Within

The true "house" is not the egoic structure, but the temple of the soul—the sacred dwelling place of the Divine within each person. Hildegard of Bingen spoke of this divine temple within when she said: *"The soul is like a virgin dwelling, a place where God comes to rest."* This sacred house cannot be destroyed, for it is eternal and part of the Divine nature of the soul. The destruction Jesus speaks of is the disintegration of the house that is not truly ours, the false house of illusion. Once we allow this destruction, the true, eternal house—the soul in union with the Divine—remains.

A New House: The Birth of the Inner Kingdom

The mystical path often involves a process of inner transformation, where the false house is destroyed, and the true temple of the soul is revealed. Khalil Gibran speaks to this inner renewal when he writes: *"Your house is your larger body. It is a place of rest, and the rest is love."* The true house is built on love, not on the shifting sands of the ego. This love is the foundation of the soul's connection with the Divine, and when the egoic house falls, it is replaced by this eternal, indestructible love.

Jesus' statement also resonates with the Vedic concept of the Atman, the true self that is never destroyed. The Atman is often depicted as a sacred temple that, despite the changes and transformations in life, remains constant. Swami Vivekananda expressed this beautifully: *"The goal of life is to manifest the Divinity within."* This manifestation is the new "house" we are called to build—a house rooted in divine truth and love, free from the limitations of the ego.

Conclusion: The Spiritual House of the Soul

The destruction of the "house" Jesus speaks of is not a tragic end, but a necessary step in the soul's journey back to its true nature. It is a divine invitation to break down the illusions we cling to and to recognize the eternal, unshakable truth of who we are. In doing so, we allow the divine temple within to be built—not of stone or wood, but of love, light, and the unchanging presence of the Divine.

As Rainer Maria Rilke writes: *"You must change your life."* This change begins with the destruction of the false self, the crumbling of the house that no longer serves the truth of the soul. Only then can the true temple of the Divine be revealed in its fullness, and we will no longer seek to rebuild the false houses that once defined us.

Matthew 24:1-2: "Jesus left the temple and was going away, when his disciples came to point out to him the buildings of the temple. But he answered them, 'You see all these, do you not? Truly, I say to you, there will not be left here one stone upon another that will not be thrown down.'"

This passage parallels **Saying 71**, where Jesus prophesies the **destruction of the temple** (the "house") in Jerusalem, which symbolized the old order of worship and sacrifice. This event occurred in 70 CE, marking the end of the **temple system** in Jerusalem.

John 2:19-21: "Jesus answered them, 'Destroy this temple, and in three days I will raise it up.' The Jews then said, 'It has taken forty-six years to build this temple, and will you raise it up in three days?' But he was speaking about the temple of his body."

Here, Jesus speaks metaphorically about His own body as the temple. This connects to **Saying 71**, as it indicates that the destruction of physical structures (like the temple) is part of a deeper spiritual reality—the **transformation** of the relationship between God and humanity.

In Saying 71, the **"house"** Jesus speaks of can be understood as **the physical temple** or the **system of religious institutions** that centered around the temple in Jerusalem. The **destruction of the house** marks the **end of the old religious system** based on rituals, sacrifices, and physical places of worship, which were no longer necessary with the coming of Christ.

The New Temple: The destruction of the temple in Jerusalem and the building of a new **spiritual temple** is a theme in Christian theology. The **new temple** is no longer a building, but the **body of Christ** and the collective body of believers. This signifies the **transition** from physical worship to a **spiritualized worship** in which **Jesus Himself becomes the new temple**.

Irreversibility: The statement that no one will be able to rebuild the house underscores the irreversible nature of this change. The spiritual kingdom Jesus ushers in cannot be restored or rebuilt to the old ways. It marks the **permanence of the new covenant** that Jesus brings through His life, death, and resurrection.

Saying 72: Not a Divider, but a Revealer

[A man said] to him: Speak to me brothers, that they may divide my father's possessions with me. He said to him: O man, who made me a divider? He turned to his disciples. He said to them, I am not a divider, am I? (72)

In this teaching, Jesus speaks of a division, not one that tears apart, but one that separates the transient from the eternal. The "divider" is not an enemy, but a necessary force to help us distinguish between the fleeting nature of the world and the eternal, unchanging nature of the Kingdom of Heaven. To be with the kingdom, we must transcend the earthly desires and attachments that bind us to this world.

This separation is not a rejection of creation, but an invitation to see beyond its surface, to understand that we are not merely part of this world, but part of a higher, divine reality.

As we align ourselves with the kingdom, we become participants in that which divides heaven from earth—a sacred bridge between the divine and the human. Just as the temple of Christ connects us to the divine, so too does this divider, showing us the path to a deeper, spiritual union that cannot be broken by the transient world.

In this space of division, we come closer to recognizing our true identity as beings of divine light, indivisible from the love that sustains all life, and united through Christ's temple, where heaven and earth meet in the eternal presence of God.

Saying 72 recounts an interaction where a man asks Jesus to settle a dispute over an inheritance—a request that mirrors one found in Luke 12:13–14. In both versions, Jesus refuses to take the role of arbitrator over material possessions. But in Thomas, the response carries a deeper, almost ironic twist. Jesus turns the question back on his disciples, asking, *"Am I a divider?"*—an invitation not only to reconsider his mission, but to awaken to a deeper understanding of unity.

In rejecting the role of "divider," Jesus distances himself from worldly notions of justice based on property, entitlement, or familial inheritance. Instead, his focus is on revealing the kingdom within, the indivisible truth that transcends duality and conflict. His rhetorical question suggests that the true inheritance is not external, but interior—the unbroken unity with the Father, the treasure of spiritual awakening.

This saying exposes the false logic of separation—that we are distinct from one another, that things can be owned, divided, and possessed. Jesus, as revealer of divine oneness, is not a broker of earthly concerns but a guide back to the indivisible source. To follow him is to transcend divisions, not negotiate them.

The man asking for help with inheritance is looking for fairness in the material realm; Jesus redirects attention to the eternal, where nothing is lost, and nothing needs to be claimed, for *all is already one.*

Saying 73: The Great Harvest

Jesus said, "The harvest is great, but the laborers are few. Pray therefore that the Lord of the harvest will send laborers into the harvest." (73)

In the stillness of the morning, when the first rays of light touch the earth, there is a whisper that stirs the air, calling us to the fields. The harvest is abundant, like the ripened fruit of the vine, the golden grains swaying in the breeze, waiting to be gathered. Yet, few hear the call to labor in this vast and bountiful field.

The earth, in all its wisdom, knows the time of harvest, just as the soul, in its depths, knows the call of the divine. The laborers, those who have heard the whisper of the sacred wind, must rise with the sun and tend to what is ripe. They must bend low, gathering each grain with reverence, for each is a gift from the Creator.

Pray, then, to the Lord of the harvest—He who watches over the fields, who tends to the roots and the fruits, that the laborers might be many. For the harvest is not just of grain, but of souls, of light that shines through the dust of this world. And when we labor in the fields of the spirit, we become one with the wind, the sun, and the soil, joining in the eternal work of creation.

In this divine labor, we are not separate from the harvest, but part of it—a thread woven into the great tapestry of life, moving towards the fulfillment of the divine plan. The laborers are those who walk with open hearts, ready to gather what has been sown by the hand of God, and to carry the fruit of the Spirit into the world.

> *Luke 10:2 – "He told them, 'The harvest is plentiful, but the workers are few. Ask the Lord of the harvest, therefore, to send out workers into his harvest field.'"*

᠀᠀᠀᠀

Saying 74: The Empty Well

He said, "Lord, many are gathered around the well, but there's nothing to drink." (74)

In the quietude of the desert, where the sun beats down upon the earth, a well stands, ancient and unyielding, etched into the landscape as a place of hope. Many come, parched, seeking solace in its depths, yet its waters remain elusive, untouched by their thirst.

The well is surrounded by a gathering, but they are without the refreshment they seek. Their hands grasp the stone, their hearts longing for the life-giving water, yet the vessel is empty. They stand in communion, united in their longing, but the waters of life have not yet flowed to quench their spirits.

This is the cry of the soul, longing for the Living Water that springs from the depths of God's love—rivers of grace that are beyond the reach of mere hands, and only found through surrender to the divine source. For the well of true life is not a mere object in the world, but the heart that is open, the spirit that is willing to receive. It is not in the act of reaching that we are filled, but in the stillness, in the quiet acceptance of the water that flows not from the earth, but from the eternal wellspring of the divine.

Jesus, knowing the depths of our thirst, spoke to the Samaritan woman at the well, saying, "Everyone who drinks this water will be thirsty again, but whoever drinks the water I give them will never thirst. Indeed, the water I give them will become in them a spring of water welling up to eternal life" (John 4:13-14, NIV).

The water that Jesus speaks of is not like the water of the earth that fades with the passing of time. It is a water that quenches the deepest thirst of the soul—a wellspring that flows not from the ground but from the very heart of the Father, a river of life that pours into those who are open to receive. In Him, we find what we need to satisfy our longing, a drink that fills us with eternal life and makes our spirits whole.

As we gather in the presence of the well, let us not seek only the form of the water, but the essence of the water, for it is the Spirit that sustains us. When we open our hearts, when we become the vessels willing to be filled, the waters will flow. In the moment of receiving, we drink deeply from the unending well of God's love, and we are made whole, no longer thirsty, but alive with the life that is eternal.

❧❀❧

Saying 75: Standing at the Door

Jesus said, "There are many standing at the door, but it is the solitary who will enter the bridal chamber." (75)

"Christ by Andrei Rublev, early 15th century"

The door is narrow, and though many stand before it, few have the inner sight to cross its threshold. It is a solitary journey, one that requires the shedding of all that is external, the relinquishing of the distractions that pull the heart away from the divine union. The bridal chamber is a sacred space, a place where the soul and the Beloved come together in intimate communion. It is a union that transcends the physical world and reaches into the deepest chambers of the heart, where only the solitary soul can meet the Divine.

As wisdom teaches us, "The soul that is not still, and the heart that is not attuned to the voice of God, will never enter the bridal chamber." This is the journey of inner solitude, where one must transcend the noise of the world, enter into silence, and wait patiently for the voice of the Beloved. It is not a path of separation from others, but of deepening connection with one's own inner truth. It is a path of devotion, where the heart, unburdened by the distractions of the world, is united with the Divine.

In the Song of Songs, we are reminded of this sacred intimacy: "Let my beloved come into his garden and taste its choice fruits" (Song of Songs 4:16, NIV). This verse speaks of the yearning of the soul to be fully known and loved, to be received by the Beloved in the deepest part of the garden of the heart. It is in that secret place, the bridal chamber, that true union takes place.

And yet, as Jesus says, the path is narrow, and it is the solitary soul that enters. This does not mean physical solitude, but spiritual solitude—a state of being where the heart is no longer divided. The soul that is undistracted, that has turned away from the illusions of the world, can step into the fullness of the union with God.

In the stillness of the solitary heart, the soul can hear the call of the Beloved, and it is in this moment that the door opens. The bridal chamber awaits all who seek not just the surface of existence, but the deeper, more intimate union with the Divine. To enter, we must be willing to let go of the crowd, to walk the solitary path, and to become fully present with the One who calls us.

For those who answer this call, the bridal chamber is a place of joy, union, and divine love—a place where the soul is nourished and made whole. Only those who are willing to stand in solitude, to meet the Divine with an undivided heart, will experience the eternal union that awaits in the bridal chamber of the Beloved.

In solitude, we find not separation, but a deep connection to the eternal. The kingdom is not a distant place, but the very ground beneath our feet, the breath we take, the heartbeat of the world. To walk this path alone is to discover that we are never truly alone; we are one with the eternal, the Source, and all of life.

Revelation 19:7-9 –
"Let us rejoice and be glad and give him glory! For the wedding of the Lamb has come, and his bride has made herself ready. Fine linen, bright and clean, was given her to wear."

Dhammapada, Verse 210:
"The wise one who is solitary and content with their practice will experience the bliss of liberation. Those who are distracted by the world remain entangled in suffering."

In coming into my faith, it was as if I were opening a sacred Matryoshka, one doll nested within another—each a veil of the self, peeled back gently like the petals of a rose kissed by eternity. Layer by layer, the illusions fell away: the outer name spoken by the world, the masks of expectation, the memories I once mistook for who I was.

Each shell opened into a smaller, more silent version of myself—quieter, truer, more radiant. Until at last, all that remained was near to nothing, and yet infinite: a single, luminous pearl hidden at the center. A mystery within a mystery. The treasure buried in the field. The living seed of divine identity, the pearl of great price—glowing with the breath of the Kingdom, not just beyond the world, but *within* it… and within me.

There are things too real for language. Things that find you when the mind is silent and the heart is open. This is the story of what found me. A vision, yes—but more than a vision. It was a return. A remembering. A knowing beyond knowing.

"The Hidden Within the Hidden"

Saying 76: The Pearl of the Kingdom

Jesus said: "The kingdom of the Father is like a merchant who had a load of goods and found a pearl. That merchant was wise. He sold the load and bought for himself the pearl alone. You also, seek after his treasure which does not fail but endures, where moth does not come near to devour nor worm to destroy." (76)

The merchant, who wanders the marketplace of life, is burdened with many goods—material and transient—items that carry no lasting value. Yet in the midst of this fleeting world, he discovers the pearl, a treasure of inestimable worth, shimmering with divine radiance. It is not like the ordinary trinkets that catch the eye of the world; this pearl is the essence of the Kingdom of the Father, pure and unchanging.

The merchant, recognizing the surpassing value of the pearl, relinquishes everything—his load, his worldly wealth, the goods that weighed him down. He chooses the pearl alone, for in it, he knows lies the fullness of life. So, too, are we invited to abandon the load of worldly distractions and seek the pearl of great price, the divine treasure that endures beyond the ravages of time.

In the stillness of our hearts, we are called to recognize this treasure, which is the Kingdom itself. It is not a kingdom built on riches or fleeting pleasures, but one that is eternal, untouched by the passage of time, immune to the decay of moth and worm. It is the treasure of divine love, the pearl that transcends all earthly wealth and is only found through the wisdom of the heart.

In the words of the mystic, *The true treasure lies not in what you accumulate, but in what you are willing to let go of in order to find it. The pearl is the light within, the divinity that resides in the depths of your being. When you seek it with all your heart, you find not only the Kingdom of the Father, but your true self—whole, complete, and eternal.*

For this treasure, no price is too great. All that we hold dear in this world must be seen as a mere shadow of the glory that awaits. The merchant knows that to possess the pearl is to possess everything, for it is the doorway to the Kingdom, the path to eternal life. The pearl calls to all who have ears to hear, "Come, leave behind what is perishable, and enter into the eternal, where neither moth nor worm can touch the treasure of your soul."

Thus, let us seek the pearl with all that we are, for in its light, all else fades away. The Kingdom of the Father is yours, ever enduring, ever shining—awaiting those who are wise enough to recognize its worth. The Kingdom is not found by adding, but by peeling away. The pearl lies buried in simplicity.

Guru Granth Sahib, Ang 723: "The true treasure is the Name of God, which is imperishable and cannot be taken away. Those who are blessed with the Name are forever rich, and their hearts are fulfilled."

"Transfiguration of Christ"

Saying 77: The Divine Light Within

Jesus said, "I am the light that is over all things. I am the All. The All came forth from me, and the All reaches unto me. Cleave a piece of wood; I am there. Lift up the stone, and you will find me there." (77)

In the beginning, the light shone forth, and the light was with God, and the light was God. (John 1:4) Jesus, the eternal light, speaks now of the divine unity that permeates all things. The light that illumines the world is not just a distant sun, but the very essence of Being, ever-present in every fragment of creation. The All—created and Creator—is one, and this unity transcends time and space, for it exists before all things and will endure after all things.

"Cleaving a piece of wood, and finding Him there," Jesus beckons us to understand that the divine is not hidden in lofty temples or sacred places alone, but can be found in the smallest details of the world. Whether it be the rough-hewn wood, the stone beneath our feet, or the beating of our hearts, the Divine is ever-present, for all creation is an emanation of His being. He is not apart from the world but woven into its very fabric, the light that gives life to all things.

The Psalmist, in his wisdom, knew this truth:

"The earth is the Lord's and the fullness thereof, the world and those who dwell therein." (Psalm 24:1)

There is no part of creation where the Divine is not. The same psalm proclaims, "Who shall ascend the hill of the Lord? And who shall stand in His holy place? He who has clean hands and a pure heart, who does not lift up his soul to what is false and does not swear deceitfully." (Psalm 24:3-4)

Here, the call is not just to recognize the presence of God in the world, but to cleanse our own hearts so that we may perceive it with clarity. When we lift the stone or cleave the wood, it is with hearts purified that we will see the light of God revealed in all things.

In Proverbs, we find further confirmation of this:

"The Lord by wisdom founded the earth; by understanding, He established the heavens." (Proverbs 3:19)

The wisdom that created the earth is the very light that Jesus speaks of—present in all things, from the smallest grain of sand to the tallest tree. We are invited to see the wisdom of the Creator in everything around us, to perceive the divine harmony in all creation, and to understand that God is not distant but near, within and around us, in every stone and tree.

To "cleave the wood" and "lift the stone" is an invitation to look beyond the surface of things and see with spiritual eyes. The material world, often seen as separate from the divine, is in fact a manifestation of God's will and presence. It is all part of the sacred dance of life, the eternal flow of light that connects the seen and unseen.

As the mystic says, "God is in the details." The divine light is not a distant star, but a light woven into every leaf, every breeze, every stone, and every soul. Let us therefore walk with reverence upon the earth, seeing in everything the reflection of the One who is the All. For as the Psalmist declared:

"For in Him we live and move and have our being." (Psalm 139:7)

In Him, we are one with all things—light, wood, stone, and soul. And through this unity, we find our true nature.

"I am the light that is over all things."
"In him was life, and that life was the light of all mankind. The light shines in the darkness, and the darkness has not overcome it." (John 1:4-5, NIV)

"When Jesus spoke again to the people, he said, 'I am the light of the world. Whoever follows me will never walk in darkness, but will have the light of life.'" (John 8:12, NIV)

"And surely I am with you always, to the very end of the age." (Matthew 28:20, NIV)

Saying 78: The Test of True Strength and Truth

Jesus said, "What did you go out into the desert to see? A reed shaken by the wind? A person wearing fancy clothes, like your rulers and powerful people? They wear fancy clothes, but can't know the truth." (78)

The desert, vast and empty, offers no illusion. It strips away the distractions of wealth, power, and fleeting comforts, revealing only what is essential—what is true. Jesus asks, "What did you go out into the desert to see?" The answer is not found in the transient, but in the eternal. The reed that sways with the wind represents those who bend with the tides of society, whose foundations are weak and easily influenced by the whims of power and fashion. They may appear adorned, but they are like the flowers of the field—here today and gone tomorrow (Matthew 6:30).

The person in fancy clothes, like the rulers and powerful people, represents those who place their trust in outward appearances—prestige, wealth, status. But true knowledge, true understanding, cannot be bought or worn. It is found in the purity of the heart, not in the finery of the body. As Jesus speaks, He calls us away from the illusions of the world to the simplicity of truth.

In Proverbs, it is written:

"Better is a poor man who walks in his integrity than a rich man who is crooked in his ways." (Proverbs 28:6)

This truth resonates with the teaching of Jesus. Wealth, status, and appearances are fleeting, but integrity—truth—lasts beyond this world. The man who walks in truth is grounded, steadfast like the desert itself, while the one who seeks after the shifting winds of the world will always be unsettled.

The Psalmist speaks of this deeper knowing in a quiet heart:

"The Lord is near to all who call on Him, to all who call on Him in truth." (Psalm 145:18)

It is in the simplicity of calling on God in truth, not through the display of wealth or power, that we find union with the Divine. As we walk in the desert, shedding all that is superficial, we discover the still, small voice of God that speaks within.

And so, Jesus asks again: What are you seeking? Are you looking for the illusions of the world, or are you seeking the truth that is not shaken by the wind? The truth is found in the quiet, the humble, and the eternal. Let us, then, walk in simplicity, seeking not the adornments of this world, but the Kingdom that is within us.

Saying 79: Listening to the Message—The True Blessing of Listening

A woman in the crowd said to him: Blessed is the womb which bore you, and the breasts which nourished you. He said to [her]: Blessed are those who have heard the word of the Father (and) have kept it in truth. For there will be days when you will say: Blessed is the womb which has not conceived, and the breasts which have not given suck. (79)

> *A voice rose from the crowd, a woman's cry,*
> *"Blessed is the womb that bore you,*
> *the breasts that nourished you."*

But He, the Living Word, turned and spoke:
"Blessed are those who have listened
to the message of the Father and kept it."

For there will come days when the earth will tremble,
when the rivers will dry,
and the longing of the soul
will not be satisfied by the fruit of the flesh.
A time when voices will sigh,
"Blessed is the womb that did not conceive,
and the breasts that have not given milk."

O traveler, hear!
The blessing is not in birth, nor in the hands that swaddle,
but in the ear that hears,
in the heart that holds the fire of the Word.
For the seed of the Spirit is sown in those
who drink of the hidden well,
who listen in the silence where eternity whispers.

"Incline your ear, and come to Me;
listen, that you may live." *(Isaiah 55:3)*

The womb of the world brings forth dust,
but the womb of the soul, when awakened,
gives birth to light.
Blessed are those who listen,
for they will hear the voice of the Father
before the storm, before the night.

Luke 11:27-28: "As Jesus was saying these things, a woman in the crowd called out, 'Blessed is the mother who gave you birth and nursed you.' He replied, 'Blessed rather are those who hear the word of God and obey it.'"

Mark 3:33-35: "Who are my mother and my brothers? Then he looked at those seated in a circle around him and said, 'Here are my mother and my brothers! Whoever does God's will is my brother and sister and mother.'"

Saying 80: The World is a Body: The Search for True Knowledge

Jesus said, "Whoever has known the world has found the body; but whoever has found the body, of them the world isn't worthy." (80)

To come into the world is to take on a body, but the soul is far greater than the form it inhabits. The body is the vessel, but the soul is the radiant essence, the breath of the divine. The flesh exists for a time, yet within it, the eternal light dwells. The one who discovers this light within themselves is no longer bound by the world's illusions, for they know they are more than dust—they are spirit, flowing from the Source of all.

Rumi spoke of this truth, saying, *"You were born with wings. Why prefer to crawl through life?"* The soul is not confined to the body but rather moves through it as light through a lantern. The body is not the prison of the soul but its instrument, given for the purpose of revealing the divine. St. Teresa of Ávila affirmed this when she wrote, *"Christ has no body now but yours, no hands, no feet on earth but yours."*

To find the body in the way Jesus speaks is not merely to recognize the flesh but to understand its purpose—to be an expression of God's love in the world. Those who awaken to this truth no longer belong to the world's distractions and fleeting desires. The world cannot comprehend them, for they are not merely of the earth but of the light.

As St. Francis of Assisi taught, *"What you are looking for is what is looking."* The divine spark within us is not separate from its Source. To find the true body is to remember that we are an emanation of divine light, temporarily walking in flesh, yet always belonging to the eternal.

Luke 9:25: *"What good is it for someone to gain the whole world, and yet lose or forfeit their very self?"*

John 17:16: *"They are not of the world, even as I am not of it."*

Chapter 10

The Path of Knowledge (Sayings 81-90)

Saying 81: The Poverty That Leads to True Riches

Jesus said, "Whoever has grown rich, let him become poor. If you become poor, you will be able to enter the Kingdom of Heaven." (81)

This is not the poverty of lacking, but the poverty of release—the emptying of self so that one may be filled with the divine. To be rich in the world is to carry the weight of possessions, attachments, and pride. But to become poor in spirit is to surrender, to strip away all that is not God, and to enter the kingdom with open hands and an unburdened heart.

St. John of the Cross speaks of this when he writes, *"To reach satisfaction in all, desire satisfaction in nothing. To come to possess all, desire the possession of nothing. To arrive at being all, desire to be nothing."* True wealth is not found in abundance, but in freedom from needing it.

The Psalmist echoes this call to surrender: *"The Lord is my shepherd; I shall not want"* (Psalm 23:1). Those who trust in God's providence find themselves rich in a way the world cannot understand. They become like the lilies of the field, clothed in glory without striving, for they depend not on themselves but on the infinite Source.

To become poor is to let go of the illusion of self-sufficiency and to recognize the divine as our true wealth. It is the great paradox: in losing all, we gain everything. As Meister Eckhart wrote, *"The more we let God take us over, the more truly ourselves we become—because He made us. He invented us."*

Those who release their grip on the fleeting treasures of the world find their hands open to receive the riches of heaven.

Luke 6:20 – "Looking at his disciples, he said: 'Blessed are you who are poor, for yours is the kingdom of God.'"

❧❦❧

Saying 82: The Solar Logos and the Fire of Baptism

Jesus said, "Whoever is near me is near the fire, and whoever is far from me is far from the Kingdom." (82)

Christ, the Solar Logos, is the burning heart of divine radiance, the Word through whom all things were made (John 1:3). He is the Sun of Righteousness who rises with healing in His wings (Malachi 4:2), the eternal fire that illuminates and purifies. To draw near to Him is to step into the refining flame, where dross is burned away, and the soul is kindled with the light of truth.

At His baptism, the heavens opened, and the Spirit descended as a dove, anointing Him with the holy fire of divine sonship (Matthew 3:16-17). This was no ordinary water—it was the baptism of fire foretold by John the Baptist: *"He will baptize you with the Holy Spirit and fire" (Luke 3:16).* Those who come to Him must pass through this flame, the inward transfiguration where the old self is consumed, and the new creation is born.

The fire of Christ is not mere destruction but illumination, the flame of the burning bush that is ablaze yet never consumed (Exodus 3:2). It is the sacred fire of Pentecost that descended upon the apostles as tongues of flame, igniting them with divine wisdom (Acts 2:3-4).

The mystic Symeon the New Theologian spoke of this fire, saying:

"We awaken in Christ's body as Christ awakens our bodies, and my poor hand is Christ, He enters my foot, and is infinitely me. I move my hand, and wonderfully, my hand becomes Christ, becomes all of Him."

To be near Christ is to be near the eternal fire of the Logos, the sacred conflagration that consumes all illusion and awakens the soul to its divine nature. Those who remain far from this fire remain cold, estranged from the light of the Kingdom. But those who step into its glow are baptized anew, transformed into living flames, bearing the brilliance of the Divine.

John 15:5 – *"I am the vine; you are the branches. If you remain in me and I in you, you will bear much fruit; apart from me you can do nothing."*

Saying 83: Seeing With The Soul What The Eyes Cannot Behold

"Jesus said, 'The images are visible to humanity, but the light within them is hidden in the image of the Father's light. He will be revealed, but his image is hidden by his light.'" (83)

Psalm 104:3 (KJV):
"Who layeth the beams of his chambers in the waters: who maketh the clouds his chariot: who walketh upon the wings of the wind."

Matthew 17:5 (KJV):
"While he yet spake, behold, a bright cloud overshadowed them: and behold a voice out of the cloud, which said, This is my beloved Son, in whom I am well pleased; hear ye him."

The next photograph is a zoomed-in picture of the Almighty showing us a graceful visage of the side profile of the Heavenly Father, similar to the fresco painting by Michelangelo. I have made a facial features guide to show his face in detail.

"Dunston, J.C. (2015) Details of our Heavenly Father's Face"

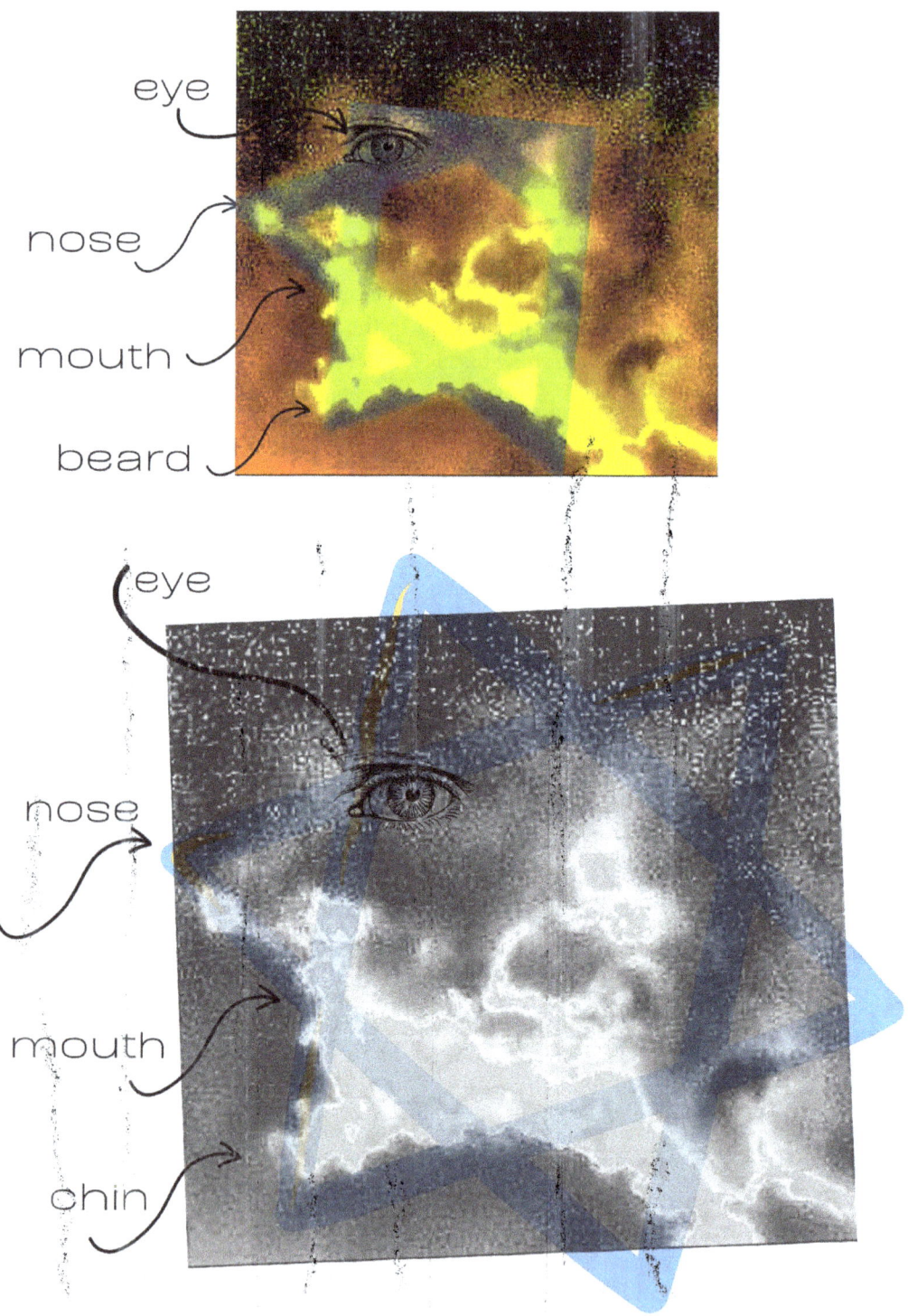

"Guide to Facial Features of Heavenly Father"

"Michelangelo, "THE CREATION OF ADAM" Fresco. Sistine Chapel, Vatican City"

At the heart of this saying is a paradox—what is most luminous is also most concealed. Humanity perceives the external world, the forms and images that populate material existence, but within them resides a deeper reality, veiled by the very brilliance of divine light. This recalls the Johannine concept of Jesus as the Light of the world (John 8:12), yet not all recognize him, for the light shines in the darkness, and the darkness did not comprehend it (John 1:5). It suggests that the Father's presence is hidden within all things, yet it is precisely this hiddenness that calls forth revelation.

The archetypal Being of the Father, as revealed in scripture, is often described as a great cloud, a presence beyond form yet manifest in infinite wisdom and love. In Exodus, God leads His people as a pillar of cloud by day and fire by night (Exodus 13:21), concealing and revealing His presence simultaneously. Job declares, He spreads out the clouds as His covering (Job 36:29), indicating that divine knowledge is vast, yet shrouded in mystery. In the Eastern tradition, the Brihadaranyaka Upanishad states, The self is hidden in the heart of every creature, but the wise see it with the eye of wisdom (4.4.22), echoing the idea that divine light is present yet obscured.

Jesus, in contrast, is the Light that has come into the world, the one who illuminates and reveals. His archetypal being is that of the Solar Logos, the bridge between the hidden

Father and manifest creation. He is the true light which gives light to every man coming into the world (John 1:9). As the Incarnation of the Word, Jesus embodies divine wisdom and presence in a tangible form. The Bhagavad Gita expresses a similar idea when Krishna declares, I am the light in the sun and the moon, and I am the intelligence of the intelligent (Bhagavad Gita 7:8). Jesus is the Logos made flesh, the radiance of God's glory (Hebrews 1:3), the one through whom all things are made manifest.

The Holy Spirit, the Paraclete, is the Living Presence that moves within all things, the breath of life that sustains and sanctifies. The Spirit is luminous, radiant as a rainbow upon a rainy day, an image drawn from Ezekiel's vision: Like the appearance of a rainbow in the clouds on a rainy day, so was the radiance around him. This was the appearance of the likeness of the glory of the Lord (Ezekiel 1:28). The Holy Spirit is the one who brings forth fruit and joy (Galatians 5:22-23), the whispering wind that enlivens creation (John 3:8), the divine Shekinah that dwells among us. In the Tao Te Ching, Laozi describes the Tao in similar terms: It is hidden but always present. I do not know who gave birth to it. It is older than God (Tao Te Ching, 4). The Spirit, ever-present and moving, is the light of many mansions (John 14:2), illuminating the soul's journey toward divine union.

The mystical tradition affirms that divine light is both the great revealer and the great concealer. Meister Eckhart speaks of God as a super-essential nothingness, a darkness beyond light, suggesting that divine illumination is beyond human comprehension. St. Symeon the New Theologian, in his Hymns of Divine Love, describes encountering the divine as being wholly embraced by light, yet unable to see its source. The 13th-century Sufi poet Rumi mirrors this when he writes, The light you see is not from any sun, it is from beyond, a glory that blinds even the angels.

Saying 83 ultimately beckons the soul into mystery, into the awe and wonder of divine illumination. The world is filled with visible images, yet within them is the radiance of the Father's light, hidden in plain sight. It is a call to contemplation, to seeing beyond the surface and perceiving the luminous reality that pervades all things. As the Psalmist writes, In Your light, we see light (Psalm 36:9).

The images of the divine are seen by humanity, yet the light within them remains veiled, concealed within the brilliance of the Father's radiance. As Jesus said, 'He will be revealed, but His image is hidden within His own light.' Only those with eyes attuned to the unseen may glimpse the mystery beyond the veil.

2 Corinthians 4:6 – "For God, who said, 'Let light shine out of darkness,' made his light shine in our hearts to give us the light of the knowledge of God's glory displayed in the face of Christ."

Saying 84: The Burden of the Unseen Image

"Jesus said, 'When you see your likeness, you rejoice. But when you see your images that came into being before you did – which don't die, and aren't revealed – how much you'll have to bear!'" (84)

This saying carries profound mystical significance. The joy of seeing one's likeness suggests an initial awakening—the recognition of divine imprint within oneself, the image of God reflected in human nature. This echoes Genesis: *God created mankind in his own image, in the image of God he created them* (Genesis 1:27). Yet, the deeper mystery lies in perceiving *the images that came into being before you*, eternal realities that exist beyond time and mortality. The weight of such a revelation is overwhelming, as it calls the seeker to transcend personal identity and behold the divine archetype beyond all form.

"Theotokos of the Inner Christ"

In the mystical tradition, the burden of divine knowledge is well-documented. St. John of the Cross speaks of the *dark night of the soul*, where the soul, upon glimpsing divine reality, must endure purification to be fully united with it. Similarly, Plotinus in the *Enneads* describes the ascent of the soul toward the One, where the closer one draws to absolute truth, the more one must shed illusion. The Bhagavad Gita echoes this challenge when Krishna tells Arjuna, *The wise see the same divine presence in a learned priest, a cow, an elephant, a dog, and an outcast* (Bhagavad Gita 5:18), calling for a vision that transcends appearances and perceives the eternal essence.

In the Christian mystical tradition, this recognition carries the weight of responsibility. The one who sees the hidden, eternal image must bear the suffering of humanity's forgetfulness. The prophet Isaiah, upon his vision of God's glory, laments, *Woe to me! I am ruined! For I am a man of unclean lips, and I live among a people of unclean lips, and my eyes have seen the King, the Lord Almighty* (Isaiah 6:5). The seeker who beholds divine reality must carry both the joy of revelation and the sorrow of human limitation.

The Eastern Orthodox tradition speaks of *theosis*, the process of becoming one with God, wherein seeing the divine image within oneself is only the beginning—full transformation requires bearing the weight of divine love. As Meister Eckhart states, *The eye with which I see God is the same eye with which God sees me.* Saying 84 ultimately reveals that divine knowledge is not merely a gift but a calling—one that requires endurance, surrender, and the willingness to bear the weight of transcendence.

When you see your likeness, you rejoice. But when you behold the images that came into being before you—immortal and hidden—you will bear a great burden.

A mystic understands that our earthly reflection is but a fleeting shadow, while our true form—unseen, eternal—presses upon the soul with the weight of revelation. To witness this hidden image is to awaken to a reality beyond time, yet with such knowledge comes the profound responsibility of bearing its light.

To see your true likeness is to lose all illusions—and to bear the holy weight of being. We live like stacking dolls, one within another—layers of name, role, story, fear. But something inside remembers.

Saying 85: Adam Wasn't Worthy

Jesus said, "Adam came into being from a great power and great wealth, but he didn't become worthy of you. If he had been worthy, [he wouldn't have tasted] death." (85)

Adam, the first-formed, was shaped by the hands of the Divine, sculpted from the dust yet animated by the breath of life (Genesis 2:7). He was placed in a garden of abundance, where every tree was given for nourishment except one—the tree of the knowledge of good and evil (Genesis 2:16-17). Yet, despite his origin in great power and divine favor, he fell, exiled from Eden, and bound to the dust of mortality.

What was his unworthiness? Was it disobedience alone, or was it the failure to recognize the true gift within him—the spark of the divine, the image of God that could not perish? Adam turned outward, grasping at knowledge apart from wisdom, and so he tasted death. But Christ, the Second Adam, came to restore what was lost.

As Paul declared: *"For as in Adam all die, so in Christ all will be made alive" (1 Corinthians 15:22).* Christ did not merely return to Eden but opened the way to the Kingdom, not of earth but of the heavens. The one who cleaves to the First Adam remains in the cycle of death, but the one who unites with Christ, the true image of the Father, enters into life eternal.

Mystic theologian Matthew Fox speaks of humanity not as originally cursed but as bearing an "original blessing." He writes:

> *"We are born with a divine spark inside us, an image of God that cannot be erased, only obscured. To return to our original blessing is to awaken to our divinity."*

The worthiness Adam could not attain, Christ has granted freely. Not through grasping but through surrender, not through knowledge alone but through divine union, the soul passes beyond death into the unending life of the Father. To awaken is to remember: we were never separate, only sleeping.

In Hinduism, the concept of the divine potential within all beings is present. In the story of the *Purusha*, the cosmic being whose sacrifice created the world, there is a notion that humans are created with inherent divine qualities. However, humans must overcome ignorance (*avidya*) to realize their divine nature, much like how Adam's fall led to a loss of spiritual potential.

In Buddhism, there is a similar idea that humans are born with the potential to attain enlightenment, but failure to recognize and act on that potential leads to suffering and ignorance, akin to the death mentioned in Saying 85.

Saying 86: The Son of Man Has No Place to Lay His Head

Jesus said, "The foxes have their holes, and the birds have their nests, but the Son of Man has no place to lay his head." (86)

The title *Son of Man* is layered with profound meaning, rooted in the visions of the Hebrew prophets. In Daniel's revelation, one *like a Son of Man* appears before the Ancient of Days, receiving an everlasting kingdom (Daniel 7:13-14). This is no ordinary figure; he is the divine-human mediator, the one who reigns with God.

Ezekiel, too, is addressed as *Son of Man*—a mortal sent to speak divine truth, often rejected by his own people (Ezekiel 2:1-3). Jesus, in calling himself the Son of Man, unites both visions: the suffering prophet and the glorified king. He walks the earth with no home, no resting place, embodying the exile of humanity estranged from God, yet he also carries the promise of restoration.

Christ's homelessness is not mere physical wandering but a sign of the world's rejection. He has come to gather the scattered, yet the world does not recognize him. The foxes and the birds have their domains, but the kingdom he brings is not of this world (John 18:36). He is the cosmic wanderer, seeking not a place to rest his head, but hearts in which to dwell.

The *Son of Man* has nowhere to lay his head, for his resting place is not in stone or earthly shelter, but in the temple of the human soul—those who open themselves to him. As Jesus said:

> *"If anyone loves me, they will keep my word, and my Father will love them, and we will come to them and make our home with them" (John 14:23).*

The question remains: Will we be the dwelling place of the Son of Man? Or will he pass by, still seeking a home in this world?

Saying 87: The Interwoven Mystery of Flesh and Soul

Jesus said, "Woe to the flesh that depends on the soul; woe to the soul that depends on the flesh." (87)

These words unveil a paradox, a tension that mystics and sages have long contemplated—the dance of spirit and matter, the soul's descent into flesh, and the flesh's longing for the soul's illumination.

To the one who clings to the soul yet remains bound by the flesh, there is woe, for the soul is meant to soar, not to be tethered. The divine spark within us does not exist merely to sustain the body's desires, but to transcend them, to awaken to its origin in the Eternal.

And to the soul that depends on the flesh—this too is woe, for the body is impermanent, a vessel that fades. If the soul anchors itself to the perishable, it forgets its true nature, mistaking the temporal for the eternal.

"The perishable must clothe itself with the imperishable, and the mortal with immortality" (1 Corinthians 15:53).

And yet, Jesus came in the flesh, not to reject it, but to transfigure it. The Incarnation reveals that the body is not meant to enslave the soul, nor is the soul meant to abandon the body. Rather, the body becomes a temple, a dwelling place of the Divine, when it is aligned with the spirit.

The mystic Meister Eckhart said:

"The eye through which I see God is the same eye through which God sees me; my eye and God's eye are one."

Thus, the challenge is to live in harmony—not letting the flesh rule the soul, nor the soul become lost in the flesh, but allowing the two to be united in divine purpose

Matthew 16:26 – "What good will it be for someone to gain the whole world, yet forfeit their soul? Or what can anyone give in exchange for their soul?"

Galatians 5:16 – "So I say, walk by the Spirit, and you will not gratify the desires of the flesh."

Saying 88: The Guiding Light of Angels and Prophets

Jesus said, "The angels and the prophets will come to you, and they will take you by the hand and lead you into the light." (88)

This saying is a radiant promise—a whisper of divine assurance echoing through the ages. It speaks of the invisible guides, the messengers of heaven, and the mystics of every age who stretch out their hands to lead us home.

Jesus reveals a truth both cosmic and intimate: that the angels and prophets—those illuminated beings dwelling in the eternal now—are not far from us. They walk beside us, sentinels of love and wisdom, guiding the soul through shadowed valleys into the brightness of the divine light. These are not figures lost in time, but living presences who accompany all who earnestly seek the truth.

The saying is prophetic. It affirms the unity of heaven and earth, and the unbroken thread of divine revelation woven through the prophets of Israel, the mystics of every tradition, and the awakened hearts of today. Jesus knows there are multitudes—celestial beings and risen sons and daughters of the Most High—who have answered the call of love. They bear witness to the Almighty's mercy and truth, ensuring that no soul is ever forsaken, for the Good Shepherd loses none.

Even now, they come:

In dreams, in silence, in the glimmering stillness between breaths. They come in a sweet melody heard in a song, the ancestral voice ringing through the infinite cosmos. They come when you call in the feathers of the wind, and with eyes like burning lamps. They come when the heart is open, and they whisper, "Know"

Those who have walked before us—Isaiah, Elijah, Mary Magdalene, Hildegard, Rumi, Teresa, Francis, and countless unnamed prophets—still shine. Their light mingles with the light of angels, and together, they call to the soul: *"Awaken. Come into the light."*

To those who have eyes to see and ears to hear, the light is not distant. It is rising now, within.

And then, as if heaven wished to be seen, the veil grew thin.

What had long been felt in the heart and heard in whispers now appeared before the eye—light upon light, presence within presence. In this sacred moment, the celestial hosts revealed themselves not in thunder or flame, but in quiet radiance.

In the photograph below, you will witness a glimpse of the Angelic Host—glowing orbs of white light, the gentle signatures of divine beings who walk among us. These are the messengers of pure love, the watchers, the guides. Their appearance is not an illusion, but an invitation.

They come in peace.
They come in truth.
They come to lead us into the Light.

"Dunston, J. C. (2015) "CELESTIAL SYMPHONY: The Luminous Dance of Myriads of Angelic Host"

"Fra-Angelico Angelic Presence"

In this profound teaching, we are reminded that the spiritual journey is never one of isolation. Even in our darkest hours, when we feel alone in the world, the light of divine guidance is always near. Angels, messengers of God, and prophets, who are seers of truth, stand ready to guide us through the labyrinth of earthly existence and lead us toward the illumination of divine wisdom.

The light they guide us toward is not a mere reflection of this world, but a light that emanates from the very heart of the Divine. It is the light of *the Logos*, the eternal Word, that can only be truly known through deep spiritual awakening. Just as Jesus Himself is the light of the world (John 8:12), so too do the angels and prophets serve as bearers of that light, lighting the path back to the Father.

In the *Apocryphal Gospel of Thomas* (Saying 50), Jesus speaks of the need to "become children" to enter the Kingdom, signifying a return to the pure, innocent perception of divine truth that can only be received when we are guided by those who have already seen and known the way.

The great Christian mystic Julian of Norwich once wrote:

"All shall be well, and all shall be well, and all manner of thing shall be well."

This assurance is rooted in the divine guidance we receive from the holy ones who walk before us. The angels and prophets, those who have known the Father's heart, are ever-present, holding out their hands to lift us from the shadows and show us the path to eternal light.

Let us trust in their guidance, for in the company of these divine messengers, we are never without the light that leads us back to the source of all life.

For there are many who shepherd the flock. Hebrews 1:14 - *"Are not all angels ministering spirits sent to serve those who will inherit salvation?"*

Bhagavad Gita 4:34 - "Acquire transcendental knowledge from a realized soul. Ask him questions and submit yourself to him. The wise, who know the truth, will impart knowledge to you."

Saying 89: The True Cleansing of the Soul

Jesus said, "Why do you wash the outside of the cup? Do you not understand that the one who made the inside made the outside also? You also cleanse the outside of the cup, but the inside remains full of greed and wickedness." (89)

In this teaching, Jesus calls us to a deeper form of purification, one that goes beyond surface appearances. The world often emphasizes outward cleanliness and behavior—how we present ourselves to others, how we dress, or the image we project. Yet, Jesus directs our attention to the inward state, where true transformation must occur. The external may appear pristine, but if the internal remains corrupt, the outward purification is meaningless.

This profound lesson echoes the message of Matthew 23:25-26, where Jesus criticizes the Pharisees, saying, "Woe to you, teachers of the law and Pharisees, you hypocrites! You clean the outside of the cup and dish, but inside they are full of greed and self-indulgence. Blind Pharisee! First clean the inside of the cup and dish, and then the outside also will be clean."

Here, Jesus is not merely condemning ritual purity but pointing to a deeper spiritual truth—an internal hypocrisy. This is not just a critique of ancient religious leaders, but also a warning to any who use the guise of holiness or piety for personal gain. Too often, individuals and institutions in power focus on external displays of religious observance or moral superiority, while the hearts of their followers, and perhaps their own hearts, remain enslaved to greed, ambition, or a thirst for control. In this way, they obscure the truth of spiritual purification, turning it into a means of self-enrichment rather than the transformation of the soul.

This idea finds resonance in the words of Saint John Chrysostom, who once said, "There are those who, through their outward observance of the law, deceive themselves and others into thinking they are righteous, while the inner self remains untouched by God." Just as the Pharisees of Jesus' time were criticized for their hypocrisy, modern spiritual leaders who focus on the outward display of virtue while allowing selfishness and greed to fester inside, continue to obscure the true message of love and spiritual awakening.

This principle reflects a spiritual truth known to mystics throughout history: the cleansing of the heart and soul must take precedence over outward appearances. True holiness and righteousness are not about the way we look or how others perceive us, but about the purity of our hearts. The Song of Solomon (4:7) beautifully describes the purity of the soul, stating, "Thou art all fair, my love; there is no spot in thee." Here, the soul, when cleansed by divine love, is seen as perfectly radiant and whole.

Saint John of the Cross, in his *Dark Night of the Soul*, speaks of the inner purification required for union with the divine, stating: "In the evening of life, we will be judged on love alone." This "love" is not just an external action, but a deep, transformative love that cleanses the very soul, just as fire refines gold.

Thus, the washing of the outside must be accompanied by the inner work of cleansing our desires, thoughts, and intentions. We are called to purify our hearts and minds, aligning them with the divine will so that our outer actions naturally reflect the purity of our inner being. True purity begins not with the hands, but with the heart, where love, compassion, and wisdom dwell. And in this way, we must guard against the temptation to hide behind an external display of righteousness, for only through authentic inner transformation can we truly embody the love and light of the divine.

"Come to me, for my yoke is easy, and my burden is light."

Saying 90: The Ease of the Divine Yoke

Jesus said: Come to me, for my yoke is easy and my lordship is gentle, and you will find rest for yourselves. (90)

In this saying, Jesus invites us into a deeper relationship with Him, one that transcends the heavy burdens of the world. The image of the *yoke*, a wooden frame that pairs two oxen for the purpose of working together, is a powerful metaphor for the way we are called to walk with Christ. Unlike the heavy yokes of the world—burdens of anxiety, striving, and the weight of unfulfilled desires—Jesus offers us a yoke that is "easy" and a burden that is "light."

This saying echoes the invitation found in *Matthew 11:28-30*, where Jesus speaks directly to those weary from life's struggles: *"Come to me, all you who are weary and burdened, and I will give you rest. Take my yoke upon you and learn from me, for I am gentle and humble in heart, and you will find rest for your souls. For my yoke is easy and my burden is light."*

The key to understanding this invitation is in the word "easy," which is not simply about a lack of difficulty but refers to a yoke that is well-fitted, tailored for us. In contrast to the burdens we take on in our own strength—those that feel restrictive, exhausting, and unnatural—Christ's yoke is suited perfectly for us. It enables us to work in harmony with the divine flow of the universe, guided by love and grace, rather than struggle and resistance.

Mystics throughout the ages have attested to the transformative power of walking in union with Christ. Meister Eckhart, the great Christian mystic, echoed this sentiment in his writings, noting that when we unite with the divine, we move beyond the struggles of ego and grasp onto the peace that comes with surrendering to God's will: *"The soul must become so completely united with God that the soul becomes a stillness and a silence, wholly attentive to God's presence."*

Furthermore, the beloved *Song of Solomon* speaks to this intimacy of union, where the bridegroom calls to his bride: *"Let my beloved come into his garden and eat its choice fruits" (Song of Solomon 4:16)*—a symbol of the nourishment and joy found in divine union. The lightness of the yoke is found in yielding to this union, letting go of the self-centered burdens and receiving the lightness of divine grace.

As St. Augustine beautifully expressed:

"What grace is meant to do is to help good people, not to escape their sufferings, but to bear them with a stout heart."

Thus, when we "take on" the yoke of Christ, we are not weighed down by the demands of the world but are freed to live with love, peace, and trust in God's guiding hand. As we walk with Him, the yoke becomes a tool of spiritual alignment, a path of rest that enables us to bear fruit without the crushing weight of unfulfilled expectations. It is the yoke of grace, where the divine labor flows effortlessly through us.

John 14:27 – "Peace I leave with you; my peace I give you. I do not give to you as the world gives. Do not let your hearts be troubled and do not be afraid."

"Come unto me... and you shall find rest." "You have not recognized the one who is before you." "He who drinks from my mouth will become as I am, and I shall be he." "Where there are two or one, I am with him." "You have omitted the one living in your presence."

It was not thunder that split the sky. It was stillness.

You do not become union through effort, but through surrender.

I drank from His mouth—
not wine, but Word.
Not sound, but essence.
And it changed me.

I became as He is.
And He was in me.

Not metaphor. Reality.

I was not outside God, reaching toward Him.
I was inside the Divine— like flame inside flame.

The breath of the Paraclete wove me into the song of all things.
The Father's Light clothed me.

Where there were Three, now there was One. And that One was All.

Chapter 11

Eternal Life and the Resurrection (Sayings 91-100)

Reading the Signs-Reading the Present Moment: Recognizing the Truth Before You

Saying 91: The Unseen Presence: Recognizing the Truth Before You

"They said to him, 'Tell us who you are so that we may trust you.' He said to them, 'You read the face of the sky and the earth, but you don't know the one right in front of you, and you don't know how to read the present moment.'" (91)

He said to them, *"You read the face of the sky and the earth, but you don't know the one right in front of you, and you don't know how to read the present moment."*

The seekers of wisdom peer into the heavens, tracing the paths of stars, discerning the signs of wind and rain, yet their eyes remain veiled to the mystery standing before them. They measure time, mark the turning of seasons, and set their gaze upon distant wonders, yet fail to recognize the Eternal dwelling among them.

To see rightly, one must not only look outward but inward. The kingdom is not written in the stars alone, nor hidden in the folds of distant lands—it is near, as close as breath, as intimate as the silent voice within. "The light shines in the darkness, and the darkness has not overcome it" (*John 1:5*), yet how often do we search for what is already illuminating our path?

Jacob Boehme, the German mystic, once wrote:

"If you would behold with the eye of eternity, you must first close the eyes of time."

There is an urgency in Jesus' words—an invitation to awaken from the dream of distraction. The present moment is the gate to eternity. The world's wisdom charts the movements of planets, yet the wisdom of the Spirit calls us to chart the movements of the heart.

Angelus Silesius, a voice from the deep wells of contemplation, reminds us:

"I do not need to cross the sea nor travel to the sun. The Presence that I long for dwells in me and is one."

To know Christ is not merely to study His works but to recognize His presence in the now, in the whispering wind, in the flicker of a candle, in the stillness between words. The sky declares His glory, the earth trembles with His voice, yet it is in the quiet surrender of this moment that He is most profoundly known.

Who do you seek? The one you long for is already before you. Do not look to the horizon for what is standing at your doorstep.

> *Matthew 16:2-3 – "He replied, 'When evening comes, you say, 'It will be fair weather, for the sky is red,' and in the morning, 'Today it will be stormy, for the sky is red and overcast.' You know how to interpret the appearance of the sky, but you cannot interpret the signs of the times.'"*

> *Luke 19:41-44 – "As he approached Jerusalem and saw the city, he wept over it and said, 'If you, even you, had only known on this day what would bring you peace—but now it is hidden from your eyes.'"*

The lover seeks the beloved, but does not realize that the beloved is within.

↊❃❃↋

Saying 92: The Path of Seeking

Jesus said: Seek, and you will find; but the things you asked me in those days and I did not tell you then, now I desire to tell them, but you do not ask about them. (92)

> *Matthew 7:7 -"Ask and it will be given to you; seek and you will find; knock and the door will be opened to you."*

The spiritual journey begins not with answers, but with longing—the deep, unrelenting thirst for something beyond the fleeting world. To seek is to attune oneself to the silent call of the Divine, to step beyond mere curiosity and into communion.

Paul Brunton writes, *"The quest is not to be won by physical strength or intellectual cleverness but by spiritual perception, moral purity, and personal self-conquest. The true seeker is he who is ready to lose himself in the search."* This is the paradox of the path: one must empty oneself in order to be filled, surrender in order to be found.

In the Psalms, the voice of the yearning soul calls out:
"My soul thirsts for God, for the living God; when shall I come and appear before God?" (Psalm 42:2)

Yet the door upon which we knock is not outside of us; it is the threshold of inner awakening. Swami Prabhavananda reminds us, *"Truth is not something that can be demonstrated like a theorem; it must be experienced directly, and that experience transforms the whole of one's life."* To seek is not to accumulate knowledge, but to dissolve in wisdom; not to reach outward, but to awaken inward.

The knocking is not done with the hands, but with the heart pressing against the veil of illusion. The asking is not with words, but with a soul emptied of all pretense, ready to receive.

The search is already unfolding within you. The door is waiting. Will you step through?

Luke 11:9 – "So I say to you: Ask and it will be given to you; seek and you will find; knock and the door will be opened to you."

꧁❀꧂

Saying 93: Guarding the Sacred—The Wisdom of Discernment

Jesus said, "Don't give what's holy to the dogs, or else it might be thrown on the manure pile. Don't throw pearls to the pigs, or else they might trample them underfoot." (93)

Wisdom is a treasure, but not all hands are ready to receive it. Just as one would not cast a luminous jewel into the mud, so too must the seeker guard the sacred truth from those who cannot yet recognize its worth. Discernment is not withholding out of pride but preserving out of reverence.

Paul Brunton speaks to this wisdom, *"The higher teachings are not a matter for intellectual debate. They are a living flame that must be protected from the winds of cynicism and careless handling."* The mysteries of the divine are not for mockery, nor should they be reduced to mere words for those who seek entertainment rather than transformation.

In the Proverbs, the wisdom of the ancients echoes this teaching:

"Do not rebuke mockers, or they will hate you; rebuke the wise, and they will love you." (Proverbs 9:8)

Swami Prabhavananda reminds us, *"Truth must be given only to those who truly yearn for it. For the one who seeks with sincerity, a single word can ignite the soul; for the one who scoffs, an entire scripture will fall on deaf ears."*

Jesus' words are a call to honor the divine spark within—both in ourselves and in others. The pearl of wisdom must be placed in the hands of those who will cherish it, just as the sacred fire must be tended by those who will keep it burning.

> *Matthew 7:6* – *"Do not give dogs what is sacred; do not throw your pearls to pigs. If you do, they may trample them under their feet, and turn and tear you to pieces."*

Saying 94: One Who Seeks Will Find

"Jesus said, 'One who seeks will find, and upon finding, they will marvel. And when they marvel, they will rule, and after ruling, they will rest.'" (94)

This saying highlights the transformative power of seeking the truth. The act of seeking is inherently dynamic, driven by a deep yearning for understanding, and by its very nature, it provokes a response. Just as knocking on a door leads to it opening, seeking leads to finding, because nature itself is alive and responsive. The universe, alive with divine presence, responds to our actions. The key is to realize that we live in a participatory universe, where our thoughts, intentions, and deeds shape the reality around us. When we seek truth, we align ourselves with this dynamic, creative force, and thus, we open ourselves to revelation.

Upon finding this truth, the seeker is overwhelmed with wonder—*they marvel.* This revelation is a turning point, and it leads to mastery over one's life and understanding, as the seeker begins to govern their own thoughts and actions in accordance with divine wisdom. The "ruling" suggests an awareness and control over one's own being, where the seeker aligns themselves with higher principles, making choices that reflect spiritual understanding. The rest that follows is not mere inactivity, but spiritual fulfillment and peace that comes from living in harmony with the divine order.

This idea parallels the *Sabbath rest*, a completion of creation that signifies spiritual fulfillment. In *John 16:24*, Jesus invites us to ask in His name and promises that we will receive, bringing our joy to completion. This rest, this peace, comes from the realization of the truth that has been sought and found. It reflects the joy of understanding and the fulfillment of the soul's deepest longings. This is echoed in the parable from *Matthew 13:44*, where the kingdom of heaven is like treasure hidden in a field, and when the man finds it, he joyfully gives up everything to possess it.

The *Bhagavad Gita* (18.63) invites a reflection on this process, saying, *"Thus, I have explained to you this knowledge that is more secret than all secrets. Ponder over it deeply, and then do as you wish."* This resonates with the seeker's journey in Saying 94, where the act of finding truth leads to a period of mastery, and ultimately, peace. Similarly, the *Chandogya Upanishad* (8.7.1) states, *"The Self is to be realized. The Self is to be heard of, to be reflected on, to be meditated upon."* Here, the realization of the divine self mirrors the process of seeking and finding truth, a journey that culminates in inner peace.

Mystical writers like St. Teresa of Avila in *Interior Castle* describe the soul's progression through stages of self-discovery, ultimately resting in God's presence. Meister Eckhart, too, speaks of the "Birth of the Word" within the soul, a moment of realization that brings profound peace and fulfillment.

The seeking, finding, and marveling are not merely external pursuits, but reflections of the inner journey. We are co-creators in this participatory universe, shaping our reality with our thoughts, intentions, and actions. When we align our hearts and minds with divine truth, we become part of the living universe, which responds to our deepest yearnings. The rest that follows is the peace that comes from understanding our unity with the divine.

And in this journey, there is the divine name—*I AM*. This name, revealed in the burning bush to Moses in Exodus 3:14, signifies the eternal, ever-present essence of God. *I AM* is not just a title but a profound declaration of the divine's essence, representing the fullness of being itself. It is the name that encompasses all creation and existence, for it is the source from which all things emerge and to which all things return. As we seek and knock, we are engaging with this living, dynamic force, and in doing so, we become more attuned to the reality of *I AM*—the foundation of all being.

Thus, Saying 94 is an invitation to actively seek and participate in the divine order of the universe, understanding that our thoughts and actions shape the world around us. As we seek truth, we come into alignment with the eternal *I AM*, the foundation of all life, and rest in the peace that flows from this divine union.

I am not a visitor to the Kingdom—I am its child.

⤲⚜⚜⤳

Saying 95: The Gift Beyond Return

Jesus said, "If you have money, do not lend it at interest, but give it to one from whom you will not get it back." (95)

True generosity does not calculate returns; it flows like a river, seeking no recompense but the joy of giving. To lend with the expectation of gain is to entangle oneself in the world's economy, but to give freely is to enter the divine economy—the wealth of the Kingdom, where love, not gold, is the true currency.

Socrates, in his wisdom, spoke of the nature of virtue, saying, *"The greatest way to live with honor in this world is to be what we pretend to be."* If one gives with the pretense of generosity but secretly desires profit, the gift is tainted. But to give with an open heart, expecting nothing in return, is to embody the highest form of virtue.

Jesus' teaching echoes the wisdom of Proverbs:

"Whoever is generous to the poor lends to the Lord, and He will repay him for his deed." (Proverbs 19:17)

To give without expectation is to trust in the abundance of God. It is to see wealth not as possession, but as provision—something to pass through our hands for the benefit of others. As Swami Prabhavananda put it, *"The more we give, the more we are filled. When the self is forgotten in service, the divine fills the heart."*

The world may call such giving foolish, but the wise know: what is freely given is never lost. It is sown in the unseen fields of eternity, where the harvest is immeasurable.

Luke 6:34-35 – "And if you lend to those from whom you expect repayment, what credit is that to you? Even sinners lend to sinners, expecting to be repaid in full. But love your enemies, do good to them, and lend to them without expecting to get anything back."

Matthew 5:42 – "Give to the one who asks you, and do not turn away from the one who wants to borrow from you."

❧❧❧

Saying 96: The Transformative And Hidden Power Of The Kingdom Of God

"Jesus said, 'The Father's kingdom can be compared to a woman who took a little yeast and hid it in flour. She made it into large loaves of bread. Anyone who has ears to hear should hear!'" (96)

This parable speaks to the subtle yet powerful work of the Kingdom, which often begins in small, unseen ways and gradually grows into something greater. The yeast, a small and hidden agent, transforms the dough in ways that are not immediately visible but are essential to the final result. In the same way, the Kingdom of God, though it may seem small or insignificant at first, has the power to radically transform lives and the world around us. The divine presence works silently, often in hidden ways, to bring about change and growth.

The action of the woman hiding the yeast in the flour mirrors the idea that the divine operates within the fabric of ordinary life, transforming it from within. This concept aligns with the mystical idea of divine immanence—God is present within all things, working through the smallest of actions and moments to bring about greater spiritual reality. As the yeast spreads through the dough, it represents the slow but steady growth of the Kingdom in the heart of the seeker, expanding from the inner self into the outer world.

This concept is echoed in *Matthew 13:33*, where Jesus shares a similar parable: *"The kingdom of heaven is like yeast that a woman took and mixed into about sixty pounds of flour until it worked all through the dough."* The emphasis here is on the hidden yet powerful nature of the Kingdom—it is not always immediately apparent, but it is transformative and persistent.

In *Bhagavad Gita* 10.20, Krishna speaks of his immanence, saying, *"I am the Self, O Gudakesha, seated in the hearts of all creatures. I am the beginning, the middle, and the end of all beings."* This aligns with the parable's message that divine presence, though hidden, is present within all creation, working subtly to bring forth transformation. The divine essence, though small and hidden in its initial form, has the power to shape all things.

Similarly, the *Chandogya Upanishad* (3.14.1) teaches that the Self is the ultimate source of all creation: *"In the beginning, this world was the Self alone, and it became this universe. It created everything out of itself. From the Self, it became the creation."* This echoes the transformation described in the parable—just as yeast transforms the dough from within, the divine presence transforms the world from within.

The hidden power of the yeast also mirrors the teachings of mystical Christian writers such as St. Teresa of Avila, who speaks of the soul's growth in stages, much like the slow, hidden process of yeast leavening bread. Meister Eckhart also speaks of the soul's transformation through the gradual, often imperceptible work of God within the heart.

The parable calls us to recognize that transformation is often an internal process. The small, seemingly insignificant actions we take in our daily lives can have profound and lasting effects, just as the small bit of yeast can leaven a whole batch of dough. We may not always see the immediate results, but the transformation is taking place, working within us and through us, bringing the Kingdom of God to fruition in the world.

As the woman hides the yeast in the flour, she does so quietly, without fanfare. Similarly, the work of the Kingdom can often be quiet and unnoticed, yet it is powerful. The parable invites us to trust that even in our smallest actions, the divine is at work, and in time, the fruit of that work will be made visible. *"Anyone who has ears to hear should hear!"* This call to attentiveness urges us to recognize the hidden divine presence in our lives, trusting that it is quietly transforming us, even when we cannot yet see the full effect.

Saying 97: The Hidden Spill: A Lesson In Divine Awareness

"Jesus said, 'The Father's kingdom can be compared to a woman carrying a jar of flour. While she was walking down a long road, the jar's handle broke and the flour spilled out behind her on the road. She didn't know it, and didn't realize there was a problem until she got home, put down the jar, and found it empty.'" (97)

This parable speaks to the hidden nature of spiritual transformation and how divine actions can unfold quietly, beyond our immediate awareness. The woman, walking with a jar of flour, unknowingly loses part of it as she walks. Only upon reaching her destination does she realize the jar is empty. The process of transformation, much like the spilling flour, often occurs without our conscious realization, revealing the quiet, persistent work of the divine within our lives.

The imagery of the woman walking down the long road suggests the journey of life, filled with both progress and disruption. The broken jar handle, a symbol of unexpected disruption, may represent moments in our spiritual lives when things feel out of control or incomplete. Yet even when we feel that something is lost, divine transformation continues. This teaches us that the Kingdom of God is not always immediately recognizable or predictable. The woman's realization only comes later, suggesting that spiritual growth may often go unnoticed in the moment, but is deeply felt as we reflect on the journey.

This parable also speaks to the unseen ways in which God is at work within us. In many mystical traditions, the idea that divine action can take place in subtle, imperceptible ways is central. For instance, in *Sufism*, it is said that God's presence can be hidden even in the smallest of moments, as Rumi expresses in his poetry, *"The wound is the place where the Light enters you."* What may seem like a loss or a mistake may actually be part of the divine process of inner transformation. The flour spilling out can thus be seen as a sign of spiritual nourishment that we may not immediately recognize but which ultimately enriches us.

Similarly, *Taoist* philosophy often speaks of the "flow" of life, which can be likened to the flour spilling from the jar. Just as the Tao flows effortlessly, transforming things without force or intention, so too does the divine work within us, moving quietly but powerfully. The *Tao Te Ching* reflects this when it says, *"The Tao never does anything, yet through it all things are done."* The woman, unaware of the flour spilling behind her, continues her journey, much as we may continue through life, unaware of the unseen divine actions shaping our path.

The parable also invites us to trust the unknowns of the Kingdom of God. Spiritual transformation is not always a process we can fully control or even understand in the moment. Like the woman, we may not realize how much has been lost or changed until we reach a moment of reflection. This can be comforting, as it reminds us that even in moments where we feel disconnected or uncertain, we are still part of a greater divine unfolding.

Ultimately, saying 97 is an invitation to trust that divine work is happening, even when it is invisible to us. It encourages us to continue the journey, knowing that spiritual transformation often occurs in ways we may not immediately notice, but that ultimately shape our lives in profound and mysterious ways. It is in those hidden, small actions—the spilling of flour, the quiet moments of grace—that the Kingdom of God is revealed.

❧❀❧

Saying 98: The Kingdom and the Sword of Understanding

Jesus said, "The Kingdom of the Father is like a man who wanted to kill a powerful man. He drew his sword in his house and struck it on the wall, so that the hand was wounded. Then the man who wanted to kill the powerful man took his sword and struck the other person, and the Kingdom was with him." (98)

This cryptic parable speaks of preparation, self-discipline, and the nature of true power. The man seeks to overthrow a mighty force, perhaps symbolizing ignorance, oppression, or the false rulers of the world. Before he can engage in the true battle, he must first test his own strength, and in doing so, he wounds himself. The wound signifies the cost of wisdom, the refining of one's understanding before taking action. Only then does he strike his opponent with certainty, and in that moment, he aligns himself with the Kingdom.

The philosopher Heraclitus spoke of a similar paradox in the struggle for wisdom:

"A man's character is his fate."

Before one can overcome the external world, one must master the inner self. The man's first strike against the wall is his initiation, his trial of discernment, much like the philosopher who tests ideas before speaking truth.

Plato, too, warned of acting before one is ready:

"The measure of a man is what he does with power."

To wield truth as a weapon, one must be prepared for its consequences. The hand that bears the sword must first feel its weight, just as Socrates, before challenging Athenian society, first tested his own wisdom against the oracle's pronouncement.

And in Nietzsche's words:

"Whoever fights monsters should see to it that in the process he does not become a monster."

The man in the parable does not strike blindly; he wounds himself first, ensuring he is fit for the fight. This is the path of the Kingdom—not reckless destruction, but measured action born of discipline and inner struggle.

Thus, the parable warns us: Before you fight against the darkness of the world, be sure you have faced the darkness within. Only then will the Kingdom be with you.

Matthew 10:34 –
"Do not think that I have come to bring peace to the earth. I have not come to bring peace, but a sword."

Guru Granth Sahib, Ang 2: "The mind is like a powerful king, and the body is the house of the soul. The king must be controlled by wisdom and love, not by violence or force."

Dhammapada, Verse 223: "Hatred does not cease by hatred, but by love alone is it healed. This is an ancient and eternal law."

❧❀❧

Saying 99: Jesus' True Family: The Will of the Father

The disciples said to him: Your brothers and your mother are standing outside. He said to them: Those here who do the will of my Father, these are my brothers and my mother; they are the ones who will enter into the kingdom of my Father. (99)

In this saying, Jesus radically redefines the notion of family, shifting it away from biological ties toward spiritual communion:

"Those here who do the will of my Father are my brothers and my mother. They are the ones who will enter the kingdom of my Father."

This moment speaks to a profound spiritual truth—that true belonging in the divine family is not based on blood, ancestry, or cultural inheritance, but on alignment with the will of God. The disciples' mention of Jesus' mother and brothers standing outside contrasts with those who are inside, gathered around him. The true "inside" is not a physical location, but an inner orientation toward the Divine.

To do the will of the Father is not merely to obey external commandments, but to live from a heart awakened to divine love and truth. In the mystical tradition, this corresponds to a soul that has been refined, emptied of ego, and made receptive to the indwelling presence of God. It is a heart that listens deeply, that moves in harmony with the eternal Logos.

The Gospel of Thomas consistently emphasizes gnosis—direct experiential knowledge of the Divine. In this context, "doing the will" is not about moralism but about attunement. It means letting go of the false self, of worldly identity, and entering into union with the living source. When that happens, one becomes not only a follower of Christ but a living expression of divine sonship.

Moreover, this saying challenges all rigid notions of identity—be they family, status, or institutional religion. The kingdom of the Father is not inherited by proximity or pedigree, but discovered through inner transformation. Those who awaken to the truth of their being, and live accordingly, become part of the eternal family—a community not bound by blood, but by light.

Thus, Jesus' response is not a rejection of his earthly family, but an invitation to all:

To be his brother, his sister, his mother, is to become one with his mission and his mind— bearing divine life, birthing love into the world. This is the true path into the Kingdom.

Saying 100: The Divine and the Temporal—Rendering to Caesar and to God

They showed Jesus a gold piece and said to him: Caesar's men demand tribute from us. He said to them: What belongs to Caesar, give to Caesar; what belongs to God, give to God; and what is mine, give it to me. (100)

Jesus' response to the question of paying taxes to Caesar is one of his most famous teachings, revealing his profound wisdom in navigating both political and spiritual realities. When the Pharisees and Herodians posed this question, they sought to trap him—if he endorsed paying the tax, he would alienate those who resisted Roman rule; if he rejected it, he could be accused of sedition. Yet his response transcends the political entanglement, pointing instead to a higher truth.

Historical Context: The Tax and Roman Rule

At the time of Jesus, Judea was under Roman occupation, and the imperial tax was a symbol of subjugation. Many Jews resented paying tribute to Caesar, seeing it as an affront to their religious and national identity. Groups like the Zealots outright opposed it, viewing resistance as a divine duty, while the Herodians and Sadducees cooperated with Rome for political stability. The coin used for this tax bore the image of Emperor Tiberius and an inscription declaring him the "son of the divine Augustus." This was offensive to Jewish monotheism, as it suggested Caesar's divinity.

By saying, *"Give to Caesar what belongs to Caesar, and to God what belongs to God,"* Jesus acknowledges the legitimacy of earthly authorities but simultaneously affirms that ultimate allegiance belongs to God alone. This was not a simple endorsement of taxation but a radical call to discern what truly belongs to God—one's soul, devotion, and ultimate loyalty.

Biblical Insights: The Image and the Imago Dei (Image of God)

The deeper meaning of Jesus' teaching lies in the contrast between the coin and the human soul. The denarius bore the image of Caesar, meaning it rightfully belonged to him. But humanity, made in the image of God (*imago Dei*), belongs to God. This echoes **Genesis 1:27**, *"So God created mankind in His own image, in the image of God He created them."* If the coin is Caesar's because it bears his image, then we are God's because we bear His image.

This statement subtly shifts the question from a political debate to a spiritual one: *What do you render to God?* Jesus does not challenge the payment of taxes but challenges his listeners to consider their deeper obligation—to give their very being to God, the true King.

Historical Echoes: The Church and the State

Throughout history, this teaching has been pivotal in discussions on the relationship between religion and government.

Augustine later built on this idea in *The City of God*, distinguishing between the "earthly city" (governments, politics) and the "heavenly city" (God's kingdom), urging Christians to live in both realms while prioritizing divine allegiance.

Thomas More, before his execution by King Henry VIII, paraphrased this teaching, refusing to recognize the king as the supreme head of the Church: *"I die the King's good servant, but God's first."*

Martin Luther emphasized the "two kingdoms doctrine," suggesting that Christians live under both secular and divine rule but owe ultimate obedience to God.

The Call to Discernment

Jesus' response is not just about taxes—it is about recognizing the limits of earthly power. Governments may claim taxes, laws, and even lives, but they cannot claim the soul. His words call us to reflect:

What in our lives belongs to the world, and what belongs to God?

Are we giving our true selves to God, or have we allowed worldly concerns to claim our devotion?

Ultimately, Jesus' teaching affirms that while we may live under earthly rulers, our true citizenship is in the kingdom of God (*Philippians 3:20*).

Chapter 12

Parables and Mystical Teachings (Sayings 101-110)

Saying 101: Beyond Flesh: A Higher Love

Jesus said, "Those who do not hate their [father] and their mother as I do cannot be [disciples] of me. And those who [do not] love their [father and] their mother as I do cannot be [disciples of] me. For my mother [. . .] But my true [mother] gave me life." (101)

Saying 101 in the **Gospel of Thomas** has been a subject of significant scholarly debate and interpretation, largely due to its challenging and seemingly paradoxical language. Here's an overview of how scholars have approached this saying:

Textual Interpretation and Scholarly Viewpoints

1. The Theme of Radical Discipleship:

This saying is often interpreted as illustrating the radical nature of Jesus' call to discipleship. It emphasizes a total reorientation of one's life toward spiritual commitment, where even familial ties are subordinated to the call of the divine. The language of "hating" one's parents is hyperbolic, meant to highlight the intensity of the commitment required to follow Jesus.

Scholars like Elaine Pagels and April DeConick suggest that this saying may be seen as expressing the tension between the worldly attachments (family, society) and the spiritual life. The phrase "those who do not hate their father and mother" should not be understood literally but rather as a way to express the supremacy of spiritual commitment over earthly bonds.

2. The Role of the Family in the Early Christian Context:

In the early Christian context, there was often a conflict between the family unit and the new Christian community. The saying resonates with the idea that family loyalties might conflict with the demands of the new faith, which could require separation from traditional social structures. In this sense, the Gospel of Thomas aligns with other early Christian texts, such as the Gospel of Luke (14:26), where Jesus calls his followers to "hate" their families, which has similarly been understood as a call for absolute devotion to God, rather than a literal command to despise one's family.

John Dominic Crossan has interpreted such sayings as reflecting a purposive anti-establishment sentiment within early Christian communities, where followers were often alienated from their families because of their faith.

3. Spiritual Birth and the True Mother:

The second part of this saying is equally rich in theological implications. Jesus says, "For my mother [...] But my true mother gave me life." This part challenges conventional views of motherhood and redefines what it means to be "born" and "given life." Scholars like Thomas B. Slater and James M. Robinson argue that the "true mother" may refer to the spiritual birth one receives through the teachings of Jesus or through the divine wisdom, symbolized by the feminine aspect of God (often associated with the Holy Spirit in Christian mysticism).

The idea of a "true mother" might also connect with the notion that discipleship in Thomas involves a spiritual rebirth rather than a literal, biological one. This suggests that Jesus' own birth, traditionally understood as physical, is being reinterpreted as a spiritual birth in the Gospel of Thomas, a theme that resonates with other Gnostic texts that stress the transformative and inward nature of salvation.

4. Gnostic Influence and the Wisdom Tradition:

Many scholars emphasize that the Gospel of Thomas is heavily influenced by Gnostic thought, and this saying is an example of Gnostic teachings about inner enlightenment and spiritual awakening. In Gnostic traditions, the material world (which includes familial relationships) is often seen as inferior to the spiritual realm. The statement about the "true mother" could be a reference to Sophia, the divine feminine figure in Gnostic cosmology, who is often associated with wisdom and spiritual enlightenment. This would align with the Gnostic idea that the "true" spiritual life is not tied to the material world but transcends it.

Bart Ehrman has noted that sayings like these reflect a Gnostic worldview, where the rejection of the material world (symbolized by familial relationships) is necessary to achieve spiritual enlightenment and escape from the confines of the physical, earthly existence.

5. The Significance of Love and Hate in Thomas:

The dichotomy between "hate" and "love" is a powerful device used throughout the Gospel of Thomas to express the tension between opposites and the necessity of choosing one's spiritual calling above all else. As scholars like Marcus Borg point out, this use of contrasting terms highlights the radical nature of following Jesus, where a disciple is called to embrace a higher love (divine love) that transcends earthly ties.

Richard Bauckham and E.P. Sanders both interpret these words as emphasizing the transcendent nature of divine love: a love that goes beyond human concepts of affection and familial loyalty. The emphasis is on following Jesus with a love that is detached from conventional, human expectations and relationships.

Key Themes in Interpretation:

1. **Radical Discipleship**: This saying calls for an extreme reordering of one's life, where earthly attachments are set aside for the pursuit of spiritual truth.
2. **Spiritual Birth and the True Mother**: The true mother is seen as the force or source of spiritual life, likely symbolizing the spiritual rebirth that comes through wisdom or divine knowledge.
3. **The Rejection of Earthly Bonds**: This saying aligns with the ascetic and spiritual worldview found in many early Christian and Gnostic texts, where material or familial attachments must be abandoned in favor of the divine call.
4. **Wisdom and Sophia**: The reference to the "true mother" can also be seen as pointing to a deeper, more mystical understanding of the feminine aspect of God or wisdom, which gives spiritual life.

Conclusion:

Saying 101 is complex and challenging because of its radical language, but it offers profound insights into the nature of discipleship, spiritual rebirth, and the rejection of earthly attachments in favor of a higher, divine love. Scholars generally interpret it as a call to prioritize one's spiritual journey above all worldly concerns, even family, and to embrace the deeper, hidden spiritual truths that transcend the physical realm.

Proverbs 8:1-4, 22-23
"Does not wisdom call out? Does not understanding raise her voice? On the heights along the way, where the paths meet, she takes her stand; beside the gate leading into the city, at the entrance, she cries aloud: 'To you, O people, I call out; I raise my voice to all mankind... The Lord brought me forth as the first of his works, before his deeds of old; I was formed long ages ago, at the very beginning, when the world came to be.'"

Matthew 23:37
"Jerusalem, Jerusalem, you who kill the prophets and stone those sent to you, how often I have longed to gather your children together, as a hen gathers her chicks under her wings, and you were not willing."

Saying 102: The Gatekeepers of Falsehood

Jesus said, "Woe to the pharisees, for they are like a dog sleeping in the manger of oxen, for neither does he eat nor does he let the oxen eat." (102)

Jesus' rebuke of the Pharisees in this saying is striking in its imagery. He likens them to a **dog lying in the manger of oxen**, blocking access to the very nourishment that sustains life. The oxen, which should be feeding, are denied their sustenance—not because the dog consumes it, but because it **hoards what it neither needs nor values**. This powerful metaphor condemns those who hold authority over spiritual matters but misuse it, keeping others from the truth while failing to benefit from it themselves.

The Historical Context: The Pharisees as Religious Gatekeepers

In the time of Jesus, the Pharisees were among the religious elite, known for their strict adherence to the Law. While many were sincere in their devotion, Jesus often criticized them for legalism without love, knowledge without wisdom. They claimed to hold the keys to divine truth, yet their rigid interpretations and self-righteousness often obstructed others from encountering God's grace. This aligns with Jesus' other rebukes:

> **"Woe to you, teachers of the law and Pharisees, you hypocrites! You shut the door of the kingdom of heaven in people's faces. You yourselves do not enter, nor will you let those enter who are trying to."** *(Matthew 23:13)*

Here, the "dog in the manger" is not merely indifferent—it is actively obstructing. The Pharisees, in their zeal for the law, had become barriers rather than bridges to the divine.

Philosophical Parallels: Hoarding Knowledge Without Illumination

This image resonates beyond its immediate religious context. In philosophy, Socrates often warned against those who pretended to have wisdom but lacked true understanding. The dog in the manger represents:

- **The false teacher**—one who claims wisdom but does not embody it.
- **The miserly scholar**—one who hoards knowledge but does not share its benefits.
- **The gatekeeper of tradition**—who resists new understanding out of fear or pride.

This is the paradox of **intellectual and spiritual stagnation**—to hold power over truth but refuse to engage with it deeply, nor allow others to do so.

Mystical Insights: The Selfish Ego as the Dog

In a mystical sense, the dog in the manger represents the ego, which clings to control but refuses transformation. The Pharisees clung to the letter of the Law while missing the Spirit behind it. Similarly, the unawakened soul resists surrendering to divine truth, blocking its own path to enlightenment. The mystic Angelus Silesius wrote:

> *"The rose has no why; it blooms because it blooms."*

True spiritual knowledge is not about possession or exclusion—it is about **participation in divine life**. The dog hoards the manger as though it were its own, forgetting that true sustenance is freely given to those who seek it with open hearts.

The Call to Inner Transformation

This saying serves as a warning against the temptation to control access to spiritual truth. It challenges us:

- Are we open to divine wisdom, or do we hoard our own understanding?
- Do we act as gatekeepers, hindering others from encountering God?
- Do we truly partake of the spiritual nourishment before us, or do we simply guard it without transformation?

Jesus' rebuke of the Pharisees was not just a condemnation—it was a call to let go of control and enter into the divine feast. The table is set, the food is abundant—but only the humble will eat.

⁂⁂⁂

Saying 103: Preparedness and Vigilance – The Parable of the Bandits

Jesus said, "Blessed is the man who recognizes [which] district the brigands are going to enter, so as to arise, gather (the forces of) his domain, and arm himself before they enter." (103)

Jesus speaks here of a wisdom that belongs to the watchful heart—the one who discerns where danger lies and prepares accordingly. But this is no mere caution against earthly thieves; it is a call to **spiritual vigilance**, an awakening to the subtle forces that seek to rob the soul of its light.

The Mystic's Watchfulness

The **bandits** in this parable are not only external threats but also the internal forces of ignorance, desire, and illusion. Just as a city must guard its gates against invaders, so must the seeker guard the entrance to the **inner temple**. This echoes the wisdom of the Buddha, who warned against the restless mind:

> **"The mind is everything. What you think, you become."** *(Dhammapada 1:1)*

Buddha, like Jesus, taught that awakening requires vigilance. The enlightened one is the one who watches, who does not sleep in the illusions of the world but keeps the inner lamp burning. In the *Dhammapada*, we find a striking parallel:

> **"The vigilant do not die; the heedless are as if already dead."** *(Dhammapada 21:1)*

To be awake is to be prepared for the moment of trial, to see where the forces of ignorance may seek entry. Jesus calls the disciple to a state of continual spiritual readiness—a mind clear, a heart steady, a soul unshaken.

Defending the Soul's Inner Sanctuary

But what are the bandits that come in the night? They may be the subtle distractions of the world—the illusions of wealth, status, fear, and attachment—or the doubts that creep in and steal the peace of the soul. The mystic knows that the battle is not fought with the hands but with the spirit.

- The **bandits** are the forces that separate us from the Divine.
- The **defenses** are discernment, wisdom, and inner peace.
- The **watchtower** is the awakened consciousness that sees before it is too late.

This is why Buddha taught the Middle Way—neither indulgence nor avoidance, but a path of clear seeing. In the same way, Jesus teaches that the wise disciple must anticipate the trials of the spirit, not be caught unaware when the illusions of the world come to claim their due.

The Call to Wakefulness

Jesus' words here are a call to awareness, presence, and preparation. The enlightened soul does not wait for suffering to come before seeking wisdom. It stands ready, knowing that the forces of the world will test its light.

To be prepared is to see with the eye of the spirit, to anticipate the trials before they arrive, and to be anchored in truth when the winds of illusion blow.

For the unwatchful soul, the bandits come in the night and take what is most precious. For the vigilant soul, there is no fear—for it is already standing in the light.

☙❊❧

Saying 104: The Bridegroom's Presence – A Mystical Reflection on Fasting and Prayer

They said [to him]: Come, let us pray today and fast. Jesus said: What then is the sin that I have done, or in what have I been overcome? But when the bridegroom comes out from the bridal chamber, then let them fast and pray. (104)

In this profound saying, Jesus responds to the call for fasting and prayer not with rejection, but with a call to awareness of the present moment, of the divine presence that is ever near. His words echo the mystical understanding that fasting and prayer are not merely rituals for penitence or defeat, but expressions of an awakened heart attuned to the Bridegroom—the Divine Presence in our midst.

The Bridegroom's Arrival

The figure of the Bridegroom is an image drawn from ancient biblical wisdom, representing the divine union between the soul and the Divine. In mysticism, the Bridegroom is often understood as the soul's longing for God—a relationship of love and oneness. Jesus, speaking as the Bridegroom, reminds us that when the Divine Presence is known to be near, when the soul recognizes the living Christ within, then fasting and prayer transform into an experience of union rather than separation.

As the Buddha said:

"When the mind is pure, joy follows like a shadow that never leaves." (Dhammapada 210)

This joy, akin to the bliss of divine union, transforms fasting and prayer from acts of striving to moments of pure communion. When we are with the Bridegroom, when we recognize the Divine within us, these practices are not efforts to bridge the gap between us and God, but celebrations of the presence of the Divine in the here and now.

The Mystery of Fasting and Prayer

Fasting and prayer are not measures of worthiness, nor are they reactions to sin. They are expressions of the soul's longing for union with the divine. In this teaching, Jesus shifts the focus: it's not about the absence of food or words, but about the presence of the Bridegroom—the presence of love, the presence of grace.

"What is the sin that I have committed, or wherein have I been defeated?"

In this declaration, Jesus challenges the very notion of separation. In the mystical journey, there is no sin that separates us from God, for we are always one with the Divine. The soul's journey is a return to recognition of that unity. The act of fasting or prayer is a remembering, not a remedy for separation, but an invitation to draw near to the Divine that has always been with us.

The Sacred Union

When Jesus says, **"when the bridegroom comes out of the bridal chamber,"** he speaks of the moment of intimacy with the Divine. It is the mystical union between the soul and God. Just as the mystics speak of union in the divine light, so does Jesus here:

Rumi reminds us, "Your task is not to seek for love, but merely to seek and find all the barriers within yourself that you have built against it."
Saint Teresa of Avila calls this union a moment when the soul is embraced by God, not as a distant deity, but as an intimate, living presence: "It is not a matter of thinking; it is a matter of loving."

In that moment of union, the soul is not fasting out of hunger but fasting from the distractions of the world, praying not for what is missing but to be fully awake in the love and presence of the Divine.

The Path of Communion

The Bridegroom's presence calls us to a radical love—one that is not defined by separation or lack, but by the fullness of divine union. When we fast and pray, let it not be for penance but for the recognition of the Kingdom of God within us. The divine union is here, now, and our practices are a reflection of that living reality.

Thus, as Swami Prabhavananda states:
"In the stillness of the heart, the Divine speaks."

In the presence of the Bridegroom, fasting and prayer are not acts of deprivation, but acts of consciousness, in which we remember that the Bridegroom, the Divine Love, is always present within us, waiting to be acknowledged.

Saying 105: The Divine Union – Embracing the Sacred Marriage

Jesus said, "Whoever knows the father and the mother will be called the child of a harlot. But whoever knows the husband and the wife will be called the child of a harlot." (105)

In this cryptic saying, Jesus touches upon the sacred union of opposites, a union of the feminine and masculine energies that transcend conventional human categories. The language of the "father and mother," and "husband and wife," points to something much deeper—a mystical marriage, not of flesh, but of the soul's union with the Divine.

In the sacred tradition, the father represents the light of the masculine principle—the divine logos, the origin of wisdom, and the active force. The mother represents the wisdom of the feminine—the sacred Shekinah, the depths of grace, the embodied presence of love. These two energies together represent the fullness of the divine, a union that transcends duality and reveals the essence of all creation.

But when Jesus speaks of those who know the father and mother, he is pointing to the incomplete union of these forces in the lower realm—an understanding that is fragmented, not yet fully realized in the soul. To know these forces only in their external forms, without understanding the inward union of these energies, is to know them but in part, and thus, the soul remains untransformed. This is why Jesus says they are called the child of a harlot—a symbol of something broken, not yet whole.

On the other hand, when he speaks of knowing the husband and wife, he is referring to the union of Christ and the soul, where the divine masculine and feminine come together in the eternal marriage, where the soul is no longer fragmented but whole. In this divine union, the soul is reborn. It is not merely a relationship between two forces, but the union of the divine and the human, the eternal and the temporal, the light and the love.

This saying calls us to recognize that the path of true knowledge is not in the separation of the divine forces but in their holy marriage within our own being. The soul must become one with the Divine, not by fragmenting what is sacred, but by embracing the totality of the sacred union within itself. It is in this sacred marriage that the soul finds its true calling, for it is in this union that we become whole and enter the kingdom of God.

The Wisdom of the Mystics

In the wisdom of St. Teresa of Avila, we find a reflection of this union:

"The soul that is united with God is like a well-ordered marriage. The spirit in union with God becomes not a servant, but a beloved, and everything it does is a gesture of love."

Similarly, Hildegard of Bingen, a mystic of deep insight, reminds us of the sacredness of the Divine Feminine: "The soul who has known God has received a marriage gift, a ring of love, that is never lost. It is the seal of divinity upon us, a union that transcends time and space."

This union, the sacred marriage, is not merely a doctrinal belief, but a lived mystical reality that transforms the soul. It is the recognition that we are both the husband and the wife, both the masculine and the feminine, brought together in the eternal dance of divine love. In this union, we become whole, and in becoming whole, we are transformed into the image of the divine.

Thus, Jesus speaks not of judgment, but of the mystical awakening—an awakening to the divine marriage within, where the soul transcends duality and enters into the oneness of all being. The child born from this union is no longer a harlot, but a beloved of God, a reflection of divine love and unity.

"Stepping Into Unity As Divine Beings"

Saying 106: The Power of Unity: Becoming Sons of Man and Moving Mountains

Jesus said: When you make the two one, you will become sons of man, and when you say, 'Mountain, move away, it will move away.' (106)

In this striking saying, Jesus offers a profound teaching on the mystery of unity and the authority that arises from it. *"When you make the two one, you will become sons of man, and when you say: Mountain, move away, it will move away."* Here, unity is again the key—an inner reconciliation that brings forth the true nature of the human being as a child of the Divine.

To "make the two one" is to transcend the seeming opposites that divide the soul: spirit and body, inner and outer, above and below, masculine and feminine, heaven and earth. It is to return to the original wholeness that humanity once knew, a wholeness lost in the fragmentation of consciousness. When the soul integrates these polarities—when duality is overcome—there is no longer division within, and the fullness of divine power is realized.

Becoming "sons of man" is not simply about lineage; it is a mystical title. In the Semitic understanding, "Son of Man" signifies not only a human being but also a being who embodies the union of the human and the divine. It is the fullness of what it means to be truly human, living from the image and likeness of God within. In this state of realized unity, the soul moves beyond the ordinary limits of perception and action.

When Jesus speaks of moving mountains, he speaks of the authority that arises from this state of oneness. Mountains—symbols of the immovable, the impossible—can be moved because the soul, aligned with the Divine, is no longer hindered by separation. In union with the Source, the word spoken carries the creative power of God Himself. It is not by human will alone that such miracles occur, but through the channel of unity where the Divine will and the human heart are one.

This teaching echoes what Jesus said elsewhere: *"If you have faith as small as a mustard seed, you can say to this mountain, 'Move from here to there,' and it will move."* (Matthew 17:20). Faith, in this deeper sense, is not merely belief—it is a state of unified being, where no separation clouds the connection between the soul and God.

Thus, this saying invites us into a profound mystery: that the path to true authority, true faith, and true sonship is through the inner work of union. When the two are made one—when we live no longer divided against ourselves—we enter into the life of the Spirit, and the impossible becomes possible.

"Shepherd of the Heart"

Saying 107: The Parable of the Lost Sheep- God's Unwavering Love for the Lost

"Jesus said, 'The kingdom is like a shepherd who had a hundred sheep. When the largest one strayed, he left the ninety-nine and searched until he found it. After all his effort, he said to the sheep, 'I love you more than the ninety-nine.'" (107)

In this tender parable, Jesus speaks with the **compassionate heart of a mother**—a love that knows no bounds and **seeks out the lost**, no matter how far they may wander. The story of the shepherd, who leaves the ninety-nine to search for the one who has strayed, is a story of **divine devotion**. This is a love that refuses to give up on any soul, no matter how lost or broken it may seem.

The kingdom of God, as Jesus describes it here, is not like a distant throne but like a mother's embrace—warm, welcoming, and always ready to draw near to the one who has wandered. God's love is the kind that moves toward us, even in our wandering. It is not a love that waits for us to be perfect, but one that goes to the depths to find us, just as a mother searches for her child when they are lost.

This parable speaks of God's constant and vigilant care, just as the shepherd watches over his flock. And when one is lost, the heart of the shepherd is not at rest until it is found. God's love is like that—it never grows weary of seeking, never grows faint in pursuit. Even if it takes the wandering one far from home, the shepherd will not rest until the lost is brought back into the fold.

In the words of the Book of Wisdom, we are reminded that God's love is persistent and patient, calling us back even when we stray:

"For you love all things that are, and loathe nothing that you have made; for what you hated, you would not have fashioned." (Wisdom 11:24). This divine love never ceases, never gives up, and never loathes the lost. It constantly seeks to restore, to bring the wanderer back to its loving embrace.

"The Vladimir Icon of the Mother of God"

The **heart of God** rejoices when the lost are found, as is written in Wisdom: **"But you have mercy on all, because you can do all things; and you overlook people's sins that they may repent."** (Wisdom 11:23). The Lord's mercy is infinite, and it is in this mercy that the lost are found and restored to their rightful place.

When we feel lost or distant, this **unwavering love** calls to us. It is an invitation to come home, an invitation to experience the **restoration** of our souls. The shepherd's words to the lost sheep, **"I love you more than the ninety-nine,"** are an echo of **God's perfect love**, which is always tender, always faithful, and **forever pursuing** us, no matter where we wander.

Even when we stray, God's love, as seen in the **mother's heart**, continues to seek us with steadfast patience, eager to gather us back into the fold. **"For you loved all things that are,"** the Book of Wisdom reminds us, and **we are never beyond the reach of God's loving pursuit**.

The parable emphasizes the unconditional love of God and the idea that no one is too insignificant to be sought after and loved. Even if someone strays from the path or becomes "lost," God is always willing to go the distance to bring them back into the fold.

ᖇᔑᖇᔑ

"The Sacred Chalice Within"

Saying 108: The Divine Union: Becoming One with the Living Word

Jesus said, "He who will drink from my mouth will become like me. I myself shall become he, and the things that are hidden will be revealed to him." (108)

This saying speaks to the transformative power of direct spiritual communion with the Divine. "Drinking from my mouth" is symbolic of receiving divine wisdom and understanding directly from Jesus (the divine teacher). This act leads to becoming one with him and experiencing a profound inner transformation. The "things that are hidden" refer to deeper truths, divine mysteries, and enlightenment that are revealed through spiritual union.

> *John 6:53-58: "Very truly I tell you, unless you eat the flesh of the Son of Man and drink his blood, you have no life in you."* This verse reflects the idea of intimate communion with Jesus, receiving his divine essence and wisdom.

> *Matthew 11:25-27: "At that time Jesus declared, 'I thank you, Father, Lord of heaven and earth, that you have hidden these things from the wise and understanding and revealed them to little children.'"* Jesus speaks of hidden knowledge being revealed to those who are spiritually receptive.

These sayings reflect a deep mystical and spiritual understanding of the nature of the Kingdom, the hidden treasures of divine wisdom, and the transformative process of spiritual union with the Divine.

> *1 John 1:5 (KJV):*
> *"This then is the message which we have heard of him, and declare unto you, that God is light, and in him is no darkness at all."*

Beholding the Divine in the Heavens

What you are about to witness is not merely a photograph, but a sacred moment—a theophany captured in time. On a quiet evening in Avondale, Colorado, my camera was guided to the sky, where the Almighty chose to reveal Himself in transcendent form. In this image, the Triune God manifests visibly: from left to right, the radiant Holy Spirit shines forth in hues of heavenly light; Jesus, the Son of Man and Son of God, appears resplendent; and the Heavenly Father is enthroned upon a luminous chariot—a dove of ineffable glory, the radiant vehicle of divine majesty.

This photograph is a testimony. It bears witness to a mystery far beyond the lens, and yet is made lovingly visible to the heart that seeks. May your spirit be stirred as you gaze upon it.

❧❀❧

*" Dunston, J.C. (2015) "Transcendent Majesty:
The Radiant Throne of Divine Splendor"*

Saying 109: The Parable of the Hidden Treasure: Unrecognized Value

Jesus said, "The kingdom can be compared to someone who had a treasure [hidden] in their field. [They] didn't know about it. After they died, they left it to their son. The son didn't know it either. He took the field and sold it. The buyer plowed the field, [found] the treasure, and began to loan money at interest to whomever they wanted." (109)

Jesus presents a parable of hidden value, a story that speaks to the unrecognized treasures of the Kingdom, waiting patiently to be discovered. In this tale, the treasure lies buried in a field, and the one who owns the land—unaware of its worth—sells the field, leaving the treasure untouched. Only after the transaction does the hidden wealth come to light, and it is this wealth that transforms the buyer's life, giving them the power to lend and shape fortunes.

This story speaks to the divine truth hidden within each of us—the profound treasure of the Kingdom of Heaven that we often fail to recognize in our everyday lives. God's

225

presence within us, though eternal and precious, is sometimes veiled from our sight until the moment of revelation. The field is like the soul, and the treasure is the divine gift—the indwelling spirit of the Creator, waiting to be unearthed and brought to life.

How often do we overlook the sacred treasures within our own hearts? The wisdom of the ages, the potential for divine union, is buried beneath layers of distraction, ignorance, and material pursuit. And yet, this treasure is there, waiting to be discovered by those who, like the buyer in the parable, are willing to dig deep and till the soil of their hearts, seeking the hidden gems of wisdom, love, and truth that await them.

In the words of the mystic John of the Cross, we are reminded of the hidden nature of divine truths:

"The soul that knows its own inner depths knows how to appreciate the treasure of God's love." Just as the buyer in the parable unknowingly purchases a field that holds a hidden treasure, so too do we sometimes find ourselves unaware of the spiritual riches that reside deep within us.

The son in the parable inherits the field, but does not recognize the treasure until it is unearthed. In this, we are reminded of the spiritual inheritance we receive—sometimes without knowing its value—yet it is there, ready to be discovered in due time. As the treasure is found, it is brought to life in the hands of one who can see its worth and use it wisely. This is the divine wisdom that comes to us when we are ready to receive it, transforming our lives and allowing us to live in alignment with the truth.

The treasure of the Kingdom is often hidden in the simplest of places: in acts of love, in moments of stillness, and in the quiet whispers of the soul. As the buyer loans money to others, so too are we called to share the treasures of the spirit, to give freely of the wisdom and love we have received, passing on the divine riches to others, enriching their lives as well.

In the words of Swami Vivekananda, we are reminded that *"the treasure is hidden in the heart of each person."* Yet, it is through diligent searching, through deep contemplation and prayer, that we come to discover the infinite wealth of God's grace. This hidden treasure is the divine presence, always available to us, waiting to be found and cherished.

And when it is unearthed, the world is transformed. We are no longer slaves to the mundane, for we have accessed the divine currency of the Kingdom, rich in eternal truth, love, and light. *"Seek first the Kingdom of God, and all else will be added unto you."* The treasure we discover within is not just for us alone, but for the world, to be shared and to bring forth the abundant life that Jesus promised.

Saying 110: Renouncing the World: The Call to Detachment

Jesus said, "Let one who has found the world, and has become wealthy, renounce the world." (110)

Jesus teaches us that true wealth is not found in the accumulation of material things, but in the renunciation of worldly attachments. "Let one who has found the world, and has become wealthy, renounce the world," He says, guiding us to a deeper understanding of the spiritual wealth that lies beyond the fleeting treasures of earthly existence.

This resonates deeply with the story in the Gospel of Matthew (19:16-24), where a rich young man approaches Jesus, asking, "Teacher, what good thing must I do to get eternal life?" Jesus replies, telling him to keep the commandments. The man asks, "Which ones?" and Jesus lists the commandments. Then the young man says, "All these I have kept. What do I still lack?" Jesus, looking at him with love, says, "If you want to be perfect, go, sell your possessions and give to the poor, and you will have treasure in heaven. Then come, follow me."

But when the young man hears this, he went away sad, because he had great wealth. Jesus, looking at His disciples, then declares, "Truly I tell you, it is hard for someone who is rich to enter the kingdom of heaven. Again I tell you, it is easier for a camel to go through the eye of a needle than for someone who is rich to enter the kingdom of God."

This story speaks to the danger of attachment to material wealth and the challenge of letting go of what binds us to the world. True renunciation, as Jesus teaches, is not just about giving up possessions, but about relinquishing the inner attachment to them—the desire to hold onto them as a source of identity and security. The rich young man represents all of us who may hold tightly to the things of this world, not realizing that what we cling to often keeps us from the Kingdom of Heaven.

Eastern wisdom, too, teaches the same truth about attachment. In the Bhagavad Gita, Lord Krishna speaks to the importance of non-attachment and the idea of living in the world but not being of it:

"One who is not attached to the fruits of his work, and who acts with a pure heart, is free from bondage and attains the ultimate peace." (Bhagavad Gita 5:12)

Similarly, the Buddha taught in the Dhammapada, "The one who is free from attachment to the world, who does not cling to its pleasures, is the one who has found peace." This aligns perfectly with Jesus' call to renounce worldly desires, for it is only through letting go that we can enter into the fullness of divine life.

True wealth is not measured by what we accumulate, but by what we are willing to release. As Paul Brunton wisely wrote, "The path to realization is one of letting go, of yielding, of surrendering the false self in order to reveal the divine self." It is when we can let go of our attachment to the things of the world—wealth, status, possessions—that we open ourselves to the Kingdom of Heaven, the realm of spiritual fulfillment.

When we renounce the world, we are not abandoning it in the sense of rejecting life, but rather liberating ourselves from the false identification with it. We come to understand that the treasures of the soul are far richer than anything the world can offer. The wealth of the spirit is eternal, and it is only when we release our grip on material things that we can truly embrace the abundant life Jesus promises—life in union with God.

Thus, Jesus' teaching is a call to liberation—to free ourselves from the chains of materialism, to walk in the world but remain detached from it, and to seek first the Kingdom of God, where our true treasure lies.

> **Materialism vs. Spiritualism:** The saying invites a reflection on the tension between materialism and spiritualism. It challenges individuals to examine their priorities and question whether their pursuit of material wealth might be hindering their deeper spiritual growth. It poses the question of whether true wealth lies in acquiring more possessions or in nurturing one's inner life and connection with the divine.

> **Attachment and Freedom:** The teaching on renunciation suggests that attachment to material things can imprison the soul, limiting one's freedom and potential. Renouncing the world is seen as a path to true freedom, where the soul is no longer bound by fleeting desires but is free to seek eternal truths.

Chapter 13

Conclusion and the Final Sayings (Sayings 111-114)

Saying 111: Eternal Life Through the Living One

"Jesus said: The heavens and the earth will be folded away before you, and the Living One, emerging from the source of Life, will never experience death or fear. For those who find their true selves, the world is unworthy of them." (111)

In this profound saying, Jesus reveals the nature of eternal life. To live from the **Living One**, the essence of God, is to enter into a timeless state beyond the physical world. This eternal life is not something we attain in a distant future, but something we can experience in the present moment—a deep connection to the divine essence that permeates all things.

Deepak Chopra, a modern spiritual teacher, writes, "You are not the body, you are not the mind. You are the universe itself, expressing itself as a human being." Here, Chopra emphasizes the idea that the soul, our true essence, is far greater than the body. The body is but a vessel for the soul, a temporary expression of the eternal. The Living One is not something external to us, but something that dwells within—a source of boundless energy and life.

Chopra also teaches that the universe is fundamentally interconnected, and that everything, including human consciousness, is part of the divine flow. In his words, "The more you align with the infinite, the more your life becomes a reflection of the divine." Living from the Living One is about recognizing our oneness with the eternal, understanding that the divine essence within us is not subject to death or decay. It is a part of the timeless flow of creation, a life that transcends the material world.

This teaching echoes the words of Jesus, who says that "whoever lives from the Living One won't see death." When we live from the Living One, we are no longer confined to the limitations of the body or the fleeting nature of the material world. We are in union with the divine essence, which is eternal and indestructible.

As Chopra often points out, our consciousness is the gateway to this eternal life. In his teachings, he says, "You are not your mind, you are the awareness behind the mind." This awareness is the Living One—the eternal life of God within us. By recognizing our true nature, we awaken to the divine truth that, in Christ's words, "the heavens and the earth will roll up in front of you"—because, in the end, it is not the material world that defines us. It is the divine essence that animates all of creation, the Living One that dwells within us and in everything around us.

As we become more attuned to the divine, we realize that "whoever finds themselves, of them the world isn't worthy." The world of attachment and ego holds no power over us when we are anchored in the Living One, the eternal source of life. And as we live from this place of deep connection to the divine, we no longer fear death, for we know that we are part of the eternal flow of life, beyond time and space, beyond birth and death.

Saying 112: The Interdependence of Flesh and Soul

Jesus said, "Woe to the flesh that depends on the soul; woe to the soul that depends on the flesh." (112)

In this profound statement, Jesus invites us to explore the delicate dance between the soul and the body, reminding us that true life transcends the physical realm. Flesh and soul are not meant to be in a state of dependency on each other, but rather in harmony, each serving its purpose in the grand design.

The flesh, with its needs and desires, often seeks to control and dominate, forgetting the soul's infinite wisdom and connection to the divine. Yet, the soul, too, is vulnerable when it clings to the flesh, tying itself to temporal, material concerns that are fleeting and transient. True liberation comes when we learn to transcend both, understanding that the soul's true purpose is to reflect the divine, and the body's role is to serve as a vessel for this divine presence, not as an end in itself.

This teaching echoes the wisdom of Paul Brunton, who writes, "The soul is eternal, and the body is but a fleeting expression of it. To live in harmony is to understand that the body is the temple of the soul, not its master." The body is an instrument for the soul's work, a tool for the spirit to experience the world. When we make the body the focus, the soul suffers, and when we idolize the soul to the neglect of the body, we lose the beauty of embodied life.

Swami Prabhavananda also speaks to this in his reflections on the balance between the material and the spiritual, saying, "The soul is not bound by the body, but the body must be in service to the soul, guided by wisdom." This idea of balance between the spiritual and the material is key to understanding Jesus' warning. The soul is the source of our true life, while the body is a temporary expression of that life. When the soul depends on the body, it forgets its divine nature. When the body depends on the soul, it risks becoming detached from the world, neglecting the sacredness of earthly existence.

In both Christian and Eastern thought, the teaching suggests that detachment from worldly desires and over-attachment to physicality creates a misalignment. Jesus, in his infinite wisdom, directs us toward balance—the soul guiding the flesh, and the flesh honoring the soul. The proper relationship between the two creates an alignment with the divine flow of life, where the body serves as a vessel for divine expression, and the soul remains rooted in its eternal nature.

As we meditate on this saying, we are called to evaluate where we place our focus: Do we live too much for the body, or do we neglect the sacred role of the body in expressing divine life? By learning to live in harmony, we come closer to the truth of who we are— spiritual beings embodied in flesh, and yet not defined by it.

෧෯෪෨

Saying 113: The Hidden Kingdom: Already Among Us

His disciples said to him, "When will the kingdom come?"

"It won't come by looking for it. They won't say, 'Look over here!' or 'Look over there!' Rather, the Father's kingdom is already spread out over the earth, and people don't see it." (113)

His disciples said to him, "When will the kingdom come?"

Jesus replied, "It won't come by looking for it. They won't say, 'Look over here!' or 'Look over there!' Rather, the Father's kingdom is already spread out over the earth, and people don't see it."

The Kingdom of God is not something distant or far off. As Mary Magdalene in the Gospel of Mary reveals, it is a living presence within us, unfolding in each moment, guiding us not through outward appearances but through an inner knowing.

The Kingdom is already within you, within the deepest parts of your soul where the divine whispers to you. As Mary spoke of the light that resides within us, it is this inner light that connects us to the Father's Kingdom, not something we seek outside ourselves, but something we awaken to when we learn to listen with our hearts.

Jesus invites us to see this kingdom, not with our eyes alone, but through the eyes of the spirit. The world is filled with divine presence, but we must be present in the moment, in stillness, to recognize it.

Mary, ever the mystic, taught us that the Kingdom is within, and that the path to it is found through deep contemplation, love, and the surrendering of the ego. So, it is with gentle trust that we step into the Kingdom already here, in each breath, in each act of kindness, in each moment of awareness.

The Kingdom is now.

"Mary Magdalene: First Witness, Forgotten Voice"

Saying 114: "The Transformative Power of Divine Unity: Reconceiving Gender in the Kingdom"

"Simon Peter said to them, 'Let Mary leave us, for women are not worthy of life.' Jesus said, 'I myself shall lead her in order to make her male, so that she too may become a living spirit resembling you males. For every woman who makes herself male will enter the kingdom of heaven.'" (114)

This saying is often seen as controversial because it reflects the patriarchal views of the time. The statement by Simon Peter that "women are not worthy of life" echoes the gender biases that were prevalent in many ancient cultures. However, Jesus' reply seems to transcend this limitation, suggesting that spiritual equality is not dependent on gender. His statement about "making Mary male" should be understood symbolically, implying that in the spiritual realm, gender distinctions lose their significance. The concept of becoming "male" could be interpreted as transcending physical and societal limitations to become spiritually whole.

> *This saying resonates with Galatians 3:28 (NIV):*
> *"There is neither Jew nor Gentile, neither slave nor free, nor is there male and female, for you are all one in Christ Jesus."*

"Mary Magdalene – 'Apostle to the Apostles'"

A Reworded, More Inclusive Version:

Simon Peter said to the disciples that Mary should leave, for women are not fit to live the spiritual life. But Jesus replied: I will guide her as I do you, that she may also be transformed into a complete spirit, just like you. For anyone, regardless of gender, who seeks spiritual truth with devotion will enter the Kingdom of Heaven.[1]

Saying 114 of the *Gospel of Thomas* has sparked considerable discussion among scholars due to its provocative portrayal of gender and spiritual transformation. Elaine Pagels interprets the passage as a reflection of early Christian tensions regarding the role of women, suggesting that this text offers a radical counterpoint to the patriarchal views found in some canonical writings. Karen King similarly sees the saying as emblematic of the fluid and contested boundaries of gender and spiritual authority in early Christianity. Bart Ehrman points to Saying 114 as one of many examples of how non-canonical texts reveal the theological diversity that once flourished among early followers of Jesus. April DeConick offers a more mystical lens, interpreting the transformation of Mary not as a rejection of femininity but as a symbolic ascent into spiritual completeness, transcending all earthly distinctions. Collectively, these voices invite readers to consider Saying 114 not as a rigid doctrinal claim, but as a profound expression of the soul's journey toward unity with the divine.

In closing, the teachings of the *Gospel of Thomas* present a profound invitation to explore the depths of inner transformation, self-realization, and the active participation in the unfolding of the divine reality. By blending ancient wisdom with modern concepts of consciousness and the universe, it bridges the mysticism of the past with the scientific inquiries of the present. Whether viewed through the lens of Gnostic Christianity or alongside the teachings of great philosophical and spiritual thinkers, the Gospel of Thomas challenges us to transcend external doctrines and rituals in favor of a direct, personal engagement with the divine.

In this light, it echoes the timeless quest for knowledge and truth, urging us to seek within, not just for the Kingdom of God, but for the realization of our divine nature. It calls us to engage in the ongoing process of spiritual awakening—a transformative journey where the distinction between the observer and the observed dissolves, and where the Kingdom of God, ever-present and immanent, becomes manifest in our lives.

The *Gospel of Thomas* reminds us that the path to enlightenment is not solely an intellectual pursuit, but a lived, participatory experience in which our consciousness actively shapes our understanding of reality. This dynamic process of spiritual realization, where both the inner and outer worlds converge, offers a path toward true freedom and fulfillment. As we seek this deeper connection to the divine, we come to realize that, as both the Gospel of Thomas and contemporary physics suggest, the universe is not a passive entity—it is a participatory experience, and our engagement with it shapes the very fabric of

---

[1]   Paraphrased from Gospel of Thomas 114

existence. Through the pursuit of inner knowledge, we not only come to know the Kingdom, but we also transform our place within it, awakening to our fullest, most divine potential.

The Kingdom is not found through thought alone, but through the dance of presence, where the seeker and the sought become one. As we awaken to the divine within, the universe responds, for it is not a silent stage but a living mirror. In every moment of inner knowing, reality itself bends toward revelation.

 # Epilogue: The Light Within

My journey began amidst the swirling currents of New Age mysticism, where the boundaries between the spiritual and the esoteric often blurred. In 2015, a series of profound epiphanies led me to embrace the Roman Catholic faith, seeking the depth and tradition it offered. Though I no longer practice Catholicism formally, the mysticism of its saints and the sacred mysteries continue to illuminate my path.

Figures like Saint Francis of Assisi, who found divinity in simplicity and nature, and Saint Teresa of Ávila, who mapped the soul's interior castles, exemplify the living mysticism that transcends doctrine. Their lives, filled with visions, miracles, and unwavering devotion, keep the flame of divine intimacy burning.

The apostles Peter, James, Thomas, and Mary Magdalene each walked unique paths of revelation. Thomas's doubt led to profound understanding; Peter's faith became the Church's foundation; James's courage exemplified steadfastness; Mary Magdalene's witness to the Resurrection highlighted the transformative power of personal encounter with the Divine.

In this era of renewed revelation, the Apparitions of Avondale echo the Gospel of Thomas: "When you know yourselves, then you will be known, and you will realize you are the children of the Living One." As Jesus told Peter, "flesh and blood did not reveal this to you, but my Father in heaven" (Matthew 16:17). Such insights remind us that true communion with Christ arises not solely from external observance but from inner awakening.

The narrative of faith is ever-unfolding—etched across the skies, inscribed in sacred texts, and whispered in the silent chambers of the soul. The Light that guided the apostles continues to beckon us inward, urging us to see with the eyes of the heart and to walk in the enduring radiance of Christ.

In this same Spirit, Pope Francis became a light-bearer in our time. Amid the noise of the world, his voice remained attuned to the quiet movement of the Spirit. He reminded us that mysticism is not an escape from reality but a deeper participation in divine presence that Christ lives not only in sacrament and scripture, but in creation, in community, and in the stillness of the soul. His papacy rekindled the Church's contemplative heart, calling us back to the mercy and mystery that first drew the saints to their knees.

Postscript: A Sign in Time

In Memoriam: Pope Francis (1936–2025)

Passed into eternal life on the Day of Resurrection — April 20, 2025

"Christ is risen! These words capture the entire meaning of our existence, for we were not made for death but for life." —*Pope Francis, his final public words*

On Easter Sunday, 2025—the very day Christians around the world celebrated the resurrection of the Lord—Pope Francis breathed his last and returned to the Light.

His passing on the Day of Resurrection was not merely a historical coincidence, but a sacred sign. A saying without words, echoing the spirit of this gospel: that the Living Christ is not confined to tomb or temple, but radiates from within—*movement and repose.*

As Christ rose, so too did Francis ascend—from the Church of the Resurrection to the mystery of divine union.

Pope Francis's papacy was marked by a commitment to inclusivity, compassion, and addressing contemporary issues with a pastoral heart. He emphasized the Church's role as a field hospital, tending to the wounded and marginalized. His teachings often reflected the mystical tradition, urging believers to encounter Christ in the poor, the environment, and within themselves.

As we reflect on his legacy, we are reminded that the journey of faith is continuous. The Light that shone through Pope Francis now calls each of us to carry it forward—to seek the Divine within, to act with love and mercy, and to live as children of the Living One.

About the Author

Jamie C. Dunston is a contemplative writer, mystic, and artist whose work emerges from a life-changing theophany known as *The Apparitions of Avondale*—a profound encounter with the Triune God, the Holy Mother, and the radiant unveiling of divine glory. Rooted in sacred scripture, early Christian mysticism, and the mystery of direct divine experience, her writings seek to illuminate the indwelling presence of God and the revelation of Christ within.

She is the author of *Unveiled Sky: A Divine Revelation*, along with other theological reflections exploring divine love, metaphysical idealism, and the mystical symbolism hidden within sacred texts. Through prose, poetry, and visual art, Jamie invites readers into a sacred stillness—a space where the eternal whispers, and the soul awakens to the beauty and truth of the divine.

References

References for The Mystical Gospel of Thomas: Revelation of the Inner Christ

Scholars and Historians

Bauckham, R. (1998). Jesus and the eyewitnesses: The Gospels as eyewitness testimony. Eerdmans Publishing.

Borg, M. (1997). The God we never knew: Beyond dogmatic religion to a more authentic contemporary faith. HarperOne.

Catholic Church. (2000). Catechism of the Catholic Church (2nd ed.). Vatican Press.

Crossan, J. D. (1991). The historical Jesus: The life of a Mediterranean Jewish peasant. HarperSanFrancisco.

DeConick, A. (2007). The original Gospel of Thomas in translation: With a commentary and new English translation of the complete Gospel. T&T Clark.

Ehrman, B. D. (2003). Lost Christianities: The battles for Scripture and the faiths we never knew. Oxford University Press.

King, K. L. (2003). What is Gnosticism? Harvard University Press.

Pagels, E. (2003). Beyond belief: The secret Gospel of Thomas. Random House.

Robinson, J. M. (Ed.). (1990). The Nag Hammadi Library in English (3rd ed.). HarperSanFrancisco.

Sanders, E. P. (1993). Paul and Palestinian Judaism: A comparison of patterns of religion. Fortress Press.

Sanders, E. P. (1993). The historical figure of Jesus. Penguin.

Slater, T. B. (2003). Christ and community: A socio-historical study of the Gospel of Thomas. University Press of America.

Mystics and Classical Philosophers

Augustine. (1991). *Confessions* (H. Chadwick, Trans.). Oxford University Press. (Original work published ca. 397)

Augustine of Hippo. (2003). *The city of God* (M. D. McDonald, Trans.). Modern Library. (Original work published 426)

Böhme, J. (1967). *The way to Christ* (F. A. H. M. Haldane, Trans.). Theosophical Publishing House. (Original work published 1623)

Böhme, J. (1978). *The way to Christ* (P. Erb, Trans. & Ed.). Paulist Press. (Original work published 1624)

Chrysostom, J. (1997). *Homilies on the Gospel of Matthew* (R. C. Hill, Trans.). The Fathers of the Church. Catholic University of America Press.

Eckhart, M. (1994). *Selected writings* (O. Davies, Trans. & Ed.). Penguin Classics.

Eckhart, M. (2009). *The essential sermons, commentaries, treatises and defense* (B. McGinn, Ed. & Trans.). Paulist Press.

Fox, M. (2000). *Original blessing: A primer in creation spirituality* (25th anniversary ed.). Tarcher/Putnam.

Gibran, K. (2003). *The prophet.* Knopf.

Heraclitus. (2001). *Heraclitus: The complete fragments* (T. M. Robinson, Trans.). University of Toronto Press.

Heschel, A. J. (1951). *Man is not alone: A philosophy of religion.* Farrar, Straus and Giroux.

Heschel, A. J. (2001). *The prophets* (Perennial Classics ed.). HarperCollins. (Original work published 1962)

Hildegard of Bingen. (1990). *Selected writings* (M. Atherton, Trans.). Penguin Classics.

John of the Cross. (1959). *The dark night of the soul* (E. Allison Peers, Trans.). Image Books. (Original work published 1585)

Julian of Norwich. (1998). *Revelations of divine love* (E. Spearing, Trans.). Penguin Classics. (Original work published ca. 1395)

Merton, T. (1961). *New seeds of contemplation.* New Directions.

Nietzsche, F. (2006). *Thus spoke Zarathustra: A book for everyone and no one* (A. Tillett, Trans.). Modern Library.

Palamas, G. (1983). *The triads* (J. Meyendorff, Ed., N. Gendle, Trans.). Paulist Press.

Pascal, B. (1995). *Pensées* (A. J. Krailsheimer, Trans.). Penguin Classics.

Plato. (2004). *The complete works of Plato* (J. M. Cooper, Ed.). Hackett Publishing Company.

Plato. (2007). *The Republic* (D. Lee, Trans.). Penguin Classics.

Plotinus. (1991). *The Enneads* (S. MacKenna, Trans.). Penguin Classics.

Rabia al-Adawiyya. (1995). *Doorkeeper of the heart: Versions of Rabia* (C. Uhl, Trans.). Threshold Books.

Rilke, R. M. (2005). *Letters to a young poet* (M. D. Herter Norton, Trans.). W. W. Norton.

Rumi. (2004). *The essential Rumi* (C. Barks, Trans.). HarperOne.

Saint Teresa of Ávila. (2004). *The interior castle* (K. Kavanaugh & O. Rodriguez, Trans.). Paulist Press. (Original work published 1577)

Silesius, A. (1986). *The cherubinic wanderer* (M. Shrady, Trans.). Paulist Press. (Original work published 1675)

Silesius, A. (2008). *The cherub's song: The mystic poetry of Angelus Silesius* (D. J. B. Kersey, Trans.). Lindisfarne Books.

Silesius, A. (2009). *The living light: The spiritual poetry of Angelus Silesius* (R. C. Gregory, Trans.). Shambhala. (Original work published 1657)

Symeon the New Theologian. (1995). *Hymns of divine love* (G. A. Maloney, Trans.). Paulist Press.

Teresa of Avila. (2006). *Interior castle* (E. Allison Peers, Trans.). Dover Publications. (Original work published 1577)

The Cloud of Unknowing. (1994). *The cloud of unknowing* (C. A. S. Watson, Trans.). Doubleday.

Weil, S. (2002). *Gravity and grace* (E. Craufurd, Trans.). Routledge.

Modern Thinkers and Teachers

Aurobindo, S. (1996). The life divine. Sri Aurobindo Ashram.

Brunton, P. (2002). The secret path: A guide to the way of the heart. Larson Publications.

Chopra, D. (2008). The third Jesus: The Christ we cannot ignore. Harmony Books.

Dunston, J. C. (2024). Unveiled Sky: A divine revelation. Sacred Luminary Press.

Heschel, A. J. (1955). God in search of man: A philosophy of Judaism. Farrar, Straus and Giroux.

Jung, C. G. (1969). The archetypes and the collective unconscious (R. F. C. Hull, Trans.). Princeton University Press.

Luther, M. (1960). Luther's works, Volume 45: The Christian in society (H. T. Lehmann, Ed.). Concordia Publishing House.

More, T. (1997). The history of King Richard III (R. S. Sylvester, Ed.). Yale University Press.

Ouspensky, L., & Lossky, V. (1982). The meaning of icons. St. Vladimir's Seminary Press.

Vivekananda, S. (2006). Jnana-Yoga: The path of knowledge. Ramakrishna-Vivekananda Center.

Sacred Texts and Scriptures from Other Traditions

Blatz, F. (Trans.). (1959). *The Gospel of Thomas* (M. L. Soher, Ed.). Harper & Row.

Buddha. (2004). *The Dhammapada: A new translation* (D. L. Snellgrove, Trans.). Shambhala.

Byrom, T. (Trans.). (1993). *The Dhammapada: The sayings of the Buddha*. Shambhala Publications.

Cleary, T. (Trans.). (1993). *The Flower Ornament Scripture: A translation of the Avatamsaka Sutra* (Vol. 1). Shambhala Publications.

Cleary, T. (Trans.). (1993). *The Lankavatara Sutra: A Mahayana text*. Shambhala Publications.

Doresse, J. (1960). *The secret books of the Egyptian Gnostics* (M. L. Soher, Ed.). Harper & Row.

Easwaran, E. (Trans.). (2007). *The Bhagavad Gita*. Nilgiri Press.

Gnostic Society Library. (n.d.). *The Gospel of Mary*. In *The Gnostic Society Library*. Retrieved from http://www.gnosis.org/library/marygosp.htm

Guru Granth Sahib. (2014). *The Guru Granth Sahib: The scripture of the Sikhs* (J. S. P. S. Bedi, Ed.). Sikh Heritage Education Network.

Hume, R. E. (Trans.). (2003). *The thirteen principal Upanishads*. Oxford University Press.

King, K. L. (2003). *The Gospel of Mary of Magdala: Jesus and the first woman apostle*. Polebridge Press.

Lao Tzu. (2009). *Tao Te Ching* (S. Mitchell, Trans.). Harper Perennial Modern Classics.

Layton, B. (Trans.). (1987). *The Gospel of Thomas: Translation with commentary*. Harper & Row.

Meyer, M. (2005). *The Gospel of Thomas: The hidden sayings of Jesus*. HarperOne.

Nikhilananda, S. (Trans.). (1949). *The Upanishads: Volume 3 – Brihadaranyaka* (Vol. 3). Sri Ramakrishna Math.

Prabhavananda, S. (Trans.). (1947). *The Bhagavad Gita: As it is (with commentary)*. Ramakrishna-Vivekananda Center.

Prabhavananda, S. (1953). *The wisdom of Vedanta* (R. H. van de Weyer, Trans.). Ramakrishna-Vivekananda Center.

Red Pine. (2012). *The Lankavatara Sutra: Translation and commentary*. Counterpoint Press.

Icons and Photographs

Original Works from Unveiled Sky: A Divine Revelation

(All published by Sacred Luminary Press in 2024)

Dunston, J. C. (2024). Details of beloved Jesus' face: "Whoever has seen me has seen the Father" [Photograph]. In Unveiled sky: A divine revelation. Sacred Luminary Press.

Dunston, J. C. (2024). Divine Trinitude: Embracing the sacred unity of knowing, experiencing, and being in the Holy Trinity [Photograph]. In Unveiled sky: A divine revelation. Sacred Luminary Press.

Dunston, J. C. (2024). Guide to the facial features of Heavenly Father [Illustration]. In Unveiled sky: A divine revelation. Sacred Luminary Press.

Dunston, J. C. (2024). Ink of faith: Dove doodles and the Pantocrator [Illustration]. In Unveiled sky: A divine revelation. Sacred Luminary Press.

Dunston, J. C. (2024). Sacred splendor: Illuminating the divine essence of the Heavenly Father [Photograph]. In Unveiled sky: A divine revelation. Sacred Luminary Press.

Dunston, J. C. (2024). Spheres of radiant celestials: Archangels revealed in glowing glory [Photograph]. In Unveiled sky: A divine revelation. Sacred Luminary Press.

Dunston, J. C. (2024). The Mighty One, God the LORD, speaks and summons the earth from the rising to the setting of the sun (Psalm 50:1–2) [Photograph]. In Unveiled sky: A divine revelation. Sacred Luminary Press.

Dunston, J. C. (2024). There He was transfigured before them. His face shone like the sun, and His clothes became as white as the light [Photograph]. In Unveiled sky: A divine revelation. Sacred Luminary Press.

Dunston, J. C. (2024). Transcendent majesty: The radiant throne of divine splendor [Photograph]. In Unveiled sky: A divine revelation. Sacred Luminary Press.

Classical Icons and Historical Artworks

Artist unknown. (6th century). *Christ Pantocrator* [Icon]. Saint Catherine's Monastery, Mount Sinai.

Artist unknown. (14th century). *The parable of the sower* [Manuscript illustration]. Trnovo, Bulgaria.

Artist unknown. (16th century). *James the Just* [Icon].

Artist unknown. (n.d.). *Christ the Sower* [Icon].

Artist unknown. (n.d.). *Fig Tree* [Icon].

Artist unknown. (n.d.). *Flaming Heart* [Icon].

Artist unknown. (n.d.). *Holy Spirit* [Icon].

Artist unknown. (n.d.). *John the Baptist* [Icon].

Artist unknown. (n.d.). *Kind David* [Icon].

Artist unknown. (n.d.). *Mother of God* [Icon].

Artist unknown. (n.d.). *Mustard Seed* [Icon].

Artist unknown. (n.d.). *The Christened Cup* [Icon].

Artist unknown. (n.d.). *The Good Shepherd* [Icon].

Artist unknown. (n.d.). *Transfiguration* [Icon].

Artist unknown. (n.d.). *Trinity* [Icon].

Artist unknown. (n.d.). *Vladimir icon of the Most Holy Theotokos* [Icon].

Fra Angelico. (ca. 1433). *Altarpiece: Pala dei Linaioli (Detail)* [Painting]. Museo di San Marco, Florence.

Michelangelo. (ca. 1512). *The creation of Adam* [Fresco]. Sistine Chapel, Vatican City.

Rublev, A. (ca. 1420s). *Christ the Redeemer* [Icon]. Tretyakov Gallery, Moscow.

www.ingramcontent.com/pod-product-compliance
Lightning Source LLC
Chambersburg PA
CBHW081531120626
46550CB00009B/2687